STUDY GUIDE TO ACCOMPANY FELDMAN

UNDERSTANDING PSYCHOLOGY

SECOND EDITION

PREPARED BY

VALERIE SASSERATH ADAMS

McGRAW-HILL PUBLISHING COMPANY

New York   St. Louis   San Francisco   Auckland   Bogotá   Caracas   Hamburg
Lisbon   London   Madrid   Mexico   Milan   Montreal   New Delhi   Oklahoma City
Paris   San Juan   Sao Paulo   Singapore   Sydney   Tokyo   Toronto

1 2 3 4 5 6 7 8 9 0   SEMSEM   8 9 4 3 2 1 0 9

ISBN 0-07-020532-9

The editors were James D. Anker, David Dunham, and Maria Chiapetta; the cover was designed by Nicholas Krenitsky; the production supervisor was Leroy Young.
Cover photograph by Bohdan Hrynewych, Stock, Boston.
Semline, Inc., was printer and binder.

CONTENTS IN BRIEF

PREFACE

HOW TO USE THE STUDY GUIDE

Given the broad scope of the field of psychology, students often discover that the introductory course in psychology covers more material than they had anticipated. The purpose of this *Study Guide* is to help you understand and master the concepts presented in Robert S. Feldman's text, *Understanding Psychology,* as well as to support your efforts to perform well in your introductory course.

The *Study Guide* was designed to be closely coordinated with the text, which itself contains excellent study aids. Your systematic and conscientious use of the *Study Guide* as you read and study the text will result in the mastery that is required for both doing well on exams and appreciating the complex field of psychology. Mastery is superior to rote memorization because it signifies that you truly understand the material; consequently, it is easier to remember and apply the information you have learned. If mastery is your goal, then this *Study Guide* will take you step by step through the process involved in achieving this objective.

Each chapter in the *Study Guide,* which corresponds to a chapter in Robert Feldman's text, has the same basic structure, as described below.

CHAPTER OUTLINE

Read through the outline and skim the chapter to see how it coordinates with the outline. Use the chapter outline side by side with the text chapter as an aid to studying the relationships between major and subordinate topics and to keeping track of the more detailed material as you read and study. Note that each chapter is organized around three or four major topics.

CHAPTER OVERVIEW

After examining the chapter outline, read the overview, which is a narrative summary of the topics covered in the chapter. Each chapter overview is divided into the same sections as the text chapter to make the material easier to digest.

STUDY STRATEGY

The same study strategy is described for each chapter and provides you with a standard method for mastering the material contained in each chapter. Follow this strategy carefully for each section of each chapter.

1. Review the Chapter Outline up to Recap and Review I.

2. Read the Chapter Overview, Section I.

3. Read the chapter in the text up to Recap and Review I.

4. For any question you answered incorrectly or did not understand, go back to the parts of the text that cover that material.

5. Write your answers to the Review Questions for Section I in the *Study Guide*. Consult the answer key only after you have finished. Then correct any mistakes.

6. After you have completed the Review Questions for Section I and have corrected your mistakes, follow the Study Strategy for Section II. Do the same for each section until you have completed all Review Questions.

7. Then, answer the Integration Questions at the end of the chapter in the *Study Guide*. Answering these questions will help you see how the material fits together.

And, don't foget:
 Go back to the parts of the text which cover material that was difficult for you. If you still don't understand a concept, ask your teacher for clarification. Your questions in class and your teacher's answers will help other students as well.

MASTERY QUESTIONS

The mastery questions in the *Study Guide* are identical to those included toward the beginning of each text chapter (at the end of the Looking Ahead section). As you read and study, focus your attention on what you should know or be able to do after mastering the contents of the chapter. State verbally what the questions ask you to do or understand. When reading the text, keep the mastery questions in front of you as a checklist to help you determine what to emphasize as you study and review.

REVIEW QUESTIONS

The next part of each *Study Guide* chapter contains review questions corresponding to each chapter section (I, II, III, and sometimes IV). These review questions have been included to provide you with a variety of ways to test your mastery. Answer all the questions. Getting answers wrong is the first step in a useful review process. When your answer is wrong (check the answer key at the end of each section), go back to the part of the text that explains the concept you have missed. The following types of questions are included: Fill in the Blanks, Multiple Choice, and Matching Questions.

INTEGRATING THE MATERIAL

This section contains essay questions that help you put the pieces together. Psychology is a vast and complex field, and when students first encounter the variety of topics, the field may seem disconnected. However, the various subtopics in the field of psychology are held together by many important threads. The questions in this section help you to identify those threads and integrate material among chapters so that the field may be viewed as unified.

ACTIVITIES FOR CHAPTER REVIEW

This last section of the *Study Guide,* containing exercises that apply to the chapter as a whole, are to be done outside of class. These exercises call for an understanding of basic concepts and an ability to apply this understanding. Your instructor may assign activities, or you may choose to do them on your own to enhance your mastery of the material.

Before beginning your journey through the field of psychology, you might find it useful to examine the following section on effective study techniques that explains how to:

1. get organized

2. study actively

3. set goals, and

4. plan your time.

For some of you, this information will serve as a review of methods you already use when approaching a new body of knowledge. For others, it will open new doors. In either case, read this information as part of your preparation for the introductory course in psychology.

I have enjoyed preparing this *Study Guide* and hope that you will use it as an active aid in mastering the material in Robert Feldman's *Understanding Psychology,* second edition.

Valerie Sasserath Adams

EFFECTIVE STUDY TECHNIQUES

GET ORGANIZED

One of the first steps in effective studying is organization. If possible, set aside a few hours each day for study, preferably the same hours every day. And stick to your study time. If it is not possible for you to follow this suggestion, the key is still to be organized and to take your study time seriously. Change your schedule for study only when absolutely necessary.

To study effectively, you will need the following:

1. *Your study place.* Just as you eat in a dining hall and program in a computer center, you should study in a set place. The exact type of place that is best for studying will vary from person to person, and possibly from subject to subject. Explore potential study environments at the beginning of the term, asking yourself critical questions about the work you have accomplished in various settings:

Do I read best under conditions of extreme silence, or do I need background noise (such as soft music or office sounds)?

Am I distracted by the presence of other students?

Do pleasant environments with many things to look at distract me from studying and entice me to finish earlier than I had planned?

Do I need to sit in a straight, hardback chair, or is a comfortable armchair better for me?

Do the lighting conditions cause eyestrain and force me to quit studying earlier than I had planned?

Use your common sense in selecting the best study place for you. Make sure it has a minimum of distractions. Take study breaks, but at appropriate times. Don't set yourself up to take more breaks for food, drink, and conversation than you had planned. It is okay to study with a friend, as long as you are both really studying.

2. *Your study time.* Make sure you set aside enough time to read an entire chapter, if possible. Or, scan the material and set a goal to complete a major portion of a chapter so that you will not end your reading in the middle of a discussion of an important concept. In *Understanding Psychology*, natural breaks occur at the end of each Recap and Review section.

3. *A good dictionary.* Have a dictionary nearby and look up all words that you do not understand. Write down their meanings so that you will not have to look up the same words over and over again. Learning unfamiliar words will help you in studying and in passing exams.

4. *A pencil, a highlighter, and a pad of paper.* Having these tools handy will make it easier for you to take notes from the text, write down questions that you want to ask in class, or even write down information that you find particularly interesting and want to explore further. If you have this equipment when you begin to study, you will save time and avoid the frustration of having to scrounge around for them at the last minute.

Now that you are organized, you need to study in an active, rather than in a passive, way.

STUDY ACTIVELY

Read the section in the text (Using *Understanding Psychology,* second edition: Strategies for Effective Study, on pages xxix to xxxi) which describes in detail the SQ3R method for achieving mastery. SQ3R stands for *survey, question, read, recite,* and *review.* Using these steps, you will become actively engaged in a learning process that will help you learn and retain the material in a more meaningful way and for a longer period of time.

The *Study Guide* may be used in carrying out all the steps of the SQ3R process. When *surveying* what is to be learned, use the outline and mastery questions in the *Study Guide* and read the chapter overview. As a result, you will have some idea of what you will be reading about and how that material is organized. You will then be able to organize the material in your mind and relate it to information you already have from previous experience and reading. Then, *question* yourself before each new section of a given chapter about the things you will be learning, how they relate to concepts you already understand, and what you should know when you have completed this section of the chapter. The mastery questions in the *Study Guide* can help you in the questioning process.

Now you are ready for the three R's. When *reading* the chapter, keep the outline and mastery questions nearby as aids. Read everything completely, even if it seems familiar and obvious. Feldman presents concepts in the text in a variety of different ways, and reading all the examples will help reinforce your understanding. If you find it helpful, underline or highlight key concepts. But don't underline everything because this will just lead to confusion. As you read, try to actively relate the new material to what you already know so that the information hangs together. When *reciting* and *reviewing* material, use the review questions and answers in the *Study Guide.* When you look up an answer, recite it out loud. Hearing yourself say the answer can help you remember it. Try all the questions when you review. Then, go back and reread, recite, and review information from the text that you may have missed or not understood. Then, if you still have difficulty in understanding particular concepts or topics, use your classroom time as a valuable resource by asking your professor for clarification.

SET GOALS

On the first day of class, you will probably receive a syllabus that will list which chapters should be read by what date, when tests will be given, and when papers are due. Rather than putting this important document somewhere where you may never find it again, keep it handy and use it as a guide for goal-setting in your psychology course. Being prepared each week for the chapter or pages assigned involves setting *short-term goals,* whereas preparing yourself for exams and writing papers involves setting *long-term goals.* Both short-term goals and long-term goals will have to be broken down into smaller subgoals so that you can accomplish them efficiently and without panic.

It is helpful to make a list of your goals. There are several ways to do this. One effective method involves drawing a right triangle and dividing it up into time blocks, with specific dates indicated on the horizontal line. Along the hypotenuse, list the goals you wish to achieve by each date. You can have one figure for long-term goals, which should match the long-term goals in your syllabus, and one for shorter-term goals, which should cover less time and be arranged in concrete, realistic, and achievable steps. Once you have set up your goal chart, stick to it and try to determine how effective it is. Are your steps too big? If they are, revise them into more realistic steps. Don't be afraid to revise your goals. The important thing is to create a plan that works.

PLAN YOUR TIME

Now that you have set your goals and have written them down, you should begin to decide how you will plan your time to accomplish them. Managing your time is a major part of goal achievement.

Long-range planning. Get a large calendar with space to note events and activities for each day. The desk blotter type of calendar is excellent for this purpose. Then, plot out your semester, listing dates for midterms, finals, and vacations, due dates for term papers and library books, and other relevant information. Using the syllabi for your psychology class and your other classes, note the assignment and reading deadlines on the calendar. Also note upcoming concerts, sports events, plays, and other social events so that you will be able to budget your time around them.

Short-range planning. You should engage in short-range planning on a weekly basis. Using your semester calendar as a guide, block out the week ahead on a sheet of paper by listing classes, meetings, extracurricular events, and regularly scheduled study time first. Then list special or one-time events, such as dances, TV specials, due dates, and appointments of other kinds. Keep this short-range planning calendar on your desk and check off events as you complete them.

You may also want to jot down a short list each morning, noting what you want to accomplish in the course of the day in an order that will save you time and energy. Cross off items as they are finished, and redistribute leftover events to your weekly schedule.

When you are planning your short-term goals, consider what time of the day you are most productive and schedule your most important and difficult tasks for those times.

Remember—don't overschedule. Leave room for the unexpected and the spontaneous in your life. Be efficient, but don't be compulsive. Breaks and leisure time are important, and without them you will exhaust yourself and thwart your study efforts.

Now you can get to work.

CHAPTER
1

INTRODUCTION TO PSYCHOLOGY

1

CHAPTER OVERVIEW

Chapter 1 introduces the field of psychology, which is defined as the scientific study of behavior and mental processes. Although psychologists study many diverse topics and work in a variety of settings, the common link among them is the attempt to explain, predict, modify, and improve the lives of people and the world through scientific methods.

Chapter 1 is divided into three sections.

I. The first section focuses on psychologists at work and different aspects of the field. Biopsychologists study the biology underlying behavior with a focus on how the brain, the nervous system, and the body interact with the mind to influence behavior. Experimental psychologists study the processes of sensing, perceiving, learning, and thinking. Developmental psychologists study how people grow and change intellectually, emotionally, and socially throughout life. Personality psychologists examine individual differences in traits and behavior patterns and try to answer the question ''What is the common bond among us and what makes us unique?'' Health psychologists explore the relationship between psychological factors and physical ailments—for example, how stress can affect health. Clinical and counseling psychologists diagnose and treat abnormal behavior as well as crises in daily living. Social psychologists study how people's thoughts, feelings, and actions are affected by others and try to unravel such issues as human aggression and attitude change. Industrial and organizational psychologists focus on behavior in the workplace, whereas environmental psychologists examine people in other physical environments. Emerging areas of psychology include forensic psychology (legal issues), consumer psychology (buying habits, impact of advertising), and program evaluation (assessment of the value and effectiveness of large-scale government programs, such as Head Start). Most psychologists are employed by institutions of higher learning. Others are employed by hospitals, clinics, and community health centers or are engaged in private practice.

II. The second section of the chapter focuses on the history, development, and current direction of the field of psychology. The major models of present-day psychology have their roots in structuralism, functionalism, and gestalt psychology. Structuralism, a model developed by Wilhem Wundt, who set up the first psychology laboratory in Leipzig Germany in 1879, studied the fundamental elements of thinking, consciousness, and emotions. The idea was to identify, through scientific means, the structure of the mind. As psychology evolved, human functioning was perceived more as a process than as a set of elements, and functionalism replaced structuralism. Gestalt psychology, which emerged in the early 1900s as another reaction to structuralism, examined how perception is organized. Today, five basic models form the foundation of the field of psychology:

1. The biological model (the physiological underpinnings of human behavior)

2. The psychodynamic model (the unconscious determinants of human behavior)

3. The cognitive model (the nature of thought processes and understanding the world)

4. The behavioral model (the observable part of human functioning)

5. The humanistic model (reaching human potential and self-fulfillment)

In the future, psychologists will probably become more specialized, new models will emerge, psychological treatment will become more acceptable and available, and more emphasis will be placed on the applications of psychological principles.

III. The third and final section of the chapter focuses on psychological research. Discovering the principles underlying human behavior is dependent on asking the right questions. The formulation of theories and hypotheses helps psychologists ask useful questions, which can then be tested through scientific research methods. Research can take a variety of forms, including the case study, the study of existing records, naturalistic observation, survey research, and experimental research. The only way that psychologists can establish cause-and-effect relationships through research is by carrying out experiments. The process of experimentation begins with the formulation of one or more hypotheses to be tested. Then the hypotheses are operationalized, or translated into actual procedures that can be used in an experiment. Subjects are randomly assigned to groups—an experimental group and a control group. The experimental group or groups receive special treatments that vary, while the control group does not. Then the differences in scores or behaviors between the experimental groups and the control group can be analyzed to determine whether the treatments (cause) were responsible for group differences (effects). Threats to experiments include experimenter expectations and subject expectations. Because research has the potential to violate the rights of participants, psychologists adhere to a strict set of ethical guidelines aimed at protecting subjects. Although it is important to beware of exaggerated claims and faulty research, it is also important to appreciate the contributions that the field of psychology has made in improving the quality of our lives.

STUDY STRATEGY

Follow this strategy for *each* section of the chapter.

1. Review the CHAPTER OUTLINE up to Recap and Review I.

2. Read the CHAPTER OVERVIEW, Section I.

3. Read the chapter in the text up to Recap and Review I.

4. For any question you answered incorrectly or did not understand, go back to the parts of the text that cover that material.

5. Write your answers to the REVIEW QUESTIONS for Section I in the *Study Guide*. Consult the answer key only after you have finished. Then correct any mistakes.

6. After you have completed the REVIEW QUESTIONS for Section I and have corrected your mistakes, follow the STUDY STRATEGY for Section II. Do the same for each section until you have completed all REVIEW QUESTIONS.

7. Complete the INTEGRATING THE MATERIAL questions at the end of the *Study Guide* chapter. Answering these questions will help you see how the material fits together.

And, don't forget:

Go back to the parts of the text that cover material that was difficult for you. If you still don't understand a concept, ask your teacher for clarification. Your questions in class and your teacher's answers will help other students as well.

MASTERY QUESTIONS

After mastering Chapter 1, you will be able to answer the following questions:

What is psychology and why is it a science?

What are the different kinds of psychologists?

What assumptions do psychologists make about the world?

How do psychologists use theory and research to answer questions of interest?

What are the different forms of research employed by psychologists?

REVIEW QUESTIONS: SECTION I

FILL IN THE BLANKS

1. Psychology is the study of _____ and _____ _____ .

2. Biopsychologists focus on the operation of the _____ and the _____ _____ .

3. Sensing, perceiving, learning, and thinking are studied by _____ psychologists.

4. _____ psychology explores the relationship between psychological factors and physical ailments.

5. _____ psychology is the branch of psychology that focuses on educational, social, and career adjustment problems.

6. Industrial-organizational psychology is concerned with the psychology of the _____ .

7. A _____ psychologist would play a role in determining whether a person is competent to testify at a trial.

8. The majority of psychologists are found in _____ settings.

MULTIPLE CHOICE

9. An architect interested in designing an inner-city apartment building that would not be prone to vandalism might consult with a(n)

   a. clinical psychologist.
   b. school psychologist.
   c. forensic psychologist.
   d. environmental psychologist.

10. Questions such as how we are influenced by advertising and why we form relationships with each other are studied by _____ psychologists.

   a. counseling
   b. social
   c. clinical
   d. health

11. A forensic psychologist would be particularly interested in

    a. the nature of stress.
    b. the study of perception.
    c. human relationships.
    (d.) legal issues.

12. The effectiveness of government programs such as Head Start and Medicaid would be the focus of psychologists interested in

    a. experimentation.
    (b.) evaluation.
    c. forensics.
    (d.) cognition.

13. The ways in which people respond to advertisements is an area of study for

    (a.) consumer psychologists.
    (b.) industrial psychologists.
    c. clinical psychologists.
    d. social psychologists.

14. Of the following, an environmental psychologist would be most likely to study

    a. the impact of smoking on health.
    b. experimental ethics.
    (c.) the effects of crowding on behavior.
    d. program effectiveness.

(15.) Most psychologists work in

    a. hospitals.
    (b.) public schools.
    c. industry.
    (d.) universities.

MATCHING QUESTIONS

Match each type of psychologist with the correct area of study.

a	16. industrial	a.	workplace
e	17. personality	b.	abnormal behavior
i K	18. cognitive	c.	career adjustment
m	19. social	d.	learning disabilities
l	20. health	e.	individual traits
h	21. forensic	f.	brain and behavior
d	22. school	g.	perceiving and learning
j	23. educational	h.	legal issues
b	24. clinical	i.	higher mental processes
c	25. counseling	j.	developing teaching methods
f	26. biopsychologist	k.	growth throughout life
k	27. developmental	l.	stress and disease
g	28. experimental	m.	attitude shifts

ANSWER KEY: SECTION I

FILL IN THE BLANKS

1. behavior; mental processes
2. brain; nervous system
3. experimental
4. health
5. counseling
6. workplace
7. forensic
8. academic

MULTIPLE CHOICE

9. d

10. b

11. d

12. b

13. a

14. c

15. d

MATCHING QUESTIONS

16. a
17. e
18. i
19. m
20. l
21. h
22. d

23. j
24. b
25. c
26. f
27. k
28. g

REVIEW QUESTIONS: SECTION II

FILL IN THE BLANKS

1. The first psychology laboratory was set up by _Wundt_____ in _____, _Germany_____, in 1879.

2. The structuralists used a procedure known as _____.

3. _____ psychology is a model focusing on the study of how perception is organized.

4. The desire to reach potential and attain self-fulfillment is associated with the _____ model.

5. The nature of thought processes and understanding of the world around us is associated with the _____ model.

6. Subconscious processes are considered prime motivators of behavior according to the _____ approach to psychology.

7. Understanding the outer person by studying what is observable is the focus of the _____ approach to psychology.

8. Gestalt psychology and functionalism emerged as reactions to the _____ approach.

9. The functioning of the body and the role of instincts are studied within a _____ approach to psychology.

10. _____ psychology is considered the newest of the major approaches.

MULTIPLE CHOICE

11. Functionalism shifted the focus of study in psychology from elements to

    a. cognitions.
    b. processes.
    c. biological underpinnings.
    d. observable behaviors.

12. John B. Watson was the first American psychologist to follow the _____ model.

    a. behavioral
    b. humanistic
    c. cognitive
    d. psychodynamic

13. A psychodynamic psychologist would be most interested in

   a. the learning process.
   b. our perceptions of the world around us.
   c. dreams.
   d. the functioning of the brain.

14. The influence of inherited characteristics on behavior would be studied with the _____ model.

   a. cognitive
   b. psychodynamic
   c. behavioral
   d. biological

15. ''The whole is greater than the sum of the parts'' is a postulate of

   a. structuralism.
   b. functionalism.
   c. gestalt psychology.
   d. behaviorism.

16. The humanistic model places an emphasis on

   a. observable behavior.
   b. inner forces.
   c. free will.
   d. understanding concepts.

17. Sigmund Freud believed that behavior is motivated by

   a. subconscious inner forces.
   b. a desire to achieve personal fulfillment.
   c. the natural tendency to organize data through perception.
   d. inherited characteristics.

18. Gestalt psychology was developed

   a. around 1850.
   b. in 1879.
   c. during the early 1900s.
   d. in the 1950s.

MATCHING QUESTIONS

Match each name with what that person is best known for.

_____ b 19. Watson

_____ f 20. Freud

_____ e 21. Wundt

_____ a 22. Gall

_____ c 23. Descartes

_____ d 24. James

a. His theory gave rise to the science of phrenology.

b. He developed the behavioral model in America.

c. He was a philosopher who believed that animal spirits conducted impulses.

d. He established the first American psychology laboratory.

e. He established the first psychology laboratory in Leipzig, Germany, in 1879.

f. He developed the basic principles of psychodynamic thinking.

ANSWER KEY: SECTION II

FILL IN THE BLANKS

1. Wilhelm Wundt; Leipzig, Germany
2. introspection
3. gestalt
4. humanistic
5. cognitive
6. psychodynamic
7. behavioral
8. structural
9. biological
10. humanistic

MULTIPLE CHOICE

11. b
12. a
13. c
14. d
15. c
16. c
17. a
18. c

MATCHING QUESTIONS

19. b
20. f
21. e
22. a
23. c
24. d

REVIEW QUESTIONS: SECTION III

FILL IN THE BLANKS

1. Systematic inquiry aimed at the discovery of new knowledge is known as _____.

2. A(n) _____ is a prediction stated in a way that allows it to be tested experimentally.

3. A psychologist who conducts an in-depth interview of a single individual is engaged in a(n) _____ _____.

4. In _____ research, existing records are examined to confirm a hypothesis.

5. People chosen to represent a larger population are asked a series of questions about their behavior, thoughts, or attitudes in _____ research.

6. _____ research examines the relationship between two sets of factors.

7. The deliberately produced change in a formal experiment is called an experimental _____.

8. The two types of groups involved in an experiment are known as the _____ and _____ groups.

9. In an experiment, the _____ variable is manipulated and the _____ variable is measured for the effect intended to be produced.

10. In a well-designed experiment, subjects are _____ assigned to groups.

11. If two variables have a perfect positive relationship such that by knowing the value of one you could predict the value of the other, their correlation would be _____.

MULTIPLE CHOICE

12. Cause-and-effect relationships may be established through

    a. case studies.
    b. surveys.
    c. experimentation.
    d. correlation studies.

13. By examining school records, a school psychologist found that 10 percent of the students in the district were diagnosed as having a learning disability. This type of research is

    a. correlational.
    b. observational.
    c. experimental.
    d. archival.

14. Freud based his theory of psychoanalysis on in-depth examinations of the patients he was treating for psychological problems. This method of research relies on the use of

    a. case studies.
    b. correlational data.
    c. dependent variables.
    d. naturalistic observation.

15. In an experiment with two groups, the group that receives no treatment serves as a(n)

    a. control.
    b. case.
    c. independent variable.
    d. measured variable.

16. When the strength of a relationship is represented by a mathematical score ranging from +1.0 to −1.0, we are dealing with a

    a. dependent variable.
    b. manipulation.
    c. correlation.
    d. treatment.

17. A pill without any significant chemical properties that is used in an experiment is called a(n)

    a. control.
    b. placebo.
    c. dependent variable.
    d. independent variable.

18. Calling up large numbers of people to gather information concerning their attitudes toward television is a form of _____ research.

 a. case study
 b. survey
 c. experimental
 d. archival

19. Informed consent can be dispensed with if a subject

 a. is assigned to the control group.
 b. has spent time in a mental institution.
 c. is merely given a placebo.
 d. is part of a purely observational study in a public location.

MATCHING QUESTIONS

Match each term with the phrase that describes it best.

b 20. archival research

h 21. naturalistic observation

c 22. survey research

e 23. correlational research

g 24. random assignment

d 25. treatment group

f 26. control group

a 27. independent variable

i 28. dependent variable

 a. manipulated variable
 b. uses existing records
 c. used to infer to a larger group
 d. experimentally manipulated
 e. cannot determine cause
 f. receives no treatment
 g. involves chance only
 h. viewing in a normal setting
 i. the measured variable

ANSWER KEY: SECTION III

FILL IN THE BLANKS

1. research

2. hypothesis

3. case study

4. archival research

5. survey

6. correlational

7. manipulation

8. treatment; control

9. independent; dependent

10. randomly

11. +1.0

MULTIPLE CHOICE

12. c   16. c

13. d   17. b

14. a   18. b

15. a   19. d

MATCHING QUESTIONS

20. b   25. d

21. h   26. f

22. c   27. a

23. e   28. i

24. g

INTEGRATING THE MATERIAL

1. In this first chapter, a variety of models of psychology are presented and many different types of professions within the field of psychology are described. With psychologists working in settings as diverse as schools, hospitals, corporations, and laboratories, it may seem as though the field is disjointed. But there are common threads among the models, the viewpoints, and the settings. What are some of the common threads that hold psychology together as a field of study? What are some of the goals that psychologists have in common?

2. Many types of psychological research are described in this chapter—the case study, archival research, naturalistic observation, survey research, correlational research, and experimental research. Think of a topic for investigation or a general area that would be interesting to examine, and describe how you would go about using at least three of these types of approaches to research to study that topic or area. What types of questions could you ask and hope to answer by applying these different research methods to that topic?

ACTIVITIES FOR CHAPTER REVIEW

1. Using naturalistic observation, select a person or group to observe and record what you see. You might observe students immediately before taking an exam, someone on a bus or train, or a child. When you record your observations, make sure you write down behaviors—only what can be seen; do not make any inferences about what the behaviors might mean or what the person might be feeling. Recording behaviors appropriately, without drawing inferences, takes practice.

2. Obtain or borrow copies of catalogs for graduate programs in a variety of areas in the field of psychology. Look at the program requirements, course descriptions, goals of training, degrees

administered, and training of the faculty. This will give you some idea of the process required for specialization in the field of psychology.

3. Go to the library and select an article from a psychology journal in which an experiment is described. What is the format of the article? What is the investigator trying to find out? What are the independent and dependent variables? What are the treatment and control groups? What are the results and implications?

CHAPTER
2
THE BIOLOGY UNDERLYING BEHAVIOR

CHAPTER OVERVIEW

Chapter 2 examines the biological structures and functions of the body and their impact on human behavior. The relationship between biology and behavior, an important area in the field of psychology, is studied by biopsychologists, as you may recall from Chapter 1.

Chapter 2 is divided into four sections.

I. The first section of the chapter focuses on the structure and functioning of neurons, the basic elements of the nervous system. Unique among all the body's cells, neurons have the ability to communicate with other cells. The messages that travel through the neurons are electrical in nature. How neurons are activated, how they pass messages to one another, and the consequences of dysfunction provide important clues for a better understanding of human behavior and the underlying causes of certain diseases. Neurons act according to the all-or-nothing law: They are either firing or resting. The structure, operation, and functions of the neuron must be understood for an appreciation of the processes of sensation, perception, and learning.

II. The second section of the chapter deals more specifically with neuronal transmission. Although messages travel in electrical form within neurons, they travel in chemical form across synapses from one neuron to another. The chemicals that carry messages from one neuron to the next are called neurotransmitters, and they act either to excite neurons into firing or to inhibit them from firing. How neurons fit together to form the nervous system is then described. The nervous system is divided into two main parts: the central nervous system (brain and spinal cord) and the peripheral nervous system (somatic and autonomic divisions). The spinal cord provides the major route for transmission of messages between the brain and the rest of the body. The peripheral nervous system includes all parts of the nervous system other than the brain and spinal cord. The somatic division controls voluntary movements, and the autonomic division controls involuntary movements and plays an important role in emergency situations.

III. The third section of the chapter focuses on the brain—the central core, the endocrine system, and the limbic system. From the spinal cord up, the structures of the central core of the brain include the medulla (controls breathing and heartbeat), the pons (transmits motor information), the reticular formation (controls arousal and sleep), the thalamus (acts as a sensory-information relay center) and the hypothalamus (maintains homeostasis, or a steady internal environment for the body). The endocrine system, which is closely linked to the hypothalamus, secretes hormones—chemicals that circulate through the blood and affect the growth and functioning of other parts of the body. The limbic system, which connects the central core with the cerebral cortex, controls a variety of functions related to self-preservation, including eating, aggression, and reproduction. The pleasure center of the brain is located in the limbic system.

IV. The fourth and final section of the chapter focuses on the cerebral cortex, sometimes called the new brain. Its higher-order functions include reasoning, learning, memory, and language. The cortex has four main sections, called lobes—frontal, parietal, temporal, and occipital. The motor, sensory, and association areas of the cortex are described. Research using brain-scan techniques and research on patients with split brains has shown that the left and right halves of the brain are specialized in their functions even though they share structural similarity. In general, the left hemisphere specializes in language and reasoning, whereas the right hemisphere specializes in nonverbal areas such as art, music, and emotional expression. Differences in the functioning of the right and left hemispheres provide valuable information concerning the underpinnings of human behavior. The study of human psychology would not be complete without an understanding of the biological bases of behavior described in this chapter.

STUDY STRATEGY

Follow this strategy for *each* section of the chapter.

1. Review the CHAPTER OUTLINE up to Recap and Review I.

2. Read the CHAPTER OVERVIEW, Section I.

3. Read the chapter in the text up to Recap and Review I.

4. For any question you answered incorrectly or did not understand, go back to the parts of the text that cover that material.

5. Write your answers to the REVIEW QUESTIONS for Section I in the *Study Guide*. Consult the answer key only after you have finished. Then correct any mistakes.

6. After you have completed the REVIEW QUESTIONS for Section I and have corrected your mistakes, follow the STUDY STRATEGY for Section II. Do the same for each section until you have completed all REVIEW QUESTIONS.

7. Complete the INTEGRATING THE MATERIAL questions at the end of the *Study Guide* chapter. Answering these questions will help you see how the material fits together.

And, don't forget:

Go back to the parts of the text that cover material that was difficult for you. If you still don't understand a concept, ask your teacher for clarification. Your questions in class and your teacher's answers will help other students as well.

MASTERY QUESTIONS

After mastering Chapter 2, you will be able to answer the following questions:

What are the basic elements of the nervous system?

How does the nervous system communicate electrical and chemical messages?

How can an understanding of the nervous system help us to relieve disease and pain?

In what way are the structures of the nervous system tied together?

What are the major parts of the brain, and what are the behaviors for which the parts are responsible?

In what ways do the two halves of the brain operate independently of each other?

REVIEW QUESTIONS: SECTION I

FILL IN THE BLANKS

1. Psychologists who study the ways in which biological structures and body functions affect behavior are called _____.

2. _____ are the basic elements of the nervous system.

3. Just after the action potential has passed, the neuron cannot be fired again. It is in its _____ _____ period.

4. During the relative refractory period, it is more difficult than usual to _____ the neuron.

5. The long, slim, tubelike extension from the end of a neuron that carries messages is called a(n) _____.

6. The _____ are fibers at one end of a neuron that receive messages from other neurons.

7. The _____ buttons are small branches at the end of an axon that relay messages to other cells.

8. The longest part of the neuron is the _____.

9. The _____-_____-_____ law is the principle governing the state of neurons, which are either firing or resting.

10. The _____ potential is an electrical nerve impulse that changes the cell's charge from negative to positive.

11. The axon's protective coating, made of fat and protein, is called the _____ _____.

12. The myelin sheath increases the velocity with which _____ _____ travel through the neurons.

13. The part of the neuron that detects messages first is the _____.

14. The _____ of a stimulus that provokes a neuron determines how much of the potential rate is reached.

15. Although there are no differences in the strength or speed at which an impulse moves across a given neuron (all-or-nothing law), there is variation in the _____ of impulses.

MULTIPLE CHOICE

16. Fibers at one end of a neuron that receive messages from other neurons are called

    a. dendrites.
    b. axons.
    c. terminal buttons.
    d. ions.

17. According to the all-or-nothing law,

    a. either all the neurons fire or none fire.
    b. the absolute refractory period either increases action potential or stops it entirely.
    c. neurons are either firing or resting.
    d. neurons either fire 500 times per second or do not fire at all.

18. We can distinguish the feel of a drop of rain on our skin from the feel of a downpour because of the variation in the

    a. strength of neuronal impulses.
    b. speed of neuronal impulses.
    c. frequency of neuronal impulses.
    d. charge of neuronal impulses.

19. During the relative refractory period, the neuron

    a. causes ions to change their charge from positive to negative.
    b. requires more than the normal stimulus to be set off.
    c. cannot be fired because of the all-or-nothing law.
    d. prepares for another impulse.

20. As an action potential moves through a neuron, the cell charge changes to

    a. positive temporarily.
    b. positive permanently.
    c. negative temporarily.
    d. negative permanently.

21. Rabies is caused by

    a. an uneven electrical charge along the axon.
    b. a breakdown of the myelin sheath.
    c. an inability of critical neurons to fire.
    d. reverse flow along the axon from the terminal buttons.

22. Leakage from the neurons may account for

    a. rabies.
    b. ALS.
    c. epilepsy.
    d. multiple sclerosis.

23. The brain has _____ neurons.

    a. between 1 and 2 million
    b. between 100 billion and 200 billion
    c. about a billion
    d. over 500 billion

24. Most axons are

    a. 1 to 2 inches long.
    b. 1 to 2 feet long.
    c. 3 to 10 feet long.
    d. 1 to 10 centimeters long.

MATCHING QUESTIONS

Match each term with the best definition.

___h___ 25. action potential

___c___ 26. myelin sheath

___a___ 27. terminal buttons

___b___ 28. all-or-nothing law

___g___ 29. absolute refractory period

___d___ 30. relative refractory period

___f___ 31. axon

___e___ 32. dendrites

a. branches at the end of an axon

b. the principle that the neuron is either on or off

c. the protective coating

d. the time during which the neuron requires more than normal stimulation to be set off

e. fibers that receive messages from other neurons

f. a tubelike extension which carries messages through the neuron

g. a phase during which the neuron recovers

h. an electrical nerve impulse set off by a trigger that changes the cell charge

ANSWER KEY: SECTION I

FILL IN THE BLANKS

1. biopsychologists

2. neurons

3. absolute refractory

4. fire

5. axon

6. dendrites

7. terminal

8. axon

9. all-or-nothing

10. action

11. myelin sheath

12. electrical impulses

13. dendrite

14. intensity

15. frequency

MULTIPLE CHOICE

16. a

17. c

18. c

19. b

20. a

21. d

22. c

23. b

24. a

MATCHING QUESTIONS

25. h

26. c

27. a

28. b

29. g

30. d

31. f

32. e

REVIEW QUESTIONS: SECTION II

FILL IN THE BLANKS

1. A chemical connection known as a(n) _____ bridges the gap between two neurons.

2. The terminal button releases a chemical known as a(n) _____ when a nerve impulse comes to the end of an axon and reaches the terminal button.

3. Chemical messages are of two types: _____ and _____.

4. One of the most common neurotransmitters is _____, which produces contractions of skeletal muscles.

5. _____ are chemicals produced by the body that interact with an opiate receptor to reduce pain.

6. Research suggests that Alzheimer's disease is related to the production of _____.

7. Research suggests that schizophrenia may be caused by the overproduction of _____.

8. The _____ _____ is a bundle of nerves that runs along the spine and carries messages between the brain and the body.

9. The _____ division is the part of the autonomic division of the peripheral nervous system that prepares the body to respond in stressful emergency situations.

10. The _____ division is the part of the nervous system that controls voluntary movements of the skeletal muscles.

11. The _____ nervous system controls involuntary movement.

12. The _____ division brings functions back to normal after an emergency has passed.

13. Sexual arousal is controlled by the _____ division.

MULTIPLE CHOICE

14. There are about _____ known chemicals that act as neurotransmitters.

    a. 6
    b. 10
    c. 50
    d. 200

15. A deficiency of acetylcholine could result in

    a. paralysis.
    b. uncontrollable tremors.
    c. depression.
    d. schizophrenia.

16. Large concentrations of endorphins in the brain are produced when a person suffers from

    a. Parkinson's disease.
    b. severe chronic pain.
    c. paraplegia.
    d. mental illness.

17. A deficiency of dopamine in the brain is associated with

    a. Parkinson's disease.
    b. mental illness.
    c. sensitivity to pain.
    d. paralysis.

18. Which of the following is true about neurotransmitters?

    a. They carry chemical messages across a synapse.
    b. They carry messages between neurons.
    c. Both a and b.
    d. Neither a nor b.

19. The reception of acetylcholine can be blocked by

    a. curare.
    b. dopamine.
    c. both a and b.
    d. neither a nor b.

20. The spinal cord is responsible for

    a. the functioning of the peripheral nervous system.
    b. a "runner's high."
    c. preparing the body for emergency situations.
    d. simple reflex movements.

21. The autonomic division of the peripheral nervous system is responsible for all of the following *except*

    a. heartbeat while running.
    b. eye movements while reading.
    c. secretion of hormones.
    d. digestion of food.

22. Sympathetic division is to parasympathetic division as

a. fight is to flight.
b. central is to peripheral.
c. arousing is to calming.
d. helpful is to hurtful.

23. After you escape from a dangerous situation and are safe, the _____ predominates in helping you catch your breath.

a. spinal cord.
b. central nervous system.
c. sympathetic division.
d. parasympathetic division.

MATCHING QUESTIONS

Match each term with the best description.

_____ 24. central nervous system

_____ 25. sympathetic division

_____ 26. endorphin

_____ 27. parasympathetic division

_____ 28. myasthenia gravis

_____ 29. Parkinson's disease

_____ 30. somatic division

_____ 31. Huntington's chorea

a. involves a deficiency of GABA

b. reduces pain

c. involves a deficiency of dopamine

d. controls the movement of skeletal muscles

e. causes a gradual loss of muscle control

f. consists of the brain and spinal cord

g. acts during an emergency

h. calms the body after an emergency

ANSWER KEY: SECTION II

FILL IN THE BLANKS

1. synapse
2. neurotransmitter
3. excitatory and inhibitory
4. acetylcholine (ACh)
5. endorphins
6. acetylcholine (ACh)
7. dopamine
8. spinal cord
9. sympathetic
10. somatic
11. autonomic
12. parasympathetic
13. parasympathetic

MULTIPLE CHOICE

14. c   19. a

15. a   20. d

16. b   21. b

17. a   22. c

18. c   23. d

MATCHING QUESTIONS

24. f   28. e

25. g   29. c

26. b   30. d

27. h   31. a

REVIEW QUESTIONS: SECTION III

FILL IN THE BLANKS

1. The pituitary gland is regulated by the _____.

2. The process by which an organism tries to maintain an internal biological balance or steady state is called _____.

3. The _____ acts primarily as a relay station.

4. Another name for the central core is the _____ brain.

5. The _____ joins the halves of the cerebellum.

6. The cerebellum controls _____ _____.

7. The _____ _____ arouses the body to prepare it for appropriate action and screens out background stimuli.

8. The _____ is the part of the central core that controls breathing and heartbeat.

9. The _____ _____ is located just outside the new brain and controls eating and reproduction.

10. The pituitary gland is sometimes called the _____ gland because it controls the functioning of the rest of the endocrine system.

11. The job of the endocrine system is to secrete _____ that circulate through the body and affect the functioning and growth of other parts of the body.

12. The unsteady gait of someone who has had too much alcohol is caused by the depressed activity of the _____.

MULTIPLE CHOICE

13. The role of the endocrine system is to

   a. secrete hormones that affect growth.
   b. act as a pleasure center.
   c. control breathing and heart rate.
   d. act as a relay station for sensory information.

14. All of the following are brain-scan techniques *except*

   a. CAT.
   b. PET.
   c. NMR.
   d. ACh.

15. The central core is often referred to as the old brain because

   a. its functioning has been known for a long time.
   b. it is thought to have evolved early in the development of the human species.
   c. it is the first part of the brain to degenerate in old age.
   d. the functions of the central core became less vital after the evolution of the new brain.

16. Drinking too much liquor depresses the activity of the

   a. pons.
   b. endocrine system.
   c. thalamus.
   d. cerebellum.

17. When you are concentrating while reading a book and become startled because the doorbell rings, your awareness of the sound is prompted by the

   a. medulla.
   b. hypothalamus.
   c. reticular formation.
   d. cerebellum.

18. The _____ uses a computer to construct an image of the brain by combining thousands of separate x-rays taken at slightly different angles.

   a. CAT scan
   b. NMR scan
   c. EEG
   d. PET scan

19. If you prick your finger on a thorn, a sensory message will be sent through the _____ upward to higher parts of the brain.

   a. cerebellum
   b. thalamus
   c. reticular formation
   d. pons

20. A boy who is much smaller than his peers may have a problem in his

   a. cerebellum.
   b. limbic system.
   c. reticular formation.
   d. endocrine system.

Part Two: THE BIOLOGICAL FOUNDATIONS OF PSYCHOLOGY

MATCHING QUESTIONS

Match each term with the best description.

_____ 21. pons

_____ 22. homeostasis

_____ 23. CAT scan

_____ 24. central core

_____ 25. cerebellum

_____ 26. neurometrics

_____ 27. thalamus

_____ 28. limbic system

_____ 29. endocrine system

_____ 30. pituitary

a. acts as a relay station

b. is a brain-scan technique

c. is the old brain

d. secretes hormones

e. gives pleasure

f. is the master gland

g. controls balance

h. maintains a steady state in the body

i. transmits motor information

j. is a new field focusing on brain diagnosis

ANSWER KEY: SECTION III

FILL IN THE BLANKS

1. hypothalamus
2. homeostasis
3. thalamus
4. old
5. pons
6. bodily balance
7. reticular formation
8. medulla
9. limbic system
10. master
11. hormones
12. cerebellum

MULTIPLE CHOICE

13. a
14. d
15. b
16. d
17. c
18. a
19. b
20. d

MATCHING QUESTIONS

21. i   26. j

22. h   27. a

23. b   28. e

24. c   29. d

25. g   30. f

REVIEW QUESTIONS: SECTION IV

FILL IN THE BLANKS

1. _____ is the inability to perform activities in a logical way.

2. Broca's aphasia is associated with _____ and _____ speech.

3. In receptive aphasia, understanding language is a problem and results in _____ but _____ speech.

4. In the sensory area, the degree of sensitivity is directly related to the amount of _____.

5. The site of higher mental processes such as thought, language, memory, and speech is the _____ area of the brain.

6. The _____ area of the brain is responsible for voluntary movement of particular parts of the body.

7. The _____ lobe lies behind the frontal lobe.

8. The cerebral cortex is also called the _____ brain.

9. The occipital lobe is the major _____ center.

10. _____ is a procedure in which a person can learn to control physiological processes through conscious thought.

11. The largest portion of the cerebral cortex is taken up by the _____ area.

12. A disorder characterized by speech that appears to be fluent, but makes no sense is called _____ aphasia.

13. People with aphasic speech difficulties tend to have physical damage to the _____ hemisphere of the brain.

MULTIPLE CHOICE

14. Biofeedback has been used with success to control

    a. high blood pressure.
    b. emotional problems.
    c. both a and b.
    d. neither a nor b.

15. Which one of the following tasks would be best performed by the left brain?

    a. describing a Picasso painting
    b. thinking about the last time you were angry
    c. defining the word "hemisphere"
    d. playing the flute

16. Which one of the following tasks would be best performed by the right brain?

    a. following a recipe
    b. reading a short story
    c. making a speech in front of an audience
    d. recognizing the face of an old friend

17. A person who tries to cut a grapefruit in half by throwing it against the wall may be suffering from

    a. receptive aphasia.
    b. Broca's aphasia.
    c. split brain.
    d. apraxia.

18. The center for hearing is located in the _____ lobe.

    a. frontal
    b. temporal
    c. occipital
    d. parietal

19. The center for bodily sensation is located in the _____ lobe.

    a. parietal
    b. temporal
    c. occipital
    d. frontal

20. A person suffering from aphasia has difficulty with

    a. verbal expression.
    b. logical behavior.
    c. both a and b.
    d. neither a nor b.

21. The accident that injured Phineas Gage demonstrates how unusual behavioral changes can be brought about by damage to the

    a. occipital lobe.
    b. left brain.
    c. association area.
    d. corpus callosum.

22. Biofeedback is a procedure in which a person learns to

    a. produce precise bodily movements.
    b. think more clearly under stress.
    c. coordinate the two halves of the brain.
    d. control internal physiological processes.

MATCHING QUESTIONS

Match each term with the best description.

_____ 23. association area

_____ 24. occipital lobe

_____ 25. temporal lobe

_____ 26. aphasia

_____ 27. apraxia

_____ 28. biofeedback

_____ 29. somatosensory area

_____ 30. Wernicke's area

_____ 31. lateralization

a. refers to the specialization of the hemispheres

b. allows for control of involuntary functions through conscious thought

c. constitutes the hearing center

d. contains the center for sight

e. involves difficulty performing logically

f. controls higher-level thinking

g. is the same as the sensory area

h. involves difficulty with verbal expression

i. controls the understanding of language

ANSWER KEY: SECTION IV

FILL IN THE BLANKS

1. apraxia

2. halting; laborious

3. fluent; nonessential

4. tissue

5. association

6. motor

7. parietal

8. new

9. visual

10. biofeedback

11. association

12. Wernicke's

13. left

MULTIPLE CHOICE

14. c

15. c

16. d

17. d

18. b

19. a

20. a

21. c

22. d

MATCHING QUESTIONS

23. f

24. d

25. c

26. h

27. e

28. b

29. g

30. i

31. a

INTEGRATING THE MATERIAL

When you first examined Chapter 2, you might have thought, "What does biology have to do with psychology?" Now that you have studied and mastered the material in this chapter, do you have a better understanding of how biology and psychology are related? Describe and give examples of how the functioning of the nervous system is related to our psychological functioning.

ACTIVITIES FOR CHAPTER REVIEW

1. Fill in the labels that are missing from the following diagram of a neuron.

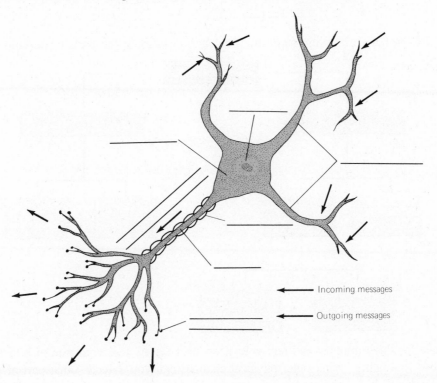

Incoming messages

Outgoing messages

2. Fill in the labels that are missing from the following diagram of the brain.

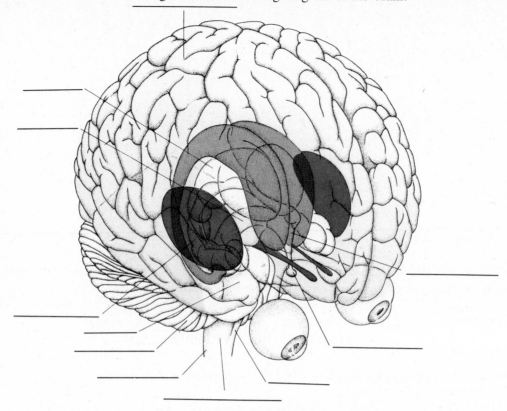

3. Fill in the labels that are missing from this flowchart describing the parts of nervous system.

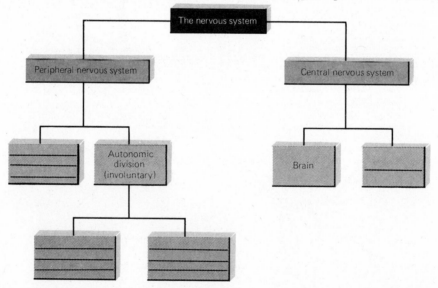

4. Run in place for three minutes and feel your heart beat faster, feel your rate of breathing increase, feel your body sweating. What other physical changes can you detect? What part of your autonomic nervous system has been activated by your running? After the three minutes are up, sit down and relax. Feel your heart rate return to normal, feel your breathing slow down to a normal rate, feel your body return to a homeostatic state. At this point, what part of your autonomic nervous system is operating?

CHAPTER 3
SENSATION

CHAPTER OVERVIEW

Chapter 3 explains how the body is able to incorporate and use outside stimuli and information. Sensation is the process by which an organism responds to a stimulus in the environment. An understanding of how physical stimulation is translated into personal sensory experience is necessary for an understanding of higher-order psychological processes such as perception, learning, memory, reasoning, and social interaction.

The chapter is divided into three sections.

I.   The first section of the chapter introduces you to the branch of psychology known as psychophysics, which studies the relationship between the physical nature of stimuli and a person's sensory responses to them. Some of the most important principles of psychophysics are absolute threshold, signal detection theory, just noticeable difference, and sensory adaptation. An absolute threshold is the smallest amount of physical intensity that must be present for a stimulus to be detected. The absolute thresholds for sight, hearing, taste, smell, and touch are described. Signal detection theory, an outgrowth of psychophysics, seeks to explain the role of psychological factors in producing variations in our ability to identify stimuli. A just noticeable difference is the smallest detectable difference between two stimuli. According to Weber's law, a just noticeable difference is a constant proportion of the magnitude of an initial stimulus. Thus, if a 1-pound increase in a 10-pound weight produces a just noticeable difference, it would take a 10-pound increase in a 100-pound weight to notice a difference (1 is to 10 as 10 is to 100). Sensory adaptation is the process of becoming accustomed to stimulation. For example, the sound of an air conditioner may seem loud to you at first, but after spending time in the room with it, you may hardly notice the sound. In fact, you may become startled if the air conditioner is turned off.

II.   The second section of the chapter explains the process of vision, including the physical aspects of light and how the eye uses light to see. The eyes are sensitive to electromagnetic radiation waves of certain lengths, and these waves register as light. The structure of the eye is described in detail, along with the mechanisms by which the eye transforms light into messages that can be interpreted by the brain. Light travels first through the cornea and then traverses the pupil, a dark hole in the center of the iris. The light then enters the lens, which bends the rays and focuses them on the retina at the rear of the eye; there the electromagnetic energy of light is converted into nerve impulses used by the brain. These impulses leave the eye through the optic nerve. The functioning of the nerve cells of the retina (the rods and cones) is described. These nerve cells play important and differing roles in vision and are responsible for dark and light adaptation. Theories of color vision and their application to the study of color blindness are described.

III.   The third and final section of the chapter discusses the ear as an organ of hearing and its relationship to motion and balance. The physical structure of sound, the movement of sound through the ear, and its modification from a physical stimulus into meaningful messages are explained. Sounds, in the form of wave vibrations, enter the auditory canal and then reach the eardrum, which vibrates; the louder the sound, the greater the vibration. The wave vibrations travel through the middle ear and vibrate the three bones there (hammer, anvil, stirrup), which transmit the vibrations to the oval window, a thin membrane leading to the inner ear. It is in the inner ear that the wave vibrations stimulate the nerve cells of the basilar membrane located in the cochlea, a coiled tube filled with fluid. The stimulation of these nerve cells transmits a neural message to the brain. Theories of hearing and their applications to helping people overcome deafness are described. The last part of the chapter covers the senses of smell and taste and the skin senses, including touch and pain. Some solutions for coping with long-term chronic pain are presented.

STUDY STRATEGY

Follow this strategy for *each* section of the chapter.

1. Review the CHAPTER OUTLINE up to Recap and Review I.

2. Read the CHAPTER OVERVIEW, Section I.

3. Read the chapter in the text up to Recap and Review I.

4. For any question you answered incorrectly or did not understand, go back to the parts of the text that cover that material.

5. Write your answers to the REVIEW QUESTIONS for Section I in the *Study Guide*. Consult the answer key only after you have finished. Then correct any mistakes.

6. After you have completed the REVIEW QUESTIONS for Section I and have corrected your mistakes, follow the STUDY STRATEGY for Section II. Do the same for each section until you have completed all REVIEW QUESTIONS.

7. Complete the INTEGRATING THE MATERIAL questions at the end of the *Study Guide* chapter. Answering these questions will help you see how the material fits together.

And, don't forget:

Go back to the parts of the text that cover material that was difficult for you. If you still don't understand a concept, ask your teacher for clarification. Your questions in class and your teacher's answers will help other students as well.

MASTERY QUESTIONS

After mastering Chapter 3, you will be able to answer the following questions:

How keen are the senses?

What is the relationship between the nature of a physical stimulus and the kinds of sensory responses that result from it?

What are the major senses, and what are the basic mechanisms that underlie their operation?

How can we deal effectively with the aches and pains we all occasionally experience in our lives?

REVIEW QUESTIONS: SECTION I

FILL IN THE BLANKS

1. An adjustment in sensory capacity following prolonged exposure to stimuli is called _____.

2. Another term meaning just noticeable difference is _____ _____.

3. _____ _____ theory addresses whether a person can detect a stimulus and whether a stimulus is actually present at all.

4. Sensation is the process by which an organism responds to a(n) _____.

5. The fact that perfume can be detected when only one drop is present in a three-room apartment is an example of a(n) _____ _____.

6. Weber's law states that the difference threshold is a constant _____ of the magnitude of the initial stimulus.

7. Psychophysics studies the relationship between the _____ nature of the stimuli and the _____ responses that are made.

8. Under perfect conditions, a candle flame can be seen _____ miles away on a dark, clear night.

9. According to signal detection theory, justice is better served when suspects on a lineup look _____ from one another.

MULTIPLE CHOICE

10. Psychophysics is the study of the relationship between the magnitude of a stimulus and

    a. its strength.
    b. its durability.
    ⓒ sensory response.
    d. adaptation.

11. You are sitting in a room trying to study, but you are distracted by the sounds of road construction outside. After a while, you find yourself absorbed in your text, unaware of the noise. The phenomenon that accounts for this change is called

    a. absolute threshold.
    b. difference threshold.
    c. Weber's law.
    ⓓ sensory adaptation.

12. If a 1-decibel increase produces a just noticeable difference in a 6-decibel sound, it would take a _____ increase to produce a just noticeable difference in a 30-decibel sound.

    a. 3-decibel
    (b) 5-decibel
    c. 6-decibel
    d. 10-decibel

13. Sensory adaptation is the same as

    (a.) getting used to a stimulus.
    b. first being aware of a stimulus.
    c. noticing a slight increase in a stimulus.
    d. sensing a stimulus that is not there.

14. The main point of signal detection theory is that our perceptions

    (a.) are influenced by such factors as motivation and expectation.
    b. depend more on excellent visual acuity than on other factors.
    c. remain unchanged after our personalities are fully formed.
    d. cannot be accurately measured because of noise factors.

MATCHING QUESTIONS

Match each term with the best description.

___g___ 15. absolute threshold

___a___ 16. sensory adaptation

___b___ (17) signal detection

___c___ (18.) Weber's law

___i___ 19. psychophysics

___h___ 20. stimulus

___d___ 21. noise

___e___ 22. difference threshold

___f___ 23. decibel

a. an adjustment following prolonged exposure to a stimulus

b. the just noticeable difference as a constant proportion

c. whether a person can detect a stimulus or whether a stimulus is detected when not present

d. background interference

e. the same as just noticeable difference

f. a unit of sound

g. the smallest amount of physical intensity by which a stimulus can be detected

h. a source of physical energy that activates a sense organ

i. the study of the relationship between a stimulus and a sensory response

ANSWER KEY: SECTION I

FILL IN THE BLANKS

1. adaptation
2. difference threshold
3. signal detection
4. stimuli
5. absolute threshold

6. proportion
7. physical; sensory
8. 30
9. different (dissimilar)

MULTIPLE CHOICE

10. c
11. d
12. b

13. a
14. a

MATCHING QUESTIONS

15. g
16. a
17. c
18. b
19. i

20. h
21. d
22. e
23. f

REVIEW QUESTIONS: SECTION II

FILL IN THE BLANKS

1. The range of wavelengths that humans are sensitive to is called the _____ _____.

2. _____ are long, cylindrical, light-sensitive receptors in the _____ that perform well in poor light but are largely insensitive to color and small details.

3. Glaucoma is a dysfunction of the eye in which _____ _____ builds up and causes a decline in visual _____.

4. The _____ nerve carries visual information to the brain.

5. Accommodation is the ability of the lens to vary in shape in order to _____ incoming images on the _____.

6. Tunnel vision occurs at an advanced stage of _____.

7. Your ability to see in a dark movie theater after not being able to see when you first walked in occurs through the process of _____ _____.

8. The size of a person's _____ increases as the amount of incoming light decreases.

9. _____ are light-sensitive receptor cells in the retina that are responsible for sharp focus and color perception, particularly in bright light.

10. As light enters the eye, it passes first through the _____.

11. According to the _____ theory of color vision, the retina has three kinds of cones, each responding to a specific range of wavelengths, with perception of color being influenced by the relative strength with which each cone is activated.

12. The stimuli that register as light in our eyes are actually _____ _____ waves.

13. The _____ is the colored part of the eye.

14. A person with normal color vision is capable of distinguishing no fewer than _____ different colors.

15. The _____-_____ theory of color vision allows us to explain afterimages very directly.

MULTIPLE CHOICE

16. The part of the eye which adjusts its size to the amount of incoming light is the

    a. cornea.
    b. pupil.
    c. iris.
    d. fovea.

17. If you want to focus on the very fine print in a contract, you will probably center the image onto the

    a. fovea.
    b. iris.
    c. rods.
    d. pupil.

18. The lens focuses light on the

    a. cornea.
    b. optic nerve.
    c. pupil.
    d. retina.

19. Which one of the following statements concerning rods and cones is *not* true?

    a. The farther away on the retina from the fovea, the smaller the number of rods becomes.
    b. The names given to the two kinds of light-sensitive receptor cells describe their shapes.
    c. There are about 7 million cones and 125 million rods in the eye.
    d. The rods are used for peripheral and night vision; the cones are used for color vision.

20. Rhodopsin is a substance involved in

    a. moisturizing the cornea.
    b. creating the blind spot.
    c. enhancing color vision.
    (d.) stimulating the rods.

21. In the most common form of color blindness, red and green objects are seen as

    a. purple.
    b. brown.
    (c.) yellow.
    d. blue.

22. When the optic nerve splits at the optic chiasma, the nerve impulses coming from the right half of the retina are sent to the

    a. right half of the brain.
    (b.) left half of the brain.

    c. left half of the brain for the right eye and right half of the brain for the left eye.
    d. left half of the brain for the left eye and right half of the brain for the right eye.

23. The blind spot is located

    a. at the center of the iris.
    b. in the fovea.
    (c.) at the opening for the optic nerve.
    d. at the corner of the lens.

24. One of the most frequent causes of blindness is

    (a.) an underproduction of rhodopsin.
    (b.) a restriction of impulses across the optic nerve.
    c. tunnel vision.
    d. an inability of the pupil to expand.

MATCHING QUESTIONS

Match each term with the best description.

_j_ 25. ganglion cells

_g_ 26. bipolar cells

_e_ 27. rhodopsin

_d_ 28. rods

_f_ 29. cones

_i_ 30. optic nerve

_a_ 31. lens

_c_ 32. cornea

_b_ 33. iris

_h_ 34. glaucoma

a. focuses images on the retina

b. is the colored part of the eye

c. is the site where light first enters the eye

d. are receptors that perform well in poor light and are insensitive to color

e. is a reddish-purple substance that causes a chemical reaction

f. are light-sensitive cells that are responsible for sharp focus in bright light

g. is comprised of nerve cells that carry visual information to the brain

h. is a dysfunction of the eye caused by fluid pressure

i. receive information directly from the rods and cones

j. collect and summarize visual information

ANSWER KEY: SECTION II

FILL IN THE BLANKS

1. visual spectrum
2. rods; retina
3. fluid pressure; acuity
4. optic
5. focus; retina
6. glaucoma
7. dark adaptation
8. pupil

9. cones
10. cornea
11. trichromatic
12. electromagnetic radiation
13. iris
14. 7 million
15. opponent-process

MULTIPLE CHOICE

16. b
17. a
18. d
19. a
20. d

21. c
22. a
23. c
24. b

MATCHING QUESTIONS

25. j
26. i
27. e
28. d
29. f

30. g
31. a
32. c
33. b
34. h

REVIEW QUESTIONS: SECTION III

FILL IN THE BLANKS

1. The function of the semicircular canals is to control _____.

2. The basilar membrane is a structure contained in the _____.

3. The _____ theory of hearing states that different frequencies are responded to by different areas of the basilar membrane.

4. Tiny bones are used for sound transmission in the _____ _____.

5. Sound is defined as the displacement of _____ _____ brought about by the vibration of an object.

6. Sound enters the inner ear through the _____ window.

7. The lowest frequency that humans are capable of hearing is _____ cycles per second.

8. The _____ theory of hearing suggests that the entire basilar membrane acts like a microphone, vibrating as a whole in response to a sound.

9. _____ cells are the receptor cells of the nose.

10. Acupuncture, nerve stimulation, and hypnosis can all provide _____ _____.

11. The _____-_____ theory suggests that particular nerve cells lead to specific areas of the brain related to pain.

12. Taste buds are located in the _____.

MULTIPLE CHOICE

13. The function of the bones of the middle ear is to transmit vibrations to the

    a. eardrum.
    b. round window.
    c. oval window.
    d. semicircular canals.

14. The sensory-receptor cells for hearing are activated in the

    a. cochlea.
    b. middle ear.
    c. semicircular canals.
    d. auditory canal.

15. The number of wave crests that occur in a second are referred to as

    a. pitch.
    b. intensity.
    c. decibels.
    d. frequency.

16. The taste buds in the tip of the tongue are most sensitive to

    a. sweetness.
    b. sourness.
    c. bitterness.
    d. saltiness.

17. Gate-control theory explains the effectiveness of

    a. hypnosis.
    b. acupuncture.
    c. nerve and brain stimulation.
    d. biofeedback.

18. It is *not* true that sense receptors

    a. are evenly distributed.
    b. detect a wide range of stimulation.
    c. play an important role in survival.
    d. transmit information to the brain.

19. The hammer, anvil, and stirrup function through the transmission of

    a. fluid.
    b. electromagnetic radiation.
    c. vibrations.
    d. implants.

MATCHING QUESTIONS

Match each term with the best description.

_____ 20. middle ear

_____ 21. basilar membrane

_____ 22. cochlea

_____ 23. anvil

_____ 24. olfactory cells

_____ 25. oval window

_____ 26. auditory cortex

_____ 27. biofeedback

a. transmits vibrations to the oval window

b. a bone of the middle ear

c. receptors in the nose

d. a technique of pain management

e. a thin membrane at the entrance to the inner ear

f. provides a map of sound frequencies

g. a coiled tube in the inner ear

h. a structure dividing the cochlea into chambers

ANSWER KEY: SECTION III

FILL IN THE BLANKS

1. balance
2. cochlea
3. place
4. middle ear
5. air molecules
6. oval

7. 20
8. frequency
9. olfactory
10. pain relief
11. gate-control
12. tongue

MULTIPLE CHOICE

13. c
14. a
15. d
16. a

17. b
18. a
19. c

MATCHING QUESTIONS

20. a
21. h
22. g
23. b

24. c
25. e
26. f
27. d

INTEGRATING THE MATERIAL

1. Part Two of the text is called ''The Biological Foundations of Psychology.'' Chapter 2, the first chapter of Part Two, covered the nervous system and the brain. Why was it necessary to master the information on the nervous system and the brain before approaching Chapter 3, which describes sensation? Would it have made sense for the chapters to be reversed in their order in the text? Why or why not?

2. In what ways is knowledge of the processes of sensation important to the understanding of psychology as a whole?

ACTIVITIES FOR CHAPTER REVIEW

1. Get two bowls or pots and fill one with cold water and one with warm water. Then place one hand in the cold water and leave the other hand out of water. After a few minutes, place both hands in the

warm water. The water will feel warm to the hand that has not been in any water, but will feel hot to the hand that adapted to the cold water first. What does this experiment reveal about our sensory experience?

2. Fill in the labels that are missing from this diagram of the eye.

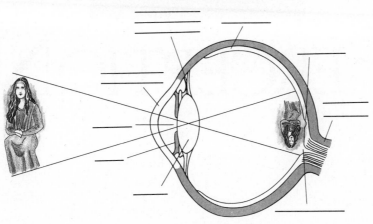

3. Fill in the labels that are missing from this diagram of the ear.

Inner Ear

Semicircular canals
(contain otolith)

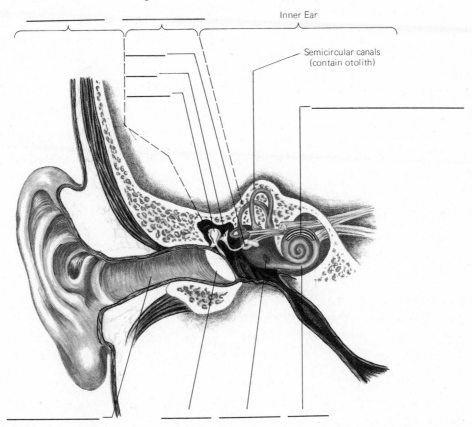

4. To appreciate the senses, try doing without one of your senses for a short time. Take a 10-minute walk with a friend while you are blindfolded. Do not talk to your friend during the 10 minutes. Use your olfactory, auditory, tactile, and other senses to become aware of the environment. Ask your friend to record your behavior while you are unable to see. How dependent are you on your sense of vision? What strategies could you use to adapt to the world if you were blind?

CHAPTER 4

PERCEPTION

CHAPTER OVERVIEW

Chapter 4 covers the topic of perception—the sorting out, interpretation, analysis, and integration of stimuli from our sensory organs. Perception is a deeper process than sensation. Whereas sensation enables us to detect stimuli in the environment, perception enables us to organize and interpret what is detected. Chapter 4 is divided into three sections.

I. The first section of the chapter explains the gestalt laws of perceptual organization, set forth in the early 1900s. These principles, which apply to both visual and auditory stimuli, include closure, proximity, similarity, and simplicity. These principles help us make sense out of our complex environment. The processes involved in the differentiation of figure and ground illustrate a key point emphasized by gestalt psychologists: We do not simply respond passively to visual stimuli that fall on the retina; rather, we actively organize and try to make sense out of what we see. Thus perception is an active, constructive process in which we go beyond the stimuli that are presented to us in an attempt to construct a meaning. Because perception involves more than merely sensing a stimulus, gestalt psychologists argue that the whole is greater than the sum of the parts; that is, our perceptions go beyond the sum of the individual elements that are sensed because meaning is imposed. One important outgrowth of the notion of active perceptual processing is perceptual constancy, a phenomenon in which physical objects are perceived as unvarying and consistent, despite changes in their appearance or in the physical environment. For example, we perceive people to be of normal size even when they are viewed from far away. In addition to size constancy, perceptual constancy occurs with shape and color. Two competing theories try to explain the phenomenon of perceptual constancy: unconscious inference theory (which suggests that we use our prior experience about the size of an object to make unconscious inferences about its location) and ecological theory (which suggests that the relationships among different objects in a scene give us clues about their size).

II. The second section of the chapter explains the perception of depth, the perception of motion, and selective attention. We are able to perceive the world in three dimensions even though our retinas are capable of sensing only two-dimensional images. Binocular disparity enables the brain to estimate distance by reconciling the discrepancy between the images that reach the retina of each eye. With only one eye we can perceive depth and distance through the use of monocular cues, including motion parallax and linear perspective. The movement of images across the retina, combined with information about head and eye movements, brings about the perception of motion. Perception occurs with both top-down and bottom-up processing. Top-down processing is guided by higher-level knowledge, experience, expectations, and motivations. Bottom-up processing consists of recognizing and processing information about the individual components of the stimuli. These two types of processing occur simultaneously and interact to help us make sense of the world around us. Selective attention—the perceptual process of choosing which stimulus to pay attention to at a particular point in time—is another process which helps us make sense out of the environment.

III. This section of the chapter places perception in the context of everyday life. Many visual illusions are described. Visual illusions are physical stimuli that consistently produce errors in perception. Among the most common are the Poggendorf illusion and the Muller-Lyer illusion. Explanations for visual illusions concentrate either on the eye's visual sensory apparatus itself or on the interpretation that is given to a figure by the brain. The perceptual problem of dyslexia is described. Dyslexia is a perceptually based reading disability which affects about 10 percent of all Americans. It is characterized by the reversal of letters, the confusion of right and left, and the making of unusual and obvious spelling errors.

STUDY STRATEGY

Follow this strategy for *each* section of the chapter.

1. Review the CHAPTER OUTLINE up to Recap and Review I.

2. Read the CHAPTER OVERVIEW, Section I.

3. Read the chapter in the text up to Recap and Review I.

4. For any question you answered incorrectly or did not understand, go back to the parts of the text that cover that material.

5. Write your answers to the REVIEW QUESTIONS for Section I in the *Study Guide*. Consult the answer key only after you have finished. Then correct any mistakes.

6. After you have completed the REVIEW QUESTIONS for Section I and have corrected your mistakes, follow the STUDY STRATEGY for Section II. Do the same for each section until you have completed all REVIEW QUESTIONS.

7. Complete the INTEGRATING THE MATERIAL questions at the end of the *Study Guide* chapter. Answering these questions will help you see how the material fits together.

And, don't forget:

Go back to the parts of the text that cover material that was difficult for you. If you still don't understand a concept, ask your teacher for clarification. Your questions in class and your teacher's answers will help other students as well.

MASTERY QUESTIONS

After mastering Chapter 4, you will be able to answer the following questions:

What principles underlie our organization of the stimuli to which our sense organs are exposed, allowing us to make sense of our environment?

How are we able to perceive the world in three dimensions when our retinas are capable of sensing only two-dimensional images?

How do we sort out auditory stimuli, paying attention to particular stimuli and ignoring others?

What clues do visual illusions give us in better understanding our general perceptual mechanisms?

REVIEW QUESTIONS: SECTION I

FILL IN THE BLANKS

1. ''The whole is greater than the sum of the parts'' is a principle of _____ psychology.

2. Elements that are _____ in appearance are grouped together.

3. The gestalt principle of _____ states that elements that are closer together are grouped together.

4. The ability to perceive a drawing consisting of a few lines as the face of a person is an example of _____.

5. The tendency to complete figures is called _____.

6. Knowing that a person who is standing far away is still of normal size even though he or she looks very small is an example of _____ _____.

7. An apple still appears red in the darkness because of _____ _____.

8. A table still appears rectangular even though its image on the retina may be trapezoidal because of _____ _____.

9. Another word for gestalt is _____.

10. When we observe a pattern, we perceive it in the most basic manner that we can according to the overriding gestalt principle of _____.

11. _____ _____ theory suggests that we use our prior experience about the size of an object to infer its location.

12. According to _____ theory, we consider the scene as a whole to bring about perceptual constancy.

MULTIPLE CHOICE

13. Closure refers to

    a. the basic element.
    b. filling in gaps.
    c. constancy.
    d. grouping together like elements.

14. The gestalt laws of organization are named for

    a. principles developed in England at the turn of the century.
    b. Dr. Hermann Gestalt, the founder of the movement.
    c. a group of German psychologists who studied patterns.
    d. the basic processes of sensory awareness.

15. "The whole is greater than the sum of the parts" refers to

    a. the mathematical nature of perception.
    b. our ability to view individual elements of a gestalt separately.
    c. our accumulated experiences in perceiving the same objects during the course of development.
    d. meaningful perceptions based on constructive processes carried out in the brain.

16. Look at these letters: *ppp ppp ppp ppp*. You see four groups, each containing three *p*'s, rather than a single row of twelve *p*'s because of the gestalt principle known as

    a. similarity.
    b. proximity.
    c. closure.
    d. constancy.

17. When we observe a pattern, we perceive it in the most basic and straightforward manner that we can, according to the gestalt principle of

    a. simplicity.
    b. constancy.
    c. closure.
    d. constancy.

18. Objects are perceived as unvarying despite changes in their appearance or the surrounding environment because of

    a. similarity.
    b. simplicity.
    c. closure.
    d. constancy.

19. According to the principle of perceptual constancy

    a. your red sports car appears to be red even in the darkness of night.
    b. your friend appears to be shrinking as she walks farther and farther down the street.
    c. both a and b.
    d. neither a nor b.

20. Unconscious inference theory suggests that

    a. we use prior experience to make perceptual judgments.
    b. our ability to make perceptual judgments is inborn.
    c. we use the relationships among the objects in a scene to make perceptual judgments.
    d. perception is a passive, unconscious process.

21. The idea that perceptual constancy is brought about by direct perception of all the stimuli in a scene is the basis of

    a. unconscious inference theory.
    b. the overriding gestalt principle of simplicity.
    c. ecological theory.
    d. the principle of proximity.

MATCHING QUESTIONS

Match each term with the best description.

_f_ 22. perceptual constancy

_a_ 23. simplicity

_b_ 24. closure

_g_ 25. similarity

_e_ 26. proximity

_d_ 27. figure

_c_ 28. ecological theory

a. the overriding gestalt principle

b. the tendency to complete figures

c. the direct perception of all stimuli in a scene

d. the object being perceived

e. the tendency to group elements that are close together

f. the principle that objects do not vary in spite of changes in their appearance

g. the tendency to group elements that look alike

ANSWER KEY: SECTION I

FILL IN THE BLANKS

1. gestalt
2. similar
3. proximity
4. closure
5. closure
6. perceptual constancy

7. perceptual constancy
8. perceptual constancy
9. pattern
10. simplicity
11. unconscious inference
12. ecological

MULTIPLE CHOICE

13. b
14. c
15. d
16. b
17. a

18. d
19. a
20. a
21. c

MATCHING QUESTIONS

22. f
23. a
24. b
25. g

26. e
27. d
28. c

REVIEW QUESTIONS: SECTION II

FILL IN THE BLANKS

1. _____ perception is the ability to view the world in three dimensions and to perceive distance.

2. Distant objects appear to be closer together than nearer objects because of _____ _____.

3. _____ listening is a procedure in which a person wears earphones through which different messages are sent to each ear at the same time.

4. Repeating a message that you are listening to is called _____.

5. _____ attention is the perceptual process of choosing a stimulus to attend to.

6. Relative size is an example of a _____ cue.

7. We can obtain a sense of _____ and _____ with just one eye through the use of monocular cues.

8. The perception of the movement of objects as the head moves is called _____ _____.

9. Different images reach the retina of each eye and allow the brain to estimate distance through _____ _____.

10. Generally speaking, the farther away a _____ is, the less the retinal disparity.

11. _____-_____ processing is guided by higher-level knowledge, experience, expectations, and motivations.

12. _____-_____ processing consists of recognizing and processing information about the individual components of the stimuli.

MULTIPLE CHOICE

13. Dichotic listening and shadowing are procedures for studying

    a. binocular disparity.
    b. selective attention.
    c. motion parallax.
    d. linear perspective.

14. Railroad tracks appear to come closer together as they move away from the observer as a result of

    a. linear perspective.
    b. figure/ground.
    c. binocular disparity.
    d. motion parallax.

15. The images projected on the retinas of both eyes are

    a. in motion even when the head is still.
    b. three-dimensional.
    c. in linear perspective.
    d. slightly different from each other.

16. Which one of the following statements concerning depth perception is true?

    a. It is not always necessary to use two eyes to perceive depth.
    b. Distant objects appear smaller because of linear perspective.
    c. The greater the discrepancy between two retinal images, the more difficult it is to reconcile depth.
    d. If two objects are the same size, the one that projects the smaller image on the retina is closer.

17. It is easiest to shadow messages that are

    a. loud.
    b. repetitious.
    ⓒ meaningful.
    d. delayed.

18. Motion parallax is

    ⓐ a monocular cue for depth perception.
    b. the change in position of an object on the retina as the head moves from side to side.
    c. neither a nor b.
    ⓓ both a and b.

19. By using two cameras to create the perception of a third dimension, people who make 3-D movies are employing the principle of

    ⓐ binocular disparity.
    b. motion parallax.
    c. top-down processing.
    d. shadowing.

20. Top-down processing allows you to

    a. perceive depth with one eye.
    ⓑ fill in the gaps.
    c. perceive motion.
    d. concentrate on individual elements of a stimulus.

MATCHING QUESTIONS

Match each term with the best description.

  _d_ 21. shadowing

  _c_ 22. binocular disparity

  _f_ 23. linear perspective

  _e_ 24. depth perception

  _b_ 25. selective attention

  _a_ 26. monocular cue

  a. motion parallax

  b. the process of filtering out information

  c. the difference between two retinal images

  d. repeating a message as it is heard

  e. perceiving three dimensions and distance

  f. a monocular depth cue

ANSWER KEY: SECTION II

FILL IN THE BLANKS

1. depth

2. linear perspective

3. dichotic

4. shadowing

5. selective

6. monocular

7. depth; distance

8. motion parallax

9. binocular disparity

10. stimulus (object)

11. top-down

12. bottom-up

MULTIPLE CHOICE

13. b   17. c
14. a   18. d
15. d   19. a
16. a   20. b

MATCHING QUESTIONS

21. d   24. e
22. c   25. b
23. f   26. a

REVIEW QUESTIONS: SECTION III

FILL IN THE BLANKS

1. In the case of visual illusions, _____ do not match the physical reality of the stimulus.

2. A visual illusion is a physical stimulus that consistently produces errors in _____.

3. Two examples of visual illusions are the _____ illusion and the _____-_____ illusion.

4. _____ is a reading disability caused by perceptual difficulties.

5. Dyslexia can result in the _____ of letters during reading and spelling.

MULTIPLE CHOICE

6. A visual illusion is a physical stimulus that is

   a. consistent in producing errors in perception.
   b. often called an optical illusion.
   c. both a and b.
   d. neither a nor b.

7. Illusions are caused by

   a. the brain's interpretive errors.
   b. poor vision.
   c. dyslexia.
   d. reading problems.

8. Dyslexia is often associated with

   a. low intelligence.
   b. spelling problems.
   c. cultural differences.
   d. selective attention.

9. About ____ percent of Americans suffer from dyslexia.

   a. 1
   b. 5
   c. 10
   d. 25

10. Someone with dyslexia would be most likely to

    a. perceive two lines of the same length as lines of different lengths.
    b. perceive a faraway object as truly smaller than a nearby object.
    c. mistake *ab* for *ad*.
    d. mistake a three-dimensional object for a two-dimensional picture.

11. The perception of visual illusions is most affected by

    a. cultural differences.
    b. age differences.
    c. sex differences.
    d. socioeconomic differences.

12. Visual illusions are caused by

    a. expectations.
    b. ambiguous stimuli
    c. both a and b.
    d. neither a nor b.

13. Confusion of left and right is most closely associated with

    a. the Muller-Lyer illusion.
    b. the Poggendorf illusion.
    c. cultural differences.
    d. dyslexia.

14. It is *not* true that dyslexia

    a. responds well to appropriate educational techniques.
    b. goes hand in hand with lower IQ scores.
    c. is associated with poor spelling.
    d. affects about 10 percent of the population.

MATCHING QUESTIONS

Match each term with the best description.

_____ 15. dyslexia

_____ 16. visual illusion

_____ 17. Poggendorf illusion

_____ 18. Muller-Lyer illusion

a. has one line that appears longer than the other

b. has lines that appear as though they would not meet

c. is a perceptual disorder

d. is a physical stimulus that produces errors in judgment

ANSWER KEY: SECTION III

FILL IN THE BLANKS

1. judgments
2. perception
3. Poggendorf; Muller-Lyer
4. dyslexia
5. reversal (confusion)

MULTIPLE CHOICE

6. c
7. a
8. b
9. c
10. c

11. a
12. b
13. d
14. b

MATCHING QUESTIONS

15. c
16. d

17. b
18. a

INTEGRATING THE MATERIAL

1. Chapter 4 is the third and final chapter in Part Two of the text, "The Biological Foundations of Psychology." Chapter 2 covered the nervous system and the brain, and Chapter 3 covered the topic of sensation. In what ways does this chapter build on the foundation provided in the two earlier chapters? Why could this chapter not have come first?

2. How is the process of perception different from the process of sensation?

3. How might the topic of perception be relevant to an understanding of the field of psychology as a whole?

ACTIVITIES FOR CHAPTER REVIEW

1. Examine this figure: **13**   Is it the letter B or the number 13? Examine it again in the

following sequences:

A   13   C   D
12   13   14   15

What makes it look like a letter in the first sentence but like a number in the second sequence? What principle of gestalt psychology does this demonstrate?

2. Look at the objects in the room you are in right now as though there were no such thing as perceptual constancy. Instead of seeing the door or table as rectangular, look at its shape as it actually appears on your retina. This is a difficult task, because perceptual constancy is taken for granted and provides us with consistency, despite natural changes in the environment. If you can let go of the constancy, describe the objects as they *really* look. What are their shapes and features? What would the world be like if we did not have the capacity for perceptual constancy?

3. Look at the Necker cube shown below. Stare at it until it reverses. What makes this visual illusion work?

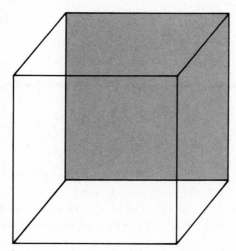

4. Look at the following figure. What do you see? Keep looking.

CHAPTER
5
LEARNING

CHAPTER OVERVIEW

Chapter 5 discusses the many aspects of learning. This is a fundamental topic for psychologists, because learning underlies such diverse areas of the field as development, motivation and emotion, personality, and social psychology. The learning process also underlies many psychotherapeutic processes which are aimed at bringing about lasting change. Although there are many different types of learning, one definition encompasses all of them: Learning is a relatively permanent change in behavior brought about by experience. This definition distinguishes learning from maturation, a natural growth process that is relatively unaffected by experience or practice.

Chapter 5 is divided into four sections.

I.   The first section of the chapter focuses on the principles of classical conditioning which apply to both animal and human behavior. Pavlov's classical conditioning experiments on dogs in the 1920s demonstrated that when a previously neutral stimulus (such as the sound of a tuning fork) is repeatedly paired with a conditioned stimulus (such as meat powder) it will eventually elicit an involuntary physiological response (such as salivation) when presented alone. Thus the dogs learned to salivate to the sound of the tuning fork because of its association with meat powder. In this case, salivation is the unconditioned response (UCR), the meat powder is the unconditioned stimulus (UCS), and the sound of the tuning fork is the conditioned stimulus (CS). Since Pavlov's experiments with animals, it has been established that the principles of classical conditioning have applications to human behavior as well and underlie many types of everyday learning, including the acquisition of emotional responses. Some of the basic phenomena of classical conditioning that are important to understand include extinction, systematic desensitization, spontaneous recovery, stimulus generalization, stimulus discrimination, and higher-order conditioning.

II. The second section of the chapter introduces the topic of operant conditioning. Operant conditioning is learning in which we make responses as a result of positive or negative consequences that are contingent upon (or dependent on) those responses. Unlike classical conditioning, in which the responses are biologically based and the learning involves making the same response to a new stimulus, operant conditioning applies to the learning of new responses that are voluntary and are produced to achieve a certain outcome. In operant conditioning, the organism operates on the environment. As in the case of classical conditioning, the principles of operant conditioning were established through experiments with animals. Thorndike's work with cats formed the basis for the law of effect, which states that responses that are satisfying are more likely to be repeated and those that are not satisfying are less likely to be repeated. B. F. Skinner is considered the founder of modern principles of operant conditioning, all based on the concept of reinforcement. A reinforcer is any stimulus that increases the probability that a preceding behavior will occur again. Food is considered a primary reinforcer because it satisfies a primary drive; money is considered a secondary reinforcer because it obtains its power through its association with obtaining primary reinforcers. What makes something a reinforcer can be individualistic. It is important to be able to distinguish among three concepts of reinforcement: a positive reinforcer (a stimulus added to the environment that brings about an increase in a preceding response), a negative reinforcer (a stimulus whose removal is reinforcing), and punishment (an unpleasant or painful stimulus that is added to the environment to decrease the probability that the preceding behavior will reoccur). Reinforcing desired behavior is a more appropriate and effective technique for modifying behavior than is using punishment.

III. The third section of the chapter goes into more detail in describing operant conditioning. There are different schedules of reinforcement which vary in terms of frequency and timing. Partial reinforcement schedules result in stronger, longer-lasting learning than continuous reinforcement schedules. There are schedules that consider the number of responses made before reinforcement is given (fixed-ratio and variable-ratio schedules), and there are schedules that consider the amount of time that elapses before reinforcement is provided (fixed-interval and variable-interval schedules). Variable-interval schedules are more likely to produce steady rates of responding. Superstitious behavior is learned through operant conditioning and may shape subsequent behavior. The Premack principle suggests that what is reinforcing to one person may be aversive to another and that higher-ranked reinforcers can be used as incentives for performing less desired activities. Other key principles of operant conditioning include generalization, discrimination, and shaping. Applications of operant conditioning, such as the use of computers in the classroom for teaching programmed instruction, are described. Although the difference between classical and operant conditioning is usually clear and should be understood, there may be some overlap in certain kinds of behaviors. This section of the chapter ends with a description of biological constraints on learning which aid, prevent, or inhibit learning.

IV. The fourth and final section of the chapter covers cognitive approaches to learning and a review of behavior modification techniques. Bandura's observational learning studies are described, emphasizing the important role of observation and imitation in the acquisition of behavior, both positive and negative. Seligman's concept of learned helplessness is then examined. The chapter ends with a discussion and illustration of how behavioral analysis and behavior modification techniques can be used to help people function more effectively in such areas as weight loss and time management.

STUDY STRATEGY

Follow this strategy for *each* section of the chapter.

1. Review the CHAPTER OUTLINE up to Recap and Review I.

2. Read the CHAPTER OVERVIEW, Section I.

3. Read the chapter in the text up to Recap and Review I.

4. For any question you answered incorrectly or did not understand, go back to the parts of the text that cover that material.

5. Write your answers to the REVIEW QUESTIONS for Section I in the *Study Guide*. Consult the answer key only after you have finished. Then correct any mistakes.

6. After you have completed the REVIEW QUESTIONS for Section I and have corrected your mistakes, follow the STUDY STRATEGY for Section II. Do the same for each section until you have completed all REVIEW QUESTIONS.

7. Complete the INTEGRATING THE MATERIAL questions at the end of the *Study Guide* chapter. Answering these questions will help you see how the material fits together.

And, don't forget:

Go back to the parts of the text that cover material that was difficult for you. If you still don't understand a concept, ask your teacher for clarification. Your questions in class and your teacher's answers will help other students as well.

MASTERY QUESTIONS

After mastering Chapter 5, you will be able to answer the following questions:

What are the different forms of learning, and how can we differentiate among them?

What is the role of reward and punishment in learning?

What is the role of thinking in learning?

How can we formally analyze behavior, and how does this lead to techniques for modifying and controlling it?

What are some practical methods for bringing about behavior change, both in others and in ourselves?

REVIEW QUESTIONS: SECTION I

FILL IN THE BLANKS

1. Learning is a relatively _____ change in behavior brought about by experience.

2. In _____ conditioning, discovered by _____ _____, an organism learns to respond to a stimulus that does not ordinarily bring about that response.

3. A potential stimulus that has no effect on a particular response is called a(n) _____ stimulus.

4. A stimulus which naturally causes a response is known as a(n) _____ stimulus, and it causes a(n) _____ response.

5. A stimulus introduced a number of times just before the natural stimulus for a certain response will eventually produce the desired response on its own; at this point it is called a(n) _____ stimulus producing a(n) _____ response.

6. When a previously conditioned response becomes weaker and eventually disappears, _____ has occurred.

7. Psychologists use a form of therapy called _____ _____ to bring about the _____ of phobias.

8. A previously extinguished response may return through _____ _____, but it will be _____ than it originally was.

9. Stimulus _____ occurs when a conditioned response follows a stimulus that is similar to the original conditioned stimulus.

10. When a conditioned stimulus established during earlier conditioning becomes paired with a neutral stimulus so that the neutral stimulus now evokes a conditioned response similar to the original one, _____ - _____ conditioning has occurred.

11. When smoke gets in your eyes, your eyes automatically blink. The blinking is an example of a(n) _____ response.

12. The sound of a bell, a neutral stimulus, is paired with blowing smoke into your eyes. After a few pairings, the sound of the bell alone makes your eyes blink. In this case, the blinking is a(n) _____ response.

MULTIPLE CHOICE

13. The changes in behavior brought about by learning are

    a. hard to measure.
    b. easily extinguished.
    c. relatively permanent.
    d. generally maturational.

14. Since we cannot actually see learning take place, it is referred to as a(n) _____ process.

    a. conditioned
    b. inferred
    c. unconditioned
    d. neutral

15. A neutral stimulus

    a. has no effect.
    b. cannot be conditioned.
    c. cannot be extinguished.
    d. is the same as an unconditioned stimulus.

16. A stimulus which automatically causes the response of interest is a(n) _____ stimulus.

    a. unconditioned
    b. conditioned
    c. neutral
    d. spontaneous

17. A child who is afraid of white mice also comes to fear white cats and rabbits. This is the result of

    a. spontaneous recovery.
    b. classical conditioning.
    c. stimulus generalization.
    d. extinction.

18. Most of Pavlov's subjects were

    a. cats.
    b. dogs.
    c. humans.
    d. rats

19. Unconditioned stimulus–unconditioned response pairings are

    a. a consequence of learning and training.
    b. unlearned and untrained.
    c. not applicable to human behavior.
    d. easily extinguished.

20. A neutral stimulus that follows an unconditioned stimulus

    a. can become very powerful in eliciting the response of interest.
    b. will elicit a conditioned response.
    c. will elicit an unconditioned response.
    d. has little chance of becoming a conditioned stimulus.

MATCHING QUESTIONS

Match each term with the best description.

_____ 21. neutral stimulus

_____ 22. conditioned stimulus

_____ 23. unconditioned stimulus

_____ 24. conditioned response

_____ 25. unconditioned response

a. can be extinguished

b. has no effect on the response of interest

c. occurs naturally

d. is not associated with previously learning

e. produces the response of interest

ANSWER KEY: SECTION I

FILL IN THE BLANKS

1. permanent

2. classical; Ivan Pavlov

3. neutral

4. unconditioned; unconditioned

5. conditioned; conditioned

6. extinction

7. systematic desensitization; extinction

8. spontaneous recovery; weaker

9. generalization

10. higher-order

11. unconditioned

12. conditioned

MULTIPLE CHOICE

13. c

14. b

15. a

16. a

17. c

18. b

19. b

20. d

MATCHING QUESTIONS

21. b

22. e

23. c

24. a

25. d

REVIEW QUESTIONS: SECTION II

FILL IN THE BLANKS

1. In _____ conditioning, people make responses because they have learned that positive consequences are _____ upon the response.

2. The term _____ emphasizes the point that organisms operate on the environment to produce some desired result.

3. Thorndike's _____ _____ _____ states that responses that satisfy are more likely to be _____.

4. Any stimulus that increases the probability that a preceding response will occur again is called a _____.

5. Reinforcements that satisfy some biological need and work naturally, regardless of a person's prior experience, are known as _____ _____.

6. We know that money is a _____ reinforcer which allows us to obtain other desirable objects, including food and shelter, which are _____ reinforcers.

7. When a stimulus brings about an increase in a preceding response, it is called a(n) _____ reinforcer.

8. When the removal of a stimulus, such as shock, leads to an increase in the probability that a preceding behavior will occur in the future, _____ _____ is occurring.

9. _____ is the administration of an unpleasant stimulus following a response and is meant to suppress behavior.

10. Punishment may consist of the removal of a(n) _____ reinforcer.

11. A(n) _____ reinforcer is effective only if a person has had prior experience with it.

12. Reinforcing desired behavior is a better technique for promoting learning than is _____.

MULTIPLE CHOICE

13. Learning in which positive or negative consequences are contingent upon a response is known as

    a. classical conditioning.
    b. Pavlovian conditioning.
    c. operant conditioning.
    d. higher-order conditioning.

14. Thorndike's law of effect is based on the principles of

    a. operant conditioning.
    b. classical conditioning.
    c. punishment.
    d. systematic desensitization.

15. Which one of the following is true?

    a. A negative reinforcer involves the introduction of an unpleasant stimulus.
    b. Punishment and negative reinforcement are the same.
    c. A primary reinforcer must be biologically satisfying.
    d. A positive reinforcement must be biologically satisfying.

16. Of the following, the most dangerous route to behavioral change is

    a. negative reinforcement.
    b. punishment.
    c. secondary reinforcement.
    d. contingency training.

17. An example of negative reinforcement is

    a. hitting a dog for tearing up a sofa.
    b. pairing a neutral stimulus with a feared stimulus to produce learning.
    c. promising to buy a child a toy for good behavior and then not buying it.
    d. letting an adolescent who has been grounded go to the movies because of improved behavior.

18. Operant conditioning applies to

    a. voluntary responses.
    b. involuntary responses.
    c. unobservable responses.
    d. biological responses.

19. Thorndike's experiments demonstrated that

    a. punishment is a dangerous way to produce behavioral change.
    b. classical conditioning is easily achieved if it is done correctly.
    c. negative reinforcement is the removal of an aversive stimulus.
    d. satisfying responses are likely to be repeated.

MATCHING QUESTIONS

Match each term with the best description.

_____ 20. reinforcer

_____ 21. primary reinforcer

_____ 22. secondary reinforcer

_____ 23. positive reinforcer

_____ 24. negative reinforcer

_____ 25. punishment

a. satisfies a biological need

b. is given to increase the occurrence of the preceding response

c. is any stimulus whose removal is reinforcing

d. becomes reinforcing because of an association

e. is any stimulus that increases the probability of the reoccurrence of the preceding response

f. results in a decrease in the probability that a behavior will occur again

ANSWER KEY: SECTION II

FILL IN THE BLANKS

1. operant; contingent (dependent)
2. operant
3. law of effect; repeated
4. reinforcer
5. primary reinforcers
6. secondary; primary

7. positive
8. negative reinforcement
9. punishment
10. positive
11. secondary
12. punishment

MULTIPLE CHOICE

13. c
14. a
15. c
16. b

17. d
18. a
19. d

MATCHING QUESTIONS

20. e
21. a
22. d

23. b
24. c
25. f

REVIEW QUESTIONS: SECTION III

FILL IN THE BLANKS

1. Schedules of reinforcement refer to the _____ and _____ of reinforcement following desired behavior.

2. In _____ reinforcement, behavior is reinforced every time it occurs; behavior that is reinforced some but not all of the time is said to be on a(n) _____ - _____ _____.

3. Patterns of responses made in reaction to a particular schedule are automatically recorded and graphed using a(n) _____ _____.

4. Reinforcement on a(n) _____ - _____ schedule occurs after a varying number of responses rather than a fixed number.

5. In a(n) _____ - _____ _____, reinforcement is given only after a certain number of responses.

6. Fixed- and variable-interval schedules focus on the amount of _____ since a person or animal was rewarded.

7. A weekly paycheck is a good example of reinforcement on a _____ - _____ schedule.

8. Slot machines in Atlantic City are on a _____ - _____ schedule.

9. Wearing a special shirt to take a test or to go on a job interview is an example of _____ behavior.

10. The Premack principle reminds us that reinforcements are _____.

11. The _____ principle states that organisms have different preferences for performing various behaviors and that preferences can be rank-ordered.

12. _____ is the process of teaching a complex behavior by rewarding closer and closer approximations of the desired behavior.

13. Carefully constructed for the computer, _____ _____ has proved to be an effective teaching technique.

14. In classical conditioning, the _____ stimulus precedes the response; in operant conditioning, the _____ is made prior to the reinforcement.

MULTIPLE CHOICE

15. When behavior is reinforced every time it occurs, a _____ reinforcement schedule is being used.

    a. cumulative
    b. constant
    c. continuous
    d. conventional

16. Slot machine payoffs are examples of

    a. primary reinforcement.
    b. partial reinforcement.
    c. fixed reinforcement.
    d. negative reinforcement.

17. Since the number of responses made by a door-to-door salesperson before reinforcement in the form of a sale is not certain, he or she is working on a

    a. variable-ratio schedule.
    b. fixed-ratio schedule.
    c. variable-interval schedule.
    d. fixed-interval schedule.

18. A high rate of response and a high resistance to extinction are provided by

    a. continuous reinforcement.
    b. any reinforcement schedule.
    c. variable-ratio schedules.
    d. fixed-interval schedules.

19. With a fixed-interval schedule, especially in the period just after reinforcement, response rates are

    a. speeded up.
    b. extinguished.
    c. relatively unchanged.
    d. relatively low.

20. Just as in classical conditioning, the principle of generalization is

    a. also applicable in operant conditioning.
    b. applicable only to partial reinforcement schedules.
    c. both a and b.
    d. neither a nor b.

21. The process of teaching a complex behavior by rewarding closer and closer approximations of the desired behavior is known as

    a. scheduling.
    b. shaping.
    c. the Premack principle.
    d. response generalization.

22. Reinforcing studying behavior with the opportunity to go to the movies is an application of

    a. the Premack principle.
    b. superstitious behavior.
    c. schedules of reinforcement.
    d. shaping.

23. Programmed instruction represents one of the most common applications of

    a. shaping.
    b. the Premack principle.
    c. variable reinforcement.
    d. classical conditioning.

MATCHING QUESTIONS

Match each example with the appropriate schedule of reinforcement. Letters may be used more than once.

_____ 24. weekly paycheck

_____ 25. slot machines

_____ 26. surprise quizzes

_____ 27. rewarding a rat every time it presses a lever

_____ 28. receiving gifts now and then

_____ 29. receiving a commission after every three sales

a. fixed-interval schedule

b. fixed-ratio schedule

c. variable-interval schedule

d. variable-ratio schedule

e. continuous reinforcement schedule

ANSWER KEY: SECTION III

FILL IN THE BLANKS

1. frequency; timing
2. continuous; variable-reinforcement schedule
3. cumulative recorder
4. variable-ratio
5. fix-ratio schedule
6. time
7. fixed-interval
8. variable-ratio
9. superstitious
10. individualistic
11. Premack
12. shaping
13. programmed instruction
14. unconditioned; response

MULTIPLE CHOICE

15. c
16. b
17. a
18. c
19. d
20. a
21. b
22. a
23. a

MATCHING QUESTIONS

24. a
25. d
26. c
27. e
28. c
29. b

REVIEW QUESTIONS: SECTION IV

FILL IN THE BLANKS

1. _____ _____ theory focuses on the thought processes that underlie learning.

2. In the phenomenon known as _____ learning, new behaviors are learned but are not demonstrated until reinforcement is provided.

3. Albert Bandura is a psychologist known for his theory of _____ learning.

4. In observational learning, new behaviors are learned through _____ of what is observed.

5. A student who feels that no matter how hard she studies, she will never get good grades may be experiencing learned _____.

6. _____ _____ is a formalized technique for promoting the frequency of desirable behaviors and decreasing the incidence of unwanted ones.

7. By using a technique known as _____ _____, we can teach ourselves to make better use of our time.

MULTIPLE CHOICE

8. Creating a schedule in which you allow yourself two hours of study time for each hour spent in class is an example of

   a. continuous reinforcement.
   b. time management.
   c. cognitive learning.
   d. modeling.

9. Formalized techniques for promoting the frequency of desired behaviors and decreasing the incidence of those which are unwanted are known as

   a. latent learning techniques.
   b. observational learning.
   c. behavior modification.
   d. cognitive learning methods.

10. Rats that appear to have learned their way through a maze but will not run it until they are rewarded demonstrate latent learning. Theorists believe that rats do this by developing

    a. a cognitive map.
    b. an observational model.
    c. learned helplessness.
    d. unmotivated behavior.

11. A 3-year-old girl does not speak because everything is done for her without her having to ask. Suddenly, when a need is not attended to, she speaks in complete sentences. This behavior is an example of

    a. modeling.
    b. learned helplessness.
    c. shaping.
    d. latent learning.

12. Psychologists specializing in behavior modification are known as

    a. cognitive psychologists.
    b. observational researchers.
    c. behavior analysts.
    d. experimental psychologists.

13. Learned helplessness results from

    a. exposure to inescapable punishment.
    b. observing aggressive behavior.
    c. the removal of continuous reinforcement.
    d. a lack of cognitive awareness.

14. The observational theory of learning was developed by

    a. Skinner.
    b. Watson.
    c. Tolman.
    d. Bandura.

15. According to observational learning theory,

    a. the observation of aggressive behavior that is reinforced will be imitated.
    b. the observation of gentle behavior that is reinforced will be imitated.
    c. both a and b are true.
    d. neither a nor b is true.

MATCHING QUESTIONS

Match each term with the best description.

_____ 16. cognitive learning theory

_____ 17. observational learning

_____ 18. learned helplessness

_____ 19. behavior modification

_____ 20. cognitive map

a. promotes increased frequency of desired behaviors

b. is the feeling of having no control over the environment

c. is concerned with unseen mental processes

d. produces behavior through imitation of a model

e. allows for latent learning

ANSWER KEY: SECTION IV

FILL IN THE BLANKS

1. cognitive learning

2. latent

3. observational

4. imitation

5. helplessness

6. behavior modification

7. time management

MULTIPLE CHOICE

8. b

9. c

10. a

11. d

12. c

13. a

14. d

15. c

MATCHING QUESTIONS

16. c

17. d

18. b

19. a

20. e

INTEGRATING THE MATERIAL

1. In what ways are classical and operant conditioning alike and in what ways are they different?

2. Give examples from your own life which demonstrate the impact of classical conditioning, operant conditioning, and cognitive learning.

3. To what extent do you think the principles of learning described in this chapter have an impact on the development of personality? On the development of emotions? On the development of social behavior? Give examples.

ACTIVITIES FOR CHAPTER REVIEW

1. Discuss with a friend a fear that you have—a fear of cats, mice, insects, being home alone, or any other fear that you can think of. How did you acquire the fear? Can you see any connection between acquiring the fear and the laws of classical conditioning? How might the fear be explained through conditioning? Has the fear reached the level of higher-order conditioning? In what ways?

2. Interview someone you know who is in sales. What happens to his or her motivation when there is a long time between successful sales of the product? How does he or she feel immediately following a sale? Does behavior change? How? For how long?

3. Observe your own behavior with a vending machine you use regularly. What happens when it doesn't respond immediately (that is, your money gets ''hung up'')? What happens if it doesn't work at all? How strongly are you conditioned to expect immediate reinforcement from the machine?

4. At your school's computer center, or with your own or a friend's personal computer, familiarize yourself with the personal computer and the methods of learning that it offers.

5. Try some modeling behavior (positive, of course) with a younger brother or sister or another young person that you know. Does the younger person seem to follow Bandura's four observational learning steps?

6. Design a time management plan for yourself. In what areas can you better manage your time?

CHAPTER
6
MEMORY

CHAPTER OVERVIEW

Chapter 6 examines the topic of memory. The storage and retrieval of information, various types of memory, theories of forgetting, and the biological foundations of memory are described.

Chapter 6 is divided into three sections.

I.   The first section of the chapter covers the three R's of memory: recording, retaining, and retrieving information. Each of these three processes represents a different aspect of remembering. Recording information puts it in a form usable by memory; retaining the information stores it for later use; and retrieving the information from storage brings it back into awareness. There are three stages of memory which vary in terms of their function and the length of time information is retained:

1.   Sensory memory (the initial momentary storage of information, lasting only an instant, where information is recorded by the person's sensory system as a raw, nonmeaningful stimulus)

2.   Short-term memory (where information is held for 15 to 25 seconds and is stored in terms of its meaning rather than mere sensory stimulation)

3.   Long-term memory (where information is relatively permanent, although it may be difficult to retrieve)

An alternative view is that rather than proceeding to sequential stages of memory, information is processed at different levels. How well it is remembered depends on how well it was initially learned and mentally analyzed. According to the levels-of-processing approach, the deeper the initial level of processing, the longer the information will be retained.

II. The second section of the chapter considers how we retrieve information from long-term memory once it is stored. One reason recall is not perfect is the vast quantity of information that is stored. One way to sort out this information and find what we need is through the use of retrieval cues, stimuli that allow us to more easily recall information that is stored in long-term memory. Retrieval cues serve as a guide. The process of recognition is easier than recall because of the retrieval cues provided by the stimuli: The search requires fewer steps. Another form of retrieval involves flashbulb memories, or memories centered around a specific, important event that are so clear they seem to represent snapshots of the event. Memories reflect, in addition, a constructive process in which they are influenced by the meaning we give to events. This constructive process often results in distorted memories, since our own expectations, motivations, and perceptions affect how the information is processed. Because memory is subject to distortions, we are prone to remember events in our lives in the way we want to rather than in the way they actually happened. This distortion can have serious consequences in witness identification.

III. The third and final section of the chapter explains the process of forgetting and explores two theories of forgetting: decay and interference. Decay, an early theory, claimed that forgetting occurred through the nonuse of information. Today, however, most research suggests that we forget things not because the memory trace has decayed, but because new memories interfere with the retrieval of old ones. Proactive interference is a process in which information learned earlier interferes with recall of newer material. Retroactive interference refers to difficulty in recall of information because of later exposure to different material. Interference theory does not explain whether the information is lost or whether it becomes difficult to retrieve. Recent research is trying to determine the biological bases for memory and forgetting. The location of an engram may be dependent on the nature of the material being learned and the specific neural system that processed the information. Affliction of forgetting, including Alzheimer's disease and different types of amnesia, are discussed. The chapter ends with a description of various techniques for improving memory: the keyword technique, the method of loci, the use of context-dependent memory, the organization of information in textbooks, good note taking, and practice and rehearsal.

STUDY STRATEGY

Follow this strategy for *each* section of the chapter.

1. Review the CHAPTER OUTLINE up to Recap and Review I.

2. Read the CHAPTER OVERVIEW, Section I.

3. Read the chapter in the text up to Recap and Review I.

4. For any question you answered incorrectly or did not understand, go back to the parts of the text that cover that material.

5. Write your answers to the REVIEW QUESTIONS for Section I in the *Study Guide*. Consult the answer key only after you have finished. Then correct any mistakes.

6. After you have completed the REVIEW QUESTIONS for Section I and have corrected your mistakes, follow the STUDY STRATEGY for Section II. Do the same for each section until you have completed all REVIEW QUESTIONS.

7. Complete the INTEGRATING THE MATERIAL questions at the end of the *Study Guide* chapter. Answering these questions will help you see how the material fits together.

And, don't forget:

Go back to the parts of the text that cover material that was difficult for you. If you still don't understand a concept, ask your teacher for clarification. Your questions in class and your teacher's answers will help other students as well.

MASTERY QUESTIONS

After mastering Chapter 6, you will be able to answer the following questions:

What is memory and how does it operate?

Are there different kinds of memory?

How are we able to recall material from long ago, yet forget information to which we have been exposed very recently?

Can we improve our memory?

REVIEW QUESTIONS: SECTION I

FILL IN THE BLANKS

1. Memory is the capacity to _____, _____, and _____ information.

2. When initially encountered, visual information is stored in _____ memory.

3. When initially encountered, auditory information is stored in _____ memory.

4. A _____ is a meaningful grouping of stimuli which can be stored as a unit in short-term memory.

5. _____ - _____ memory is a relatively permanent repository for information.

6. _____ memories are related to personal experiences rather than to factual knowledge.

7. Iconic memory involves the storage of _____ information.

8. Information is refreshed in short-term memory through the process of _____.

9. Short-term memory is sometimes referred to as _____ memory.

10. The transfer of material from short- to long-term memory proceeds largely on the basis of _____.

11. _____ are basic organizational strategies that can improve our retention of information.

12. The _____ code allows us to store information abstractly without having to rely on a specific image.

13. The _____ code is memory storage that is based on visual images.

MULTIPLE CHOICE

14. According to the levels-of-processing theory, the aspect of processing that is most critical for memory is

   a. processing of background information.
   b. depth of processing during exposure to material.
   c. length of time spent reading new information.
   d. retrieval techniques.

15. Which one of the following techniques will *not* aid in the transfer of information from short-term to long-term memory?

   a. repetition
   b. rehearsal
   c. elaboration
   d. retrieval

16. Rehearsing a phone number keeps it alive in

    a. sensory memory.
    b. iconic memory.
    c. short-term memory.
    d. long-term memory.

17. An example of episodic memory is

    a. recalling a conversation with a friend.
    b. recognizing the correct answers to math problems.
    c. reciting the letters of the alphabet backward.
    d. remembering that Columbus discovered America.

18. Which one of the following contains three chunks?

    a. T F P
    b. USACIANBC
    c. cat
    d. DAVE AL STEVE

19. Information filed in long-term memory can be retrieved when

    a. it is rehearsed.
    b. we need it.
    c. chunked.
    d. episodic.

20. About how many chunks can be held in short-term memory?

    a. three
    b. seven
    c. twelve
    d. an unlimited number

21. Iconic and echoic memory are

    a. functions of short-term memory.
    b. functions of long-term memory.
    c. both a and b.
    d. neither a nor b.

MATCHING QUESTIONS

Match each term with the best description.

_____ 22. episodic memory

_____ 23. short-term memory

_____ 24. iconic storage

_____ 25. elaboration

_____ 26. chunk

_____ 27. echoic memory

_____ 28. long-term memory

a. contains visual information

b. stores information indefinitely

c. involves auditory information

d. leads to organization

e. is the working memory

f. contains personal experience

g. is a meaningful grouping of stimuli

ANSWER KEY: SECTION I

1. record; retain; retrieve
2. iconic
3. echoic
4. chunk
5. long-term
6. episodic
7. visual

8. rehearsal
9. working
10. rehearsal
11. mnemonics
12. linguistic
13. imaginal

MULTIPLE CHOICE

14. b
15. d
16. c
17. a

18. d
19. b
20. b
21. d

MATCHING QUESTIONS

22. f
23. e
24. a
25. d

26. g
27. c
28. b

REVIEW QUESTIONS: SECTION II

FILL IN THE BLANKS

1. In _____ processes, memories are influenced by the meaning given to events.

2. In _____ reproduction, inaccuracy results from personal bias and misinterpretation.

3. A _____ cue is a stimulus that allows us to more easily recall information that is located in long-term memory.

4. Recognition is easier than _____ because it involves fewer steps.

5. _____ memories are memories of specific events that are so clear they seem like snapshots of the event.

77

6. The tip-of-the-tongue phenomenon involves difficulty recalling information from _____ - _____ memory.

7. _____ suggested that people tend to remember information in terms of schemas, or general themes that contain little detail.

8. Multiple choice questions require you to _____ material stored in memory.

9. In what has been called the soap opera effect, knowledge about _____ can lead to elaboration in memory of a prior event.

10. Unlike the serial search, searching for information all at once is a more efficient process and is called the _____ search.

11. According to the _____ effect, the more distinctive a stimulus, the more likely we are to recall it later.

MULTIPLE CHOICE

12. Serial reproduction results in

   a. the tip-of-the-tongue phenomenon.
   b. inaccuracy.
   c. flashbulb memories.
   d. greater clarity of memories.

13. Someone experiencing the tip-of-the-tongue phenomenon would be helped out by

   a. a retrieval cue.
   b. the von Restorff effect.
   c. serial reproduction.
   d. rehearsal.

14. The constructive processes used in remembering

   a. need to be rehearsed.
   b. are influenced more by recognition than by recall processes.
   c. give personal meaning to events that are remembered.
   d. make the information in long-term memory more accurate.

15. Constructive processes are associated with all of the following *except*

   a. memorization.
   b. interpretation.
   c. expectation.
   d. organization.

16. Eyewitness testimony is affected by

   a. constructive processes.
   b. retrieval cues.
   c. both a and b.
   d. neither a nor b.

17. We are more likely to be able to describe a child we saw in a group of adults than a child we saw in a group of children because of

   a. flashbulb memory.
   b. a constructive process.
   c. serial reproduction.
   d. the von Restorff effect.

18. Which of the following could be a retrieval cue?

    a. the scent of perfume
    b. a phrase from a popular song
    c. both a and b
    d. neither a nor b

19. Compared with a serial search, a parallel search is more

    a. prone to errors.
    b. efficient.
    c. exhaustive.
    d. widely used for retrieval from short-term memory.

20. Flashbulb memories have all of the following qualities *except* that they are not

    a. detailed.
    b. easily retrieved.
    c. emotional.
    d. short-lived.

MATCHING QUESTIONS

Match each term with the best description.

_____ 21. flashbulb memories

_____ 22. the von Restorff effect

_____ 23. the tip-of-the-tongue phenomenon

_____ 24. constructive processes

_____ 25. retrieval cue

_____ 26. soap opera effect

a. is a stimulus for recall

b. results in difficulty with retrieval

c. are clear, detailed memories

d. is elaboration owing to knowledge of a person's motives

e. are influenced by meaning and interpretations

f. is that distinctive stimuli are easier to recall

ANSWER KEY: SECTION II

FILL IN THE BLANKS

1. constructive

2. serial

3. retrieval

4. recall

5. flashbulb

6. long-term

7. Bartlett

8. recognize

9. motivation

10. parallel

11. von Restorff

MULTIPLE CHOICE

12. b   17. d

13. a   18. c

14. c   19. b

15. a   20. d

16. c

MATCHING QUESTIONS

21. c   24. e

22. f   25. a

23. b   26. d

REVIEW QUESTIONS: SECTION III

FILL IN THE BLANKS

1. The loss of memory through nonuse is called _____.

2. _____ involves rehearsing material beyond the point of mastery to improve long-term recall.

3. When information stored in memory interferes with recall of later-learned material, _____ interference has occurred.

4. The _____ technique can be useful for remembering vocabulary words in a foreign language.

5. The method of _____ improves the recall of words by picturing them in places.

6. Overlearning is achieved through two processes: _____ and _____.

7. Another term for memory trace is _____.

8. The first attempts to study forgetting were made about 100 years ago by _____.

9. _____ interference refers to difficulty in recalling information because of later exposure to different material.

10. _____ amnesia, or memory loss for occurrences prior to a certain event, is quite rare.

MULTIPLE CHOICE

11. If your recall of the facts of World War I (WWI) is hindered because of later exposure to the facts of World War II (WWII),

    a. a memory trace of the WWI facts will remain.
    b. a memory trace of the WWII facts will fade quickly.
    c. retroactive interference has occurred.
    d. proactive interference is operative.

12. An engram is

    a. a memory trace.
    b. an actual physical change in the brain.
    c. both a and b.
    d. neither a nor b.

13. Interference is the main cause of forgetting from

    a. sensory memory.
    b. short-term memory.
    c. long-term memory.
    d. episodic memory.

14. Which one of the following statements is *not* true?

    a. According to the theory of decay, the memory trace fades away through the passage of time.
    b. Research has shown that people often recall more information on a second test than on a first test of sequentially presented information.
    c. The theory of decay accounts for almost all the forgetting that people experience.
    d. The theory of decay assumes that when new material is learned, an actual physical change in the brain is produced.

15. To remember items on a shopping list, you might picture in your mind each item on a different piece of furniture in your house. This technique of increasing recall is called

    a. the method of loci.
    b. the keyword technique.
    c. practice.
    d. overlearning.

16. Alzheimer's disease

    a. strikes about 15 percent of the population.
    b. is the same as amnesia.
    c. causes severe memory problems.
    d. is usually curable.

17. Korsakoff's syndrome afflicts

    a. 7 percent of people over the age of 65.
    b. long-term alcoholics.
    c. nutritionally deprived infants.
    d. people who have suffered severe head trauma.

18. Patients with Alzheimer's disease have an unusually low level of

    a. intelligence.
    b. blood sugar.
    c. motivation.
    d. the neurotransmitter acetylcholine.

MATCHING QUESTIONS

Match each term with the best description.

_____ 19. keyword technique

_____ 20. Alzheimer's disease

_____ 21. retroactive interference

_____ 22. proactive interference

_____ 23. memory trace

_____ 24. decay

_____ 25. overlearning

a. is the process of rehearsing material beyond the point of mastery

b. is an engram

c. is the pairing of a foreign word with a similar-sounding English word

d. occurs when early information hinders recall of later information

e. occurs when later information hinders recall of early information

f. is the loss of information through nonuse

g. is associated with aging and includes severe memory loss

ANSWER KEY: SECTION III

FILL IN THE BLANKS

1. decay
2. overlearning
3. proactive
4. keyword
5. loci

6. practice; rehearsal
7. engram
8. Ebbinghaus
9. retroactive
10. retrograde

MULTIPLE CHOICE

11. c
12. c
13. b
14. c

15. a
16. c
17. b
18. d

MATCHING QUESTIONS

19. c

20. g

21. e

22. d

23. b

24. f

25. a

INTEGRATING THE MATERIAL

1. In what ways has your knowledge about the functioning of the nervous system and the process of perception helped you in understanding the processes involved in remembering and forgetting?

2. In what ways are short-term and long-term memory affected by the way in which information is learned in the first place?

ACTIVITIES FOR CHAPTER REVIEW

1. Describe what is meant by a flashbulb memory to a friend. Then describe to each other one of your own significant flashbulb memories. Be as specific as you can concerning details, including colors, expressions on faces, feelings, odors, and so on.

2. Use the keyword technique to memorize ten words in a foreign language. If you are currently studying a foreign language, use words that you need to remember. In the keyword technique, pair the foreign word with a common, similar-sounding English word to enhance memory of the foreign word.

3. Look at these letters for 10 seconds. Then cover them up and write down as many as you can remember.

    bep vik nes wol xat luj pum

   Now look at these letters for 10 seconds. Then cover them up and write down as many as you can remember.

    tom saw the big dog and ran

   Which series was easier to remember? Why? What is chunking, and how does it aid memory of information? Why is meaningful information easier to recall than nonsense? What is the role of organization in memory?

4. Try to remember what you were doing one year ago on this date. This task may seem impossible at first, but when you begin thinking about it, you will be able to reconstruct the memory. Verbalize out loud the processes that you are using to remember what you were doing that day as a means of seeing how you construct memories.

CHAPTER 7
COGNITION AND LANGUAGE

CHAPTER OVERVIEW

Chapter 7 focuses on two issues that are central to the field of cognitive psychology: problem solving and language. The area of cognitive psychology is broad. It includes the study of memory, covered in Chapter 6, as well as the study of intellectual processes, which is covered in Chapter 8. Cognition, then, encompasses the higher mental processes of humans, including how we know and understand the world, process information, make judgments and decisions, and describe what we know to others through language.

Chapter 7 is divided into three sections.

I.   The first section of the chapter covers thinking processes and strategies related to effective problem solving. These processes and strategies include three major steps: preparation for the creation of solutions, production of solutions, and evaluation of solutions that have been generated. The preparation stage involves understanding and diagnosing the problem. This initial stage is critical to successful problem solving because it is at this time that we develop our own personal framework for approaching the problem. The clearer we are at this first stage, the easier it will be to generate possible solutions. During the second stage, production, direct solutions may be already stored in long-term memory or may be obtained through simple trial and error. More complex problems will require the use of algorithms and heuristics. An algorithm is a set of rules which, if followed, guarantees a solution, even if the reason it works is not understood. An example is using a mathematical formula even if you don't understand how that formula was derived or why it works. Heuristics are rules of thumb or mental shortcuts that may lead to a solution but that are not guaranteed to do so. An example is studying main ideas, but neglecting to memorize details, for a test; this may work some of the time, but not all of the time. A variety of heuristics are described, including representativeness, availability, and means-end analysis. Some problems are solved through insight, a sudden awareness of the relationships among various elements that had previously appeared to be independent of one another. The final step in problem solving, evaluating the solutions, is simple if there is only one possible correct solution but becomes more difficult if there is no single correct solution.

II. The second section of the chapter discusses the obstacles to successful problem solving during the three stages of the process. During the preparation stage, it is important not to jump to conclusions and not to have a fixed mental set. During the production phase, it is important to be aware of biases in algorithms and heuristics that could lead to erroneous solutions. During the evaluation phase, be aware of confirmation bias, in which initial hypotheses are favored and contradictory information supporting alternative hypotheses or solutions is ignored. The characteristics of creativity and critical thinking are also discussed, along with the complexities of artificial intelligence. Some methods of enhancing critical thinking and creative problem solving include using analogies, engaging in divergent thinking, taking another perspective, using heuristics, and experimenting with different solutions.

III. The third and final section of the chapter deals with the components of language, the course of language development in infancy and childhood, and the relationship between language and thought. Grammar consists of three major components of language: phonology (the smallest units of sound), syntax (rules that indicate how words and phrases can be combined to form sentences), and semantics (rules governing the meaning of words and sentences). The course of language development begins with babbling and then proceeds to words and two-word combinations and the use of plurals. Much of children's language acquisition is complete by age 5. Several theories of language acquisition, including learning theory and Noam Chomsky's competing theory based on the assumption of innate mechanisms, are discussed. The use of language by animals is considered. Then the question of whether language determines thought or thought determines language is examined in some detail. The chapter ends with a discussion of concept formation. Concepts are categorizations of objects, events, or people that share certain properties. Both language and thought are used in forming and manipulating concepts. Understanding how we think and communicate our thoughts is a major undertaking in the field of cognitive psychology and relates to all other aspects of psychological functioning.

STUDY STRATEGY

Follow this strategy for *each* section of the chapter.

1. Review the CHAPTER OUTLINE up to Recap and Review I.

2. Read the CHAPTER OVERVIEW, Section I.

3. Read the chapter in the text up to Recap and Review I.

4. For any question you answered incorrectly or did not understand, go back to the parts of the text that cover that material.

5. Write your answers to the REVIEW QUESTIONS for Section I in the *Study Guide*. Consult the answer key only after you have finished. Then correct any mistakes.

6. After you have completed the REVIEW QUESTIONS for Section I and have corrected your mistakes, follow the STUDY STRATEGY for Section II. Do the same for each section until you have completed all REVIEW QUESTIONS.

7. Complete the INTEGRATING THE MATERIAL questions at the end of the *Study Guide* chapter. Answering these questions will help you see how the material fits together.

And, don't forget:
Go back to the parts of the text that cover material that was difficult for you. If you still don't understand a concept, ask your teacher for clarification. Your questions in class and your teacher's answers will help other students as well.

MASTERY QUESTIONS

After mastering Chapter 7, you will be able to answer the following questions:

How do people approach and solve problems?

What are the major obstacles to problem solving?

How do people use language, and how does it develop?

Does language produce thought—or does thinking lead to language?

Part Three: LEARNING AND THINKING

REVIEW QUESTIONS: SECTION I

FILL IN THE BLANKS

1. _____ is the sudden awareness of the relationship between various elements that had previously appeared to be independent of one another.

2. A(n) _____ is a rule of thumb that may bring about a solution to a problem but that is not guaranteed to do so.

3. A(n) _____ - _____ analysis involves repeated testing to determine and reduce the distance between real and desired outcomes in problem solving.

4. An availability heuristic is a rule for _____ the _____ that an event will occur by the ease with which it can be recalled from memory.

5. A representativeness heuristic is a rule in which people and things are judged by the degree to which they _____ a(n) _____ _____.

6. A set of rules that, if followed, guarantee a solution, although the reason they work may not be understood by the person using them, is called a(n) _____.

7. _____ psychologists specialize in the study of higher mental processes.

8. In problems of _____ _____, a person must identify the relationship that exists among the elements presented and construct a new relationship among them.

9. _____ problems consist of an initial state, a goal state, and a series of methods for changing the initial state into the goal state; the Tower of Hanoi is such a problem.

10. The _____ heuristic involves judging the probability of an event by how easily the event can be recalled from memory. According to this heuristic, we assume that events we recall _____ are likely to have occurred more frequently in the past.

MULTIPLE CHOICE

11. A heuristic is really a(n)

   a. strategy.
   b. solution.
   c. algorithm.
   d. insight.

12. The set of rules for solving geometry problems may not be fully understood by the user, but they work if used properly. Such a set of rules is called a(n)

   a. heuristic.
   b. means-ends analysis.
   c. algorithm.
   d. representation.

87

13. In the preparation stage of solving a problem, people tend to

    a. depend on insight for generating solutions.
    b. put the problem into a personal framework.
    c. generate solutions.
    d. reduce the distance between real and desired outcomes.

14. The final stage of problem solving involves

    a. preparing ideas.
    b. generating solutions.
    c. developing heuristics.
    d. making judgments.

15. Sheila remembers very clearly how she felt when she was bitten by a dog, and now she avoids dogs as much as possible. Her decision to avoid dogs is based on

    a. means-ends analysis.
    b. a representativeness heuristic.
    c. insight.
    d. an algorithm.

16. Leslie has decided not to go out at night alone because she heard about a mugging the other day. Her decision is based on

    a. an availability heuristic.
    b. insight.
    c. an algorithm.
    d. means-ends analysis.

17. Tom took apart a clock to try to fix it, but then he did not see how to put it back together. All of a sudden, seemingly out of nowhere, he saw the solution and put the clock back together with ease. His solution was generated out of

    a. insight.
    b. an algorithm.
    c. a heuristic.
    d. a trial-and-error approach.

18. Which of the following statements is *not* true?

    a. A heuristic is a rule of thumb that can fail to work.
    b. A commonly used heuristic involves dividing a problem into smaller steps.
    c. Kohler's description of insight took past experience into account.
    d. Using an algorithm properly guarantees a correct solution.

19. Heuristics are used during the _____ stage of problem solving.

    a. preparation
    b. production
    c. judgment
    d. evaluation

MATCHING QUESTIONS

Match each term with the best description.

_____ 20. cognition

_____ 21. preparation

_____ 22. production

_____ 23. algorithm

_____ 24. heuristic

_____ 25. means-ends analysis

_____ 26. insight

a. involves repeatedly testing for differences

b. guarantees a solution

c. is a rule of thumb that may solve a problem, but does not guarantee a solution

d. is the process of generating solutions

e. is composed of the higher-order mental processes, including thinking

f. is the stage of trying to understand a problem

g. is a sudden awareness of the solution

ANSWER KEY: SECTION I

FILL IN THE BLANKS

1. insight

2. heuristic

3. means-ends

4. judging; probability

5. represent; certain category

6. algorithm

7. cognitive

8. inducing structure

9. transformation

10. availability; easily

MULTIPLE CHOICE

11. a

12. c

13. b

14. d

15. b

16. a

17. a

18. c

19. b

MATCHING QUESTIONS

20. e

21. f

22. d

23. b

24. c

25. a

26. g

REVIEW QUESTIONS: SECTION II

FILL IN THE BLANKS

1. _____ _____ is the tendency to think of an object only in terms of its most typical use.

2. The availability heuristic, in which judgments of the _____ of an event are based on how easily the event can be _____, is a common source of error in problem solving.

3. To assume that a child who has a perceptual problem cannot be in an honors biology class is faulty thinking based on the _____ of _____.

4. Not realizing that a pot and a wooden spoon would make a perfectly good drum for a small child is an example of _____ _____.

5. _____ _____ is the tendency for old patterns of problem solving to persist, preventing us from seeing beyond the obvious constraints of a problem.

6. Creativity is closely related to _____ thinking, the ability to generate unusual but still appropriate responses to problems or questions.

7. Convergent thinking produces responses based on _____ and _____.

8. The question of whether computers can simulate thinking and problem solving is asked by cognitive psychologists who study _____ _____.

MULTIPLE CHOICE

9. Which of the following may be hindrances to problem solving?

   a. algorithms
   b. heuristics
   c. both a and b
   d. neither a nor b

10. When you are facing a difficult task, the best approach is

   a. redefining the problem.
   b. sticking to solutions that worked in the past.
   c. both a and b.
   d. neither a nor b.

11. Solving problems creatively involves all of the following *except*

    a. the use of analogies.
    b. experimentation.
    c. waiting for insight to take over.
    d. trying heuristics.

12. Which one of the following statements concerning problem solving is *not* true?

    a. Basic thinking skills can be improved through training.
    b. Most problems have a single correct answer.
    c. Boundaries and assumptions can be modified.
    d. The availability heuristic is a common source of error in problem solving.

13. Functional fixedness is most closely associated with

    a. fatigue.
    b. inaccuracy.
    c. poor memory.
    d. rigid thinking.

14. What often results from receiving feedback while working on a problem out loud is

    a. fuzzy logic.
    b. production of better solutions.
    c. an increase in functional fixedness.
    d. inhibition.

15. Confirmation bias is an obstacle to effective problem solving because it leads to

    a. contradictory information to be ignored.
    b. the generation of contradictory information.
    c. solutions that contradict one another.
    d. trial-and-error approaches, which often fail.

16. A construction worker who enjoys designing plans for buildings as a hobby is displaying

    a. a preparation hindrance.
    b. convergent thinking.
    c. a reasonable amount of creativity.
    d. the use of analogies.

MATCHING QUESTIONS

Match each term with the best description.

_____ 17. availability heuristic

_____ 18. functional fixedness

_____ 19. faulty assumptions

_____ 20. analogies

_____ 21. divergent thinking

_____ 22. convergent thinking

_____ 23. confirmation bias

a. ignores contradiction

b. a rule of thumb that can lead to errors

c. lead to faulty conclusions

d. is a form of creative thinking

e. focuses on solutions

f. are a useful strategy based on making comparisons

g. is a rigid approach to problem solving

ANSWER KEY: SECTION II

FILL IN THE BLANKS

1. functional fixedness

2. probability; recalled

3. heuristic; representativeness

4. functional fixedness

5. mental set

6. divergent

7. knowledge; logic

8. artificial intelligence

MULTIPLE CHOICE

9. c

10. a

11. d

12. b

13. d

14. b

15. a

16. c

MATCHING QUESTIONS

17. b

18. g

19. c

20. f

21. d

22. e

23. a

REVIEW QUESTIONS: SECTION III

FILL IN THE BLANKS

1. The theory claiming that language shapes and may even determine the way people perceive the world is called the _____ - _____ hypothesis.

2. Categorizing a table and a chair as furniture because they share common properties is an example of forming a(n) _____.

3. A neural system of the brain hypothesized by Chomsky to permit understanding of language is called a(n) _____ _____ device.

4. The existence of a universal grammar was proposed by _____.

5. Saying ''He gave me the ball'' instead of ''He gave me the ball'' is an example of _____.

6. Language is the _____ and _____ arrangement of symbols.

7. The framework of rules that determine how our thoughts can be expressed is called _____.

8. _____ is the study of the sounds we make when we speak and of how we produce meaning by forming those sounds into words.

9. _____ consists of speechlike but meaningless sounds.

10. "I show book" is an example of _____ speech.

11. The _____ - _____ approach to language acquisition follows the principles of conditioning and reinforcement.

12. Chomsky proposed the existence of a _____ grammar based on the structure and functions of the human brain.

MULTIPLE CHOICE

13. It is *not* true that babbling

    a. occurs from 3 to 6 months of age.
    b. includes words such as "mama."
    c. is speechlike.
    d. produces sounds found in all languages.

14. "See baby" is an example of

    a. babbling.
    b. overregularization.
    c. telegraphic speech.
    d. a phoneme.

15. Grammar deals with three major components of language:

    a. phonology, syntax, and semantics.
    b. acquisition, universal language, and linguistic relativity.
    c. reinforcement, conditioning, and generalization.
    d. none of the above.

16. The rules governing the meanings of words and sentences are

    a. syntax.
    b. semantics.

    c. grammar.
    d. phonemes.

17. The "i" in "bit" and the "i" in "bite" represent two different

    a. forms of syntax.
    b. grammatical rules.
    c. semantic styles.
    d. phonemes in English.

18. Which of the following statements can be supported by research?

    a. Language influences our thinking.
    b. Thinking influences our use of language.
    c. Both a and b.
    d. Neither a nor b.

19. Which of the following statements can be supported by research?

    a. Language production precedes language comprehension.
    b. Children acquire the basic rules of language by the time they reach age 5.
    c. Both a and b.
    d. Neither a nor b.

MATCHING QUESTIONS

Match each term with the best description.

_____ 20. overregularization

_____ 21. babbling

_____ 22. phoneme

_____ 23. semantics

_____ 24. syntax

_____ 25. linguistic-relativity hypothesis

a. is speechlike behavior occurring at 3 to 6 months of age

b. is a unit of speech sounds

c. are rules governing meaning

d. explains how words are joined to form sentences

e. is the belief that language affects perception

f. is the inappropriate application of rules of speech

ANSWER KEY: SECTION III

FILL IN THE BLANKS

1. linguistic-relativity

2. concept

3. language acquisition

4. Chomsky

5. overregularization

6. systematic; meaningful

7. grammar

8. phonology

9. babble

10. telegraphic

11. learning-theory

12. universal

MULTIPLE CHOICE

13. b

14. c

15. a

16. b

17. d

18. c

19. b

MATCHING QUESTIONS

20. f

21. a

22. b

23. c

24. d

25. e

INTEGRATING THE MATERIAL

1. You have so far been exposed to three chapters in the field of cognitive psychology—learning, memory, and language and thinking. What are some of the major characteristics of cognitive processes?

2. How can the use of language and mental images affect your approaches to problem solving?

ACTIVITIES FOR CHAPTER REVIEW

1. Solve a problem out loud, and record your verbalizations on a cassette as you speak. You may do any problem you like. Some possibilities: tackling a math problem, fixing an appliance, doing a puzzle, deciding how to ask your boss for a raise. Be sure to talk out what you are thinking. When the problem is solved, listen to the cassette and identify the stages of problem solving: preparation, production, and evaluation. What were your strategies? Why did you choose these particular strategies? Did you switch strategies at some point? Why? Did you solve the problem? If not, how would you change your strategies if you were trying to solve the problem now?

2. To counteract functional fixedness and to foster creativity, write down as many uses as you can for a paper clip. Limit yourself to three minutes. You can repeat this exercise for uses of a brick. Ask a friend to do the same and see how many original responses you can come up with combined.

3. Select an easily defined common noun such as ''house'' or ''tree'' and ask the following kinds of people to define it:

   child, 3 to 4 years old
   child, 9 to 10 years old
   teenager
   adult

   Write down all the responses exactly as given, and examine the definitions in terms of quantity and quality of information and stage of language development.

4. Present the evidence for and against the two major theories of language acquisition and development: the learning-theory approach and Noam Chomsky's innate approach.

	Learning Theory	*Innate Chomsky*
Underlying principles		
Evidence for		
Evidence against		
Conclusions		

CHAPTER
8
INTELLIGENCE

CHAPTER OVERVIEW

Chapter 8 examines the very broad area of intelligence. This topic deals with how people are able to adapt their behavior to a complex world and how individuals differ in their capacity to learn about and understand the world.

Chapter 8 is divided into three sections.

I.   The first section of the chapter defines intelligence and describes how it is measured. Intelligence is defined by psychologists as the capacity to understand the world, think with rationality, and use resources effectively when faced with challenges. Psychologists have relied on intelligence tests to identify levels of intelligence. Alfred Binet, a French psychologist, devised the first intelligence test to identify the "dullest" students in the Paris school system in order to provide them with remedial help. On the basis of the Binet test, children were assigned a score that corresponded to their mental age. The intelligence quotient or IQ score is derived by comparing mental age with actual or chronological age. IQ equals mental age (MA) divided by chronological age (CA) multiplied by 100. Approximately two-thirds of all individuals fall within 15 IQ points of the average score of 100. Three intelligence tests (Stanford-Binet, Wechsler Intelligence Scale for Children—Revised, and Wechsler Adult Intelligence Scale—Revised) are described. Achievement tests are distinguished from aptitude tests. Alternative formulations of intelligence that consider the phenomenon to be more than a single factor are examined. Thurstone suggested that rather than having a general factor, intelligence is composed of several primary mental abilities. He used innovative statistical techniques to identify the subcomponents of intelligence, which he felt included numerical ability, reasoning, verbal fluency, memory, and verbal comprehension. Cattell identified two different types of intelligence: fluid intelligence (the ability to deal with new problems) and crystallized intelligence (the store of acquired information and abilities). Gardner defined seven spheres of intelligence. Rather than focusing on the structure of intelligence, cognitive approaches have examined the processes underlying intelligent behavior, including the processes of drawing inferences and applying knowledge. The difference between school intelligence and practical intelligence is discussed. The section ends with a consideration of the impact of coaching on performance on standardized tests.

II. The second section of the chapter considers variations in intellectual ability, ranging from mental retardation to giftedness. Mental retardation occurs in 1 to 3 percent of the population and is defined by the American Association on Mental Deficiency as "significantly subaverage general intellectual functioning existing concurrently with deficits in adaptive behavior and manifested during the developmental period." Retardation may be mild, moderate, severe, or profound. In nearly one-third of the cases, there is a known biological cause, the most common being Down's syndrome, caused by the presence of an extra chromosome. The majority of cases of mental retardation are classified as familial retardation, in which there is no known biological defect but a history of retardation in the family. The intellectually gifted comprise 2 to 4 percent of the population and have IQ scores greater than 130. They are outgoing, well-adjusted people who are able to do most things better than the average person. Advances made in the early determination of intelligence are described.

III. The third and final section of the chapter discusses the origins of individual differences in intelligence. The basic controversy concerns heredity versus environment. The issue of whether IQ tests are biased in favor of dominant groups in society is controversial because blacks tend to average 15 IQ points lower than whites on standardized tests. Culture-fair IQ tests have been developed in an attempt to avoid discrimination against minority groups. The most important issue in this field is not really the degree to which heredity or environment is responsible for producing intelligence but rather what can be done to enrich home and school environments to help everyone reach his or her highest potential.

STUDY STRATEGY

Follow this strategy for *each* section of the chapter.

1. Review the CHAPTER OUTLINE up to Recap and Review I.

2. Read the CHAPTER OVERVIEW, Section I.

3. Read the chapter in the text up to Recap and Review I.

4. For any question you answered incorrectly or did not understand, go back to the parts of the text that cover that material.

5. Write your answers to the REVIEW QUESTIONS for Section I in the *Study Guide*. Consult the answer key only after you have finished. Then correct any mistakes.

6. After you have completed the REVIEW QUESTIONS for Section I and have corrected your mistakes, follow the STUDY STRATEGY for Section II. Do the same for each section until you have completed all REVIEW QUESTIONS.

7. Complete the INTEGRATING THE MATERIAL questions at the end of the *Study Guide* chapter. Answering these questions will help you see how the material fits together.

And, don't forget:

Go back to the parts of the text that cover material that was difficult for you. If you still don't understand a concept, ask your teacher for clarification. Your questions in class and your teacher's answers will help other students as well.

MASTERY QUESTIONS

After mastering Chapter 8, you will be able to answer the following questions:

How is intelligence conceived of and defined by psychologists?

What are the major approaches to measuring intelligence?

How can the extremes of intelligence be differentiated, and what are some of the special programs designed to help people maximize their potential?

To what degree is intelligence influenced by the environment and by heredity?

Are traditional IQ tests culturally biased?

REVIEW QUESTIONS: SECTION I

FILL IN THE BLANKS

1. The very rare condition of an individual who, despite being mentally retarded, demonstrates spectacular talent in one specific area is referred to as the _____ _____.

2. To psychologists, _____ is the capacity to understand the world, think with rationality, and use resources effectively when faced with challenges.

3. An individual's _____ _____ divided by his or her _____ _____ times 100 is that individual's _____ _____.

4. Currently, intelligence test scores are reported in a mathematically sophisticated form known as _____ _____ _____.

5. The original _____ - _____ intelligence test is still with us, though it has been revised many times.

6. The acronym WAIS-R stands for _____ _____ _____ _____—_____; its counterpart, WISC-R, stands for _____ _____ _____ _____—_____.

7. Tests designed to ascertain the level of knowledge in a certain subject area are known as _____ tests, whereas tests designed to measure a person's ability in a particular area are called _____ tests.

8. Researchers believe that _____ _____ is the ability to deal with new problems and encounters; in contrast, the store of specific information, skills, and strategies that we acquire is called _____ _____.

9. Some researchers divide intelligence into even more fine-grained subdivisions. Guilford, for instance, suggests a _____ - _____ - _____ model.

10. The way in which people approach problems and the style of their thinking is an example of _____ intelligence.

11. The first intelligence test was developed by _____.

12. The WISC-R has two major scales: _____ and _____.

MULTIPLE CHOICE

13. The ability of a mentally retarded individual to demonstrate spectacular talent in one specific area is known as

    a. an intelligence quotient.
    b. practical intelligence.
    c. savant syndrome.
    d. Binet's syndrome.

14. Which one of the following formulas for calculating IQ is correct?

    a. MA/CA $\times$ 100
    b. MA/CA
    c. CA/MA
    d. CA/MA $\times$ 100

15. The original intelligence test is called

    a. the WISC-R.
    b. the WAIS-R.
    c. the Stanford-Binet.
    d. the Binet-Simon.

16. The advantage of the deviation IQ score is that it

    a. is easier to calculate.
    b. allows us to compare adults and children.
    c. allows us to calculate the proportion of people who have similar scores.
    d. is a more accurate measure of intelligence.

17. It is difficult and time-consuming to administer the Stanford-Binet, WAIS-R, and WISC-R on a wide-scale basis because

    a. adults and children cannot be tested together.
    b. all three tests require individual administration.
    c. the tests are written in only one language.
    d. males and females cannot be tested together.

18. Which one of the following is designed to ascertain the level of knowledge in a given subject area?

    a. achievement test
    b. quotient test
    c. intelligence test
    d. aptitude test

19. Which of the following types of tests predicts ability?

    a. aptitude test
    b. achievement test
    c. both a and b
    d. neither a nor b

20. Which one of the following approaches do cognitive psychologists use to understand intelligence?

    a. structure of intellect
    b. deviation IQ
    c. aptitude testing
    d. information processing

21. According to some researchers, the store of specific information, skills, and strategies that people acquire through experience is known as

    a. fluid intelligence.
    b. practical intelligence.
    c. natural intelligence.
    d. crystallized intelligence.

22. A verbal scale and a nonverbal scale are the two major parts of

    a. the Stanford-Binet.
    b. any aptitude test.
    c. both achievement and aptitude tests.
    d. the WAIS-R and the WISC-R.

23. The first formal intelligence test was designed in

    a. the United States.
    b. the Soviet Union.
    c. France.
    d. Canada.

24. Two out of three people have an IQ score that

    a. falls between 98 and 102.
    b. falls between 85 and 115.
    c. falls between 90 and 110.
    d. cannot be determined.

MATCHING QUESTIONS

Match each term with the best description.

_____ 25. intelligence test

_____ 26. deviation IQ

_____ 27. IQ score

_____ 28. Stanford-Binet

_____ 29. WISC-R

_____ 30. WAIS-R

_____ 31. achievement test

_____ 32. aptitude test

_____ 33. fluid intelligence

_____ 34. crystallized intelligence

_____ 35. information processing

a. is a children's intelligence test that measures verbal and performance skills

b. is a cognitive approach

c. is composed of batteries

d. measures knowledge in a given subject area

e. is the ability to deal with new problems and encounters

f. was the first intelligence test

g. is calculated by MA/CA $\times$ 100

h. measures verbal and performance skills of adults

i. allows the calculation of proportion

j. predicts ability in a particular area

k. is a store of specific information, skills, and strategies

ANSWER KEY: SECTION I

FILL IN THE BLANKS

1. savant syndrome

2. intelligence

3. mental age; chronological age; intelligence quotient

4. deviation IQ score

5. Stanford-Binet

6. Wechsler Adult Intelligence Scale—Revised; Wechsler Intelligence Scale for Children—Revised;

7. achievement; aptitude

8. fluid intelligence; crystallized intelligence

9. structure-of-intellect

10. practical

11. Binet

12. verbal; performance

MULTIPLE CHOICE

13. c
14. a
15. c
16. c
17. b
18. a

19. a
20. d
21. d
22. d
23. c
24. b

MATCHING QUESTIONS

25. c
26. i
27. g
28. f
29. a
30. h

31. d
32. j
33. e
34. k
35. b

REVIEW QUESTIONS: SECTION II

FILL IN THE BLANKS

1. Mental retardation occurs in _____ to _____ percent of the American population.

2. Roughly 90 percent of retarded individuals are considered _____ retarded, with IQ scores ranging from _____ to _____.

3. IQ scores of the _____ retarded range from 40 to 54, whereas the _____ retarded score between 25 and 39. The profoundly retarded have scores below _____.

4. Nearly one-third of the cases of mental retardation have a biological cause, the most common being _____ _____.

5. In 1975, Congress ruled that the mentally retarded were entitled to a full education and must be educated in the least _____ _____.

6. Integration into regular classrooms is a process known as _____.

7. In the early 1920s _____ studied 1500 children who had IQ scores above 140.

8. Down's syndrome is caused by the existence of an extra _____.

MULTIPLE CHOICE

9. A significantly subaverage level of intellectual functioning accompanied by deficits in adaptive behavior defines

   a. savant syndrome.
   b. profound retardation.
   c. mental retardation.
   d. severe retardation.

10. Mental retardation occurs in _____ percent of the population.

    a. 2 to 4
    b. 1 to 3
    c. 3 to 4
    d. 3 to 5

11. The mildly retarded have IQ scores ranging from

    a. 45 to 75.
    b. 65 to 89.
    c. 25 to 45.
    d. 55 to 69.

12. The moderately retarded have IQ scores ranging from

    a. 45 to 54.
    b. 35 to 54.
    c. 40 to 54.
    d. 25 to 39.

13. The biological cause of Down's syndrome is

    a. temporary lack of oxygen.
    b. the presence of an extra chromosome.
    c. deprived cultural and social history.
    d. lack of medical knowledge.

14. the majority of cases of mental retardation are classified as

    a. familial retardation.
    b. Down's syndrome.
    c. severe retardation.
    d. profound retardation.

15. The process through which the retarded are integrated into regular classroom settings is known as

    a. familial instruction.
    b. special programming.
    c. provision of restrictive environments.
    d. mainstreaming.

16. Individuals with very high IQs

    a. are gifted in every academic subject.
    b. have adjustment problems later in life.
    c. should not be mainstreamed.
    d. show better social adjustment in school than the average person.

17. Psychologists feel that relatively accurate estimates of adult intelligence can be made in children as young as

    a. 1 month.
    b. 2 months.
    c. 4 months.
    d. 6 months.

MATCHING QUESTIONS

Match each term with the best description.

_____ 18. mild retardation

_____ 19. Down's syndrome

_____ 20. profound retardation

_____ 21. moderate retardation

_____ 22. familial retardation

_____ 23. severe retardation

_____ 24. the intellectually gifted

a. account for 2 to 4 percent of the American population

b. is an IQ below 25

c. is an IQ of 25 to 39

d. is the most common type of retardation

e. is biological in origin

f. is an IQ of 55 to 69

g. is an IQ of 40 to 54

ANSWER KEY: SECTION II

FILL IN THE BLANKS

1. 1; 3
2. mildly; 55; 69
3. moderately; severely; 25
4. Down's syndrome
5. restrictive environment
6. mainstreaming
7. Terman
8. chromosome

MULTIPLE CHOICE

9. c
10. b
11. d
12. c
13. b
14. a
15. d
16. d
17. d

MATCHING QUESTIONS

18. f
19. e
20. b
21. g
22. d
23. c
24. a

REVIEW QUESTIONS: SECTION III

FILL IN THE BLANKS

1. There is reason to believe that some standardized IQ tests discriminate against _____ groups.

2. _____ argued in 1969 that IQ differences between blacks and whites are based on genetic factors.

3. _____ - _____ IQ tests have been developed in an attempt to avoid discriminating against minority groups.

4. _____ is a measure of the degree to which a characteristic is related to genetic factors.

5. Intelligence is affected by both _____ and _____ factors.

MULTIPLE CHOICE

6. Culture-fair intelligence tests measure knowledge that is

   a. subject to environmental influences.
   b. unrelated to family background and experiences.
   c. based on heritability.
   d. shared by everyone.

7. The argument that the variability in IQ scores could be attributed solely to genetic factors is most closely associated with

   a. Wechsler.
   b. Binet.
   c. Jensen.
   d. Terman.

8. The use of IQ scores is most valid for

   a. comparing individuals.
   b. comparing groups of individuals.
   c. predicting job success.
   d. predicting social mobility.

9. A court in New York banned the use of Scholastic Aptitude Test (SAT) scores to determine scholarships because the SAT

   a. is a aptitude rather than an achievement test.
   b. is an achievement rather than an aptitude test.
   c. discriminates against females.
   d. discriminates against Hispanics.

MATCHING QUESTIONS

Match each term with the best description.

_____ 10. heritability

_____ 11. culture-fair tests

_____ 12. IQ scores

_____ 13. SATs

a. were banned in New York

b. is based on genetic factors

c. vary between individuals and groups

d. are designed to be unbiased

ANSWER KEY: SECTION III

FILL IN THE BLANKS

1. minority

2. Jensen

3. culture-fair

4. heritability

5. inherited (genetic); environmental

MULTIPLE CHOICE

6. b

7. d

8. a

9. c

MATCHING QUESTIONS

10. b

11. d

12. c

13. a

INTEGRATING THE MATERIAL

1. In what ways are the most widely accepted tests of intellectual functioning based on the principles of problem solving and language production discussed in Chapter 7?

2. What is your view of the heredity-versus-environment issue?

ACTIVITIES FOR CHAPTER REVIEW

1. Go to the library and find some information on Alfred Binet. Out of what political and social climate did his first tests originate? What was the intent of these early intelligence tests? Who collaborated with Binet on the first one?

2. Contact your public school district to find out the policies regarding least restrictive environment and mainstreaming. If possible, interview an administrator or teacher in the school regarding the placement of handicapped students. Do you feel these policies are adequate? What is the impact of mainstreaming on both special and regular students?

3. Ask your friends or classmates about any experiences they have had taking aptitude tests for employment. Find out how the tests were administered, the types of items they contained, and the extent to which the test taker found the tests to be relevant to the job applied for.

CHAPTER
9
MOTIVATION AND EMOTION

CHAPTER OVERVIEW

Chapter 9 is the first chapter of Part Four, ''Experiencing the World.'' Motivation examines factors that direct and energize behavior; emotion deals with the feelings we experience throughout our lives, our internal experiences at any given moment.

Chapter 9 is divided into four sections.

I. The first section of the chapter deals with various conceptions of motivation, including instinct theory, drive-reduction theory, arousal theory, incentive theory, opponent-process theory, cognitive theory, and Maslow's hierarchical theory of self-actualization. Each approach tries to explain motivation in a different way. According to the instinct theory of motivation, people and animals are born with preprogrammed sets of behaviors essential to their survival, and these instincts provide the energy that channels behavior in appropriate directions. In rejecting instinct theory, drive-reduction theorists suggest that drive, a motivational tension, energizes behavior to fulfill a need such as hunger or thirst; in this theory, homeostasis is considered a basic motivational phenomenon. Arousal theory seeks to explain motivation as the desire to maintain or increase excitement, perhaps to produce optimal performance on tasks. Incentive theory, unlike the others, explains motivation in terms of external, rather than internal, stimuli—we work to gain incentives. According to opponent-process theory, stimuli that first produce increases in arousal later produce an opposite, calming reaction in the nervous system, whereas stimuli that first produce a decrease in arousal later produce an increase in arousal. Cognitive theorists distinguish between intrinsic and extrinsic motivation; intrinsic motivation causes us to participate in an activity for our own enjoyment, whereas extrinsic motivation is based on obtaining a tangible reward. Finally, Maslow's hierarchy orders motivational needs from the need to survive up to the need for self-actualization, a state of fulfillment in which people realize their highest potential.

II. The second section of the chapter deals with specific human needs—eating, drinking, achievement, affiliation, and power. The biological and social mechanisms underlying hunger are explored, as are the factors underlying obesity, dieting, and weight control. Achievement motivation, the avoidance of failure, measuring achievement motivation, the development of achievement motivation in children, and the training of achievement motivation in adults are discussed. The section ends with a description of the need for affiliation (striving for friendship) and the need for power (striving for an impact on others).

III. The third section of the chapter deals with understanding emotional experience and theories of emotion. Emotions prepare us for action, shape our future behavior, and help us regulate social interaction. We know how we feel because of physiological changes and because of the labels we use. The James-Lange theory of emotion suggested that every emotion has a particular physiological ''gut'' reaction of internal organs—called a visceral experience—attached to it, and it is this specific pattern of visceral response that leads us to label the emotional experience. The Cannon-Bard theory rejects the view that physiological arousal alone leads to the perception of emotion. Rather, the theory assumes that both physiological arousal and the emotional experience are produced simultaneously by the same nerve impulse which emanates from the thalamus. The Schacher-Singer theory supports a cognitive view of emotion in which emotions are determined jointly by a relatively nonspecific kind of physiological arousal and the labeling of the arousal through cues from the environment. No single theory has been able to explain all the factors of emotional experience satisfactorily.

IV. The fourth and final section of the chapter deals with the role of nonverbal behavior in the expression of emotions. Convincing evidence exists for universality across cultures in the way basic emotions are displayed and interpreted. The facial-affect program, assumed to be universally present at birth, is analogous to a computer program that is turned on when a particular emotion is experienced. The facial-feedback hypothesis suggests that facial expressions not only reflect emotional experience, they also help to determine how we label and experience emotions. Although facial expressions can reveal emotions, they do not always provide an accurate representation of the emotion being experienced.

STUDY STRATEGY

Follow this strategy for *each* section of the chapter.

1. Review the CHAPTER OUTLINE up to Recap and Review I.

2. Read the CHAPTER OVERVIEW, Section I.

3. Read the chapter in the text up to Recap and Review I.

4. For any question you answered incorrectly or did not understand, go back to the parts of the text that cover that material.

5. Write your answers to the REVIEW QUESTIONS for Section I in the *Study Guide*. Consult the answer key only after you have finished. Then correct any mistakes.

6. After you have completed the REVIEW QUESTIONS for Section I and have corrected your mistakes, follow the STUDY STRATEGY for Section II. Do the same for each section until you have completed all REVIEW QUESTIONS.

7. Complete the INTEGRATING THE MATERIAL questions at the end of the *Study Guide* chapter. Answering these questions will help you see how the material fits together.

And, don't forget:
Go back to the parts of the text that cover material that was difficult for you. If you still don't understand a concept, ask your teacher for clarification. Your questions in class and your teacher's answers will help other students as well.

MASTERY QUESTIONS

After mastering Chapter 9, you will be able to answer the following questions:

What are the biological and social factors that underlie eating behavior, and what are the best strategies for dieting?

How are needs such as the needs for achievement, affiliation, and power exhibited?

What factors lead to the experience of an emotion?

What are the major emotions and their functions?

How does nonverbal behavior relate to the expression of emotions?

REVIEW QUESTIONS: SECTION I

FILL IN THE BLANKS

1. According to _____ theories of motivation, we are born with programmed sets of behaviors that are essential to our survival.

2. You are watching a sports event at a local park where there is no water fountain. It is sunny and hot, and your thirst causes you to walk across the street to a store for a soda. Your behavior fits the _____ theory of motivation.

3. The _____ theory of motivation says that if our levels of stimulation and activity are too low, we will try to increase them by _____.

4. A teacher tells a class that excellent research papers will have a strong influence on semester grades. This teacher is using the _____ theory of motivation to try to get the students to write better papers.

5. According to Maslow's theory, the state of self-fulfillment in which people reach their highest potential is known as _____ - _____.

6. Maslow's theory organizes motives into a(n) _____.

7. According to _____ - _____ theory, stimuli that first produce increases in arousal later produce an opposite, calming reaction.

8. _____ motivation causes us to participate in an activity for our own enjoyment, not for any tangible reward.

9. _____ motivation causes us to do things for tangible rewards.

10. _____ theories of motivation distinguish between intrinsic and extrinsic motivation.

MULTIPLE CHOICE

11. Maslow suggested that people need

    a. incentives.
    b. to earn extrinsic rewards to maintain positive behavior.
    c. a safe, secure environment in order to function effectively.
    d. arousal and stimulation to achieve fulfillment.

12. The view that a particular level of arousal produces optimal performance of a task is stated by

    a. the Yerkes-Dodson law.
    b. opponent-process theory.
    c. incentive theory.
    d. drive-reduction theory.

13. A need hierarchy in the shape of a pyramid is proposed by

    a. cognitive theorists.
    b. instinct theorists.
    c. Maslow.
    d. Yerkes and Dodson.

14. Which one of the following theories helps explain the motivation behind drug addiction?

    a. arousal
    b. drive-reduction
    c. cognitive
    d. opponent-process

15. Which one of the following theories is the least tied to biological mechanisms?

    a. instinct
    b. cognitive
    c. drive-reduction
    d. arousal

16. McDougall is most closely associated with the _____ theory of motivation.

    a. instinct
    b. drive-reduction
    c. cognitive
    d. opponent-process

17. Homeostasis is a basic motivational phenomenon underlying

    a. self-actualization.
    b. incentive theory.
    c. primary drives.
    d. the Yerkes-Dodson law.

18. The thrill-seeking personality is best explained through the _____ theory of motivation.

    a. instinct
    b. arousal
    c. drive-reduction
    d. cognitive

MATCHING QUESTIONS

Match each theory of motivation with the best description

_____ 19. instinct theory

_____ 20. arousal theory

_____ 21. opponent-process theory

_____ 22. drive reduction theory

_____ 23. self-actualization theory

_____ 24. cognitive theory

_____ 25. incentive theory

a. was developed by Maslow

b. is based on satisfying primary drives

c. assumes preprogrammed sets of behavior

d. accounts for thrill-seeking behavior

e. explains the cycle of addiction

f. emphasizes the importance of external stimuli

g. distinguishes between intrinsic and extrinsic motivation

ANSWER KEY: SECTION I

FILL IN THE BLANKS

1. instinct
2. drive-reduction
3. arousal; stimulation
4. incentive
5. self-actualization

6. hierarchy
7. opponent-process
8. intrinsic
9. extrinsic
10. cognitive

MULTIPLE CHOICE

11. c
12. a
13. c
14. d

15. b
16. a
17. c
18. b

MATCHING QUESTIONS

19. c
20. d
21. e
22. b

23. a
24. g
25. f

REVIEW QUESTIONS: SECTION II

FILL IN THE BLANKS

1. The _____ is the part of the brain that appears to be responsible for food intake.

2. The _____ hypothalamus is the part of the brain that signals a need for food, and the _____ hypothalamus signals that the body has consumed enough food.

3. Weight set point is the _____ _____ a body strives to maintain.

4. Obesity is the state of being more than _____ percent above one's ideal weight.

5. The rate at which energy is produced and expended by the body is known as _____.

6. Symptoms such as self-starvation and near starvation are typical of _____ _____, an eating disorder which most often strikes _____ _____.

7. The eating disorder characterized by vast intakes of food followed by self-induced vomiting is _____.

8. More than _____ percent of body weight is accounted for by water.

9. The technique used most frequently to measure a person's need for achievement is the TAT, or _____ _____ _____.

10. Since women have traditionally been raised to avoid competition and independence, there is some evidence that they may actually have a _____ _____ _____.

11. Individuals who write TAT stories that emphasize the desire to maintain friendships are showing a need for _____.

12. The tendency to seek impact on others is a type of motivation known as the need for _____.

MULTIPLE CHOICE

13. Rats that refuse offered food may be suffering from damage to their

    a. homeostasis.
    b. primary drive.
    c. lateral hypothalamus.
    d. ventromedial hypothalamus.

14. Your normal weight is 125 pounds. At which of the following weights would you qualify for obesity?

    a. 145
    b. 140
    c. 150
    d. 155

15. Each of the following has proved to be successful in weight-loss programs except

    a. lower food intake.
    b. exercise.
    c. fad diets.
    d. eliminating food cues.

16. Laboratory animals tend to eat larger quantities when their food is

    a. low in nutrients.
    b. supplemented with vitamins.
    c. both a and b.
    d. neither a nor b.

17. Jane received her college degree with honors and now has a variety of excellent job offers. Instead, she chooses graduate school so that she can acquire more advanced skills and get an even better job. Jane is demonstrating her

    a. need for affiliation.
    b. need for achievement.
    c. fear of failure.
    d. need for power.

18. Achievement motivation is most often measured by the

    a. Rorschach Test.
    b. Thematic Apperception Test.
    c. Yerkes-Dodson Scale.
    d. Scholastic Aptitude Test.

19. Linda has been working long hours for over a year in an attempt to be promoted to a job for which there is strong competition. Upon hearing that she was selected, she begins to doubt her ability and avoids the decision to accept the offer. Linda may be experiencing a fear of

    a. achievement
    b. affiliation
    c. success
    d. power

20. A man who has a high level of aggression and collects stereos and sports cars may be demonstrating his

    a. need for power.
    b. fear of failure.
    c. need for achievement.
    d. need for affiliation.

MATCHING QUESTIONS

Match each motive with the best description.

_____ 21. need for achievement

_____ 22. fear of failure

_____ 23. need for power

_____ 24. need for affiliation

_____ 25. fear of success

a. is the tendency to want to make an impact

b. results in the avoidance of tasks of intermediate difficulty of which others have been successful

c. is associated with economic and occupational success

d. is associated with women who were trained as children not to be competitive

e. results in seeking out friendships

ANSWER KEY: SECTION II

FILL IN THE BLANKS

1. hypothalamus

2. lateral; ventromedial

3. specific weight

4. 20

5. metabolism

6. anorexia nervosa; young women

7. bulimia

8. 75

9. Thematic Apperception Test

10. fear of success

11. affiliation

12. power

MULTIPLE CHOICE

13. c   17. b

14. d   18. b

15. c   19. c

16. a   20. a

MATCHING QUESTIONS

21. c   24. e

22. b   25. d

23. a

REVIEW QUESTIONS: SECTION III

FILL IN THE BLANKS

1. Feelings which have both cognitive and physiological elements and which influence behavior are known as _____.

2. According to the James-Lange theory, when you are confronted by a vicious dog, you have a _____ experience that will trigger your fear.

3. The _____ - _____ theory of emotion states that physiological and emotional arousal are produced simultaneously by the same nerve impulse.

4. The Schachter-Singer theory focuses on the role of _____ in producing emotion.

5. Cannon and Bard believed, mistakenly, that the part of the brain most closely associated with emotion was the _____.

6. It is now understood that the _____ and the _____ _____ of the brain play major roles in emotion.

7. In the Schachter-Singer experiments, people used environmental _____ to help label their arousal.

MULTIPLE CHOICE

8. Feelings which influence our behavior and which generally have both cognitive and physiological elements are known as

   a. motives.
   b. emotions.
   c. cognitions.
   d. visceral experiences.

9. The remark "I feel happy because I am laughing" is representative of the _____ theory of emotion.

   a. James-Lange
   b. Cannon-Bard
   c. Schachter-Singer
   d. Yerkes-Dodson

10. Lisa spent weeks studying for her final exam in biology. Although she felt the exam went well, she could not be sure. The gut reaction she had when she opened her grades and found she had received an A for this class was a _____ experience.

    a. cognitive
    b. emotional
    c. visceral
    d. thalamic

11. Physiological arousal and emotional arousal are produced simultaneously according to the _____ theory of emotion.

    a. Yerkes-Dodson
    b. James-Lange
    c. Schachter-Singer
    d. Cannon-Bard

12. Which of the following theories calls for an interpretation of physiological arousal on the basis of environmental cues?

    a. Schachter-Singer
    b. Cannon-Bard
    c. both a and b
    d. neither a nor b

13. A polygraph is an electronic device designed to

    a. measure irregularity in breathing patterns.
    b. measure increases in sweating.
    c. both a and b.
    d. neither a nor b.

MATCHING QUESTIONS

Match each theory of emotion with the best description.

_____ 14. James-Lange

_____ 15. Cannon-Bard

_____ 16. Schachter-Singer

a. "I'm not sure why I'm aroused, but the people around me are angry. I guess I feel angry too."

b. "My heart is racing and I'm running away. I must be really scared."

c. "I can tell I am angry because you were unfair to me *and* because I am breathing heavily and my heart is pounding."

ANSWER KEY: SECTION III

FILL IN THE BLANKS

1. emotions

2. visceral

3. Cannon-Bard

4. cognition

5. thalamus

6. hypothalamus; limbic system

7. cues

MULTIPLE CHOICE

8. b

9. a

10. c

11. d

12. a

13. c

MATCHING QUESTIONS

14. b

15. c

16. a

REVIEW QUESTIONS: SECTION IV

FILL IN THE BLANKS

1. The facial-affect program is assumed to be _____ present at birth.

2. The muscle that raises the corner of the mouth to form a smile is called the _____ _____ muscle.

3. According to the _____ - _____ hypothesis, facial expressions not only reflect emotional experience, they also help determine how we experience and label emotions.

4. Culturally, we learn _____ rules that inform us about the appropriateness of showing emotion nonverbally.

5. Zajonc theorized that there is an association between _____ _____ and blood flow to the brain, leading to emotional experience.

MULTIPLE CHOICE

6. When asked to choose a "reasonable" facial expression after hearing a story, New Guineans differed from westerners only in identifying

    a. happy faces.
    b. angry faces.
    c. fearful faces.
    d. sad faces.

7. There is convincing evidence that the way in which basic emotions are displayed and interpreted is

    a. culture-specific.
    b. universal.
    c. race-specific.
    d. learned.

8. When you are feeling down yet continue to smile, you will begin to feel better according to the

    a. facial-affect program.
    b. James-Lange theory.
    c. facial-feedback hypothesis.
    d. Cannon-Bard theory.

9. Nonverbal displays of emotion are masked and modified through the operation of

    a. display rules.
    b. the facial-affect program.
    c. the facial-feedback hypothesis.
    d. the zygomatic major muscle.

10. The term "body language" is

    a. precise.
    b. out of date.
    c. based on the syntax of language.
    d. misleading.

11. The facial-affect program is

    a. developed during early childhood.
    b. unique to American culture.
    c. the activation of nerve impulses.
    d. a technological breakthrough.

MATCHING QUESTIONS

Match each term with the best description.

_____ 12. zygomatic major muscle

_____ 13. facial-affect program

_____ 14. facial-feedback hypothesis

_____ 15. display rule

a. is the activation of a set of nerve impulses

b. causes smiling

c. is learned

d. states that expressions are involved in determining emotions

ANSWER KEY: SECTION IV

FILL IN THE BLANKS

1. universally
2. zygomatic major
3. facial-feedback

4. display
5. facial configuration

MULTIPLE CHOICE

6. c
7. b
8. c

9. a
10. d
11. c

MATCHING QUESTIONS

12. b
13. a

14. d
15. c

INTEGRATING THE MATERIAL

1. How has your knowledge of the biological foundations of behavior, particularly the functioning of nerve impulses and the brain, helped you in understanding the theories of motivation and emotion?

2. How has your knowledge about learning (conditioning and reinforcement) helped you in understanding the theories of motivation and emotion?

ACTIVITIES FOR CHAPTER REVIEW

1. The next time you experience an emotion that is clear enough to label, take the time afterward to analyze which theory of emotion best applies to your particular emotional experience. For example, would the James-Lange theory apply? Did your experience of emotion follow from physiological cues? Or did these processes happen simultaneously (Cannon-Bard)? Or did cognitive processes and labeling on the basis of context play a major role in your experience of the emotion?

2. Figure out where you fall in Maslow's hierarchy of needs. How do you know that you are at that particular level? What types of thought patterns and behaviors might you engage in during your striving to the next level in the hierarchy? You may want to construct your own hierarchy of needs or goals and develop techniques for climbing the ladder.

3. Call or write to your local community mental-health center or hospital and request information on anorexia nervosa and bulimia. According to the information sent you, what are the warning signs of these eating disorders, and what types of treatment are available?

CHAPTER
10
SEXUALITY AND GENDER

CHAPTER OVERVIEW

Chapter 10 deals with the issues of human sexuality and gender differences. Human sexual behavior involves a complex interplay between biological and psychological processes.
Chapter 10 is divided into four sections.

I.   The first section of the chapter discusses gender and sex differences. Society holds long-standing stereotypes about boys and girls and men and women. In general, these stereotypes seem more positive for men than for women. Although there are both personality and cognitive gender differences, the magnitude of these differences tends to be small, and the specific differences can change over time. Some of these differences involve degree of aggressiveness, self-esteem, and style of communication. Both environmental and biological factors underlie sex and gender differences.

II. The second section of the chapter is concerned with understanding the human sexual response. The biological aspect of sexual functioning is not all that different for humans than it is for related species. Women show a different, more complex pattern than men. What is sexually stimulating from a psychological point of view is learned largely through cultural experiences. Sexual fantasies play a major role in sexual arousal. Although the particular kinds of stimuli that produce sexual arousal are unique to each of us, we all share some basic aspects of the human sexual response. There are four phases of the sexual response: excitement, plateau, orgasm, and resolution.

III. The third section of the chapter discusses different forms of sexual behavior, including masturbation, heterosexuality, homosexuality, bisexuality, and teenage sexuality. The issue of what is normal sexuality is discussed, with the conclusion that what is normal is a matter of values and that the psychological consequences of the behavior need to be considered. Sexual behavior is considered abnormal if it produces a sense of distress, anxiety, or guilt or if it is harmful to some other person. Kinsey's extensive sex surveys are described. Masturbation, or sexual self-stimulation, is common among both men and women and is still viewed negatively by many people. Premarital sex is still governed by a double standard, although attitudes have eased over the years. Homosexuals are people attracted to members of their own sex, and bisexuals are people attracted to members of both their own sex and of the opposite sex. Many theories have been proposed to explain the origins of homosexuality, but there is no consistent explanation. Bisexuals and homosexuals have the same overall degree of mental and physical health as do heterosexuals.

IV. The fourth and final section of the chapter covers sexual difficulties and treatment. Rape is coerced sexual activity: One person forces another to submit to a sexual act such as intercourse or oral-genital sex. Rape occurs more frequently than is commonly thought. Although the causes of rape are complex, a primary motive is often anger. The sexual abuse of children is also more common than most people realize. Most often, a relative or an acquaintance, rather than a stranger, is responsible for sexually abusing a child. Both the short-term and long-term consequences of sexual abuse are negative. Sexually transmitted diseases, including AIDS, are discussed. In the United States, it is estimated that between 945,000 and 1.4 million people are infected with the AIDS virus. Common sexual problems, including erectile failure, premature ejaculation, and orgasmic dysfunction are described. Masters and Johnson's approach to treating sexual dysfunction is examined. For those seeking treatment, it is important to remember that sexual problems involve a complex interaction of physical, cognitive, emotional, social, and cultural factors.

STUDY STRATEGY

Follow this strategy for *each* section of the chapter.

1. Review the CHAPTER OUTLINE up to Recap and Review I.

2. Read the CHAPTER OVERVIEW, Section I.

3. Read the chapter in the text up to Recap and Review I.

4. For any question you answered incorrectly or did not understand, go back to the parts of the text that cover that material.

5. Write your answers to the REVIEW QUESTIONS for Section I in the *Study Guide*. Consult the answer key only after you have finished. Then correct any mistakes.

6. After you have completed the REVIEW QUESTIONS for Section I and have corrected your mistakes, follow the STUDY STRATEGY for Section II. Do the same for each section until you have completed all REVIEW QUESTIONS.

7. Then complete the INTEGRATING THE MATERIAL questions at the end of the *Study Guide* chapter. Answering these questions will help you see how the material fits together.

And, don't forget:

Go back to the parts of the text that cover material that was difficult for you. If you still don't understand a concept, ask your teacher for clarification. Your questions in class and your teacher's answers will help other students as well.

MASTERY QUESTIONS

After mastering Chapter 10, you will be able to answer the following questions:

What are the major differences between male and female gender roles?

Why, and under what circumstances, do we become sexually aroused?

What is normal sexual behavior, and how do most people behave sexually?

Why is rape *not* a crime of sex, and how prevalent is it and other forms of nonconsenting sex?

What are the major sexual difficulties that people encounter?

REVIEW QUESTIONS: SECTION I

FILL IN THE BLANKS

1. _____ _____ are based on the set of expectations, defined by society, that indicate what is appropriate behavior for men and women.

2. Forming beliefs and expectations about members of a group on the basis of their membership in that group is called _____.

3. Traits perceived as characteristic of _____ include aggressive, independent, unemotional, and direct.

4. Traits perceived as characteristic of _____ include talkative, gentle, neat, and quiet.

5. Gender stereotypes appear more _____ for men than for women.

6. Women, on the average, have _____ self-esteem than men.

7. A _____ _____ is a cognitive framework that organizes and guides a child's understanding of information relevant to gender.

8. The term _____ refers to a state in which gender roles encompass characteristics thought typical of both sexes.

MULTIPLE CHOICE

9. Sexism is caused by

   a. biological factors.
   b. stereotyping.
   c. both a and b.
   d. neither a nor b.

10. Stereotyping refers to

   a. cross-cultural beliefs.
   b. ideas that cannot be changed over a lifetime.
   c. beliefs about people that are based on bad experiences.
   d. beliefs and expectations about people because of their group membership.

11. All of the following traits are perceived as characteristic of men *except*

   a. strong need for security.
   b. ambitious.
   c. self-confident.
   d. worldly.

12. All of the following traits are perceived as characteristic of women *except*

   a. religious.
   b. dependent.
   c. aware of feelings of others.
   d. adventurous.

13. By age 2, boys tend to

    a. show better verbal skills than girls.
    b. suffer from low self-esteem more than girls.
    c. act more aggressively than girls.
    d. engage in more stereotyped behavior than girls.

14. On the average,

    a. women have lower self-esteem than men.
    b. women talk more than men.
    c. both a and b.
    d. neither a nor b.

15. In terms of styles of communication,

    a. men's speech is more precise than women's speech.
    b. women look at a partner significantly more while listening than while speaking.
    c. women are more likely to touch others than are men.
    d. men are better than women at decoding the facial expressions of others.

16. In comparing men and women in terms of cognitive abilities, it can be safely assumed that

    a. there are no differences between men and women in overall IQ scores.
    b. women do significantly better than men on tasks of verbal ability.
    c. men are superior to women in mathematics.
    d. men deteriorate more quickly with age in their cognitive functioning than do women.

MATCHING QUESTIONS

Match each term with the best description.

_____ 17. socialization

_____ 18. gender schema

_____ 19. androgynous

_____ 20. stereotype

_____ 21. sexism

a. is a cognitive framework to guide a child's understanding of gender

b. is a state in which gender roles encompass features thought typical of both sexes

c. is the process by which we learn the rules of appropriate behavior

d. is a belief about members of a group based on their membership in that group

e. involves negative attitudes and behavior toward a person on the basis of that person's sex

ANSWER KEY: SECTION I

FILL IN THE BLANKS

1. gender roles
2. stereotyping
3. men
4. women
5. positive
6. lower
7. gender schema
8. androgynous

MULTIPLE CHOICE

9. b
10. d
11. a
12. d
13. c
14. a
15. b
16. a

MATCHING QUESTIONS

17. c
18. a
19. b
20. d
21. e

REVIEW QUESTIONS: SECTION II

FILL IN THE BLANKS

1. The male hormone _____ is secreted by the _____ beginning at _____.

2. When they reach maturity at puberty, the _____ produce _____, the female hormone.

3. _____ is the monthly release of a(n) _____ from a(n) _____.

4. Many sexually arousing external stimuli have come to be labeled _____ through a process of learning.

5. Certain areas of the body known as _____ _____ are particularly sensitive because of a rich array of _____ _____.

6. _____ are thoughts and images which occur in people's minds that play an important role in _____ _____.

7. The body prepares for sexual intercourse during the _____ _____.

8. During the _____ _____, the _____ and the _____ swell with _____ as the body prepares for _____.

9. The body returns to its normal state during the _____ _____, the final phase of sexual arousal.

10. After the final arousal stage, males enter the _____ _____, during which they _____ be aroused again.

MULTIPLE CHOICE

11. Semen leaves the penis during the process known as

    a. orgasm.
    b. ejaculation.
    c. the excitement phase.
    d. the plateau phase.

12. Each time Laura recalls her first intercourse experience she becomes sexually aroused. These thoughts are _____ stimuli.

    a. orgasmic
    b. erogenous
    c. erotic
    d. vaginal

13. The small and very sensitive organ in the female external genitals is the

    a. clitoris.
    b. ovary.
    c. semen.
    d. vagina.

14. When Wendy touches John's penis, he becomes excited and begins to prepare for intercourse; however, when the doctor touches John's penis during a physical exam, there is no excitement. The difference between these two touches is

    a. one is male and one female.
    b. the reason behind them.
    c. the place in which they occur.
    d. the interpretation given to them.

15. The testes are responsible for secreting

    a. semen.
    b. androgens.
    c. estrogens.
    d. ovaries.

16. Female reproductive organs produce

    a. androgens.
    b. estrogens.
    c. ovaries.
    d. semen.

17. The greatest production of estrogen occurs during

    a. ovulation.
    b. orgasm.
    c. ejaculation.
    d. puberty.

18. During the excitement and plateau phases, the penis and clitoris swell with

    a. semen.
    b. androgen.
    c. blood.
    d. estrogen.

MATCHING QUESTIONS

Match each term with the best description.

_____ 19. testes

_____ 20. ovaries

_____ 21. genitals

_____ 22. androgens

_____ 23. estrogens

_____ 24. ovulation

_____ 25. orgasm

_____ 26. semen

_____ 27. ejaculation

_____ 28. resolution stage

_____ 29. plateau stage

a. is the peak of sexual excitement

b. contains sperm

c. occurs when the body returns to normal

d. occurs when semen leaves the penis

e. secretes androgens

f. are female organs

g. is when maximal arousal is attained

h. is the release of an egg

i. are male hormones

j. are male and female organs

k. are female hormones

ANSWER KEY: SECTION II

FILL IN THE BLANKS

1. androgen; testes; puberty

2. ovaries; estrogen

3. ovulation; egg; ovary

4. erotic

5. erogenous zones; nerve receptors

6. fantasies; sexual arousal

7. excitement phase

8. plateau phase; penis; clitoris; blood; orgasm

9. resolution stage

10. refractory period; cannot

MULTIPLE CHOICE

11. b	15. b
12. c	16. b
13. a	17. a
14. d	18. c

MATCHING QUESTIONS

19. e	25. a
20. f	26. b
21. j	27. d
22. i	28. c
23. k	29. g
24. h	

REVIEW QUESTIONS: SECTION III

FILL IN THE BLANKS

1. Fifty years ago, a physician might have told you that _____, or sexual _____ - _____, would lead to a variety of physical and mental disorders.

2. Church and Debbie have an intimate relationship that goes beyond sexual intercourse to other acts that are important between a man and a woman. Their behavior is _____.

3. Chris feels that there is nothing wrong in having intercourse with his girlfriend before they get married. However, he is appalled when she mentions that she might have other sexual relationships before settling down. Chris is operating out of a _____ _____.

4. Sexual activity between a married person and someone who is not his or her spouse is known as _____ _____.

5. Individuals attracted to members of their own sex are known as _____; those attracted to members of both sexes are _____.

6. Freud felt that homosexuality occurred as a result of inappropriate _____ with the opposite-sex _____.

7. Extensive surveys of sexual behavior were conducted about forty years ago by _____.

MULTIPLE CHOICE

8. John's mother is overprotective and dominant in her relationship with him. His father is passive and ineffective. According to the psychoanalytic view, conditions are right for John to be

   a. aggressive.
   b. bisexual.
   c. homosexual.
   d. heterosexual.

9. Although it is difficult to say what is typical or normal sexual behavior between married couples, we do know that the average frequency of intercourse is

   a. once a week.
   b. 5 times a month.
   c. 8.2 times a month.
   d. 12 times a month.

10. Which of the following statistics concerning the percentage of males and females who have masturbated at least once is the most accurate?

    a. 80 percent of males and 60 percent of females
    b. 94 percent of males and 63 percent of females
    c. 94 percent of males and 96 percent of females
    d. 97 percent of males and 83 percent of females

11. What is seen as normal and what is seen as abnormal in sexual behavior is

    a. very much a matter of values.
    b. based on comparisons with the ideal.
    c. based on statistical analysis.
    d. based on psychological consequences.

12. Research into premarital sex shows that

    a. the double standard is becoming more prevalent.
    b. the double standard is reversing.
    c. male and female attitudes are converging.
    d. male and female attitudes are moving apart.

13. Masturbation is now considered

    a. healthy and harmless.
    b. more prevalent among females than males.
    c. both a and b.
    d. neither a nor b.

14. By the time they reach age 20, about _____ percent of American women will have been pregnant at least once.

    a. 2
    b. 5
    c. 10
    d. 20

MATCHING QUESTIONS

Match each term with the best description.

_____ 15. masturbation

_____ 16. heterosexuality

_____ 17. double standard

_____ 18. extramarital sex

_____ 19. homosexuality

_____ 20. bisexuality

a. involves attraction to members of the same sex

b. makes men and women not equal in the eyes of society

c. occurs outside of marriage

d. involves attraction to members of the opposite sex

e. is sexual self-stimulation

f. involves attraction to both sexes

ANSWER KEY: SECTION III

FILL IN THE BLANKS

1. masturbation; self-stimulation

2. heterosexual

3. double standard

4. extramarital sex

5. homosexuals; bisexuals

6. identification; parent

7. Kinsey

MULTIPLE CHOICE

8. c

9. c

10. b

11. a

12. c

13. a

14. c

MATCHING QUESTIONS

15. e

16. d

17. b

18. c

19. a

20. f

REVIEW QUESTIONS: SECTION IV

FILL IN THE BLANKS

1. A newspaper article reports that a man has forced a woman to have oral-genital sex with him. If the report is true, this is all we need to know to say that _____ has occurred.

2. A sexually transmitted disease known as _____, or _____ _____ _____ _____, is caused by a virus that destroys the body's _____ _____.

3. A man's inability to achieve or maintain an erection is known as _____ _____.

4. A man seeks counseling because he has been unable to achieve or maintain an erection during the last five years of his marriage. This problem is described as _____ _____ _____.

5. _____ _____ _____ is a male's temporary inability to achieve or maintain an erection.

6. _____ _____, a male's inability to delay ejaculation, is often a(n) _____ problem, since there are rarely _____ reasons for it.

7. General relaxation techniques are often sufficient to allow a man to overcome _____ _____, or the inability to ejaculate when he wants to.

8. A female's lack of orgasm is called _____; as a long-term condition, this is known as _____ _____ _____.

9. Ellen is able to achieve orgasm only when masturbating; a therapist would treat her for _____ _____ _____.

10. In the method of sexual therapy known as _____ _____, attention is directed away from intercourse and toward other pleasurable behaviors.

MULTIPLE CHOICE

11. A long-term inability to achieve or maintain an erection is known as

    a. erectile failure.
    b. primary erectile failure.
    c. secondary erectile failure.
    d. tertiary erectile failure.

12. You are a psychoanalyst asked to speak at a conference about the motives underlying rape. You would tell your audience that the motivation on the rapist's part is frequently

    a. not sex but power and aggression.
    b. lust for and hostility toward women.
    c. rage toward the mother figure.
    d. the drive for sexual gratification.

13. In most cases of child sexual abuse, the abuse is carried out by

   a. known criminals.
   b. a relative or an acquaintance.
   c. another child.
   d. a stranger off the street.

14. Which of the following statements concerning AIDS is false?

   a. Initially confined to homosexuals, it has begun to spread to the heterosexual population.
   b. AIDS presents psychological issues which have yet to be sorted out.
   c. Some cases of AIDS are curable.
   d. AIDS has led to changes in sexual behavior.

15. A woman is capable of experiencing orgasm only under certain conditions, such as

during masturbating. This condition is known as

   a. anorgasmia.
   b. inhibited ejaculation.
   c. primary orgasmic dysfunction.
   d. secondary orgasmic dysfunction.

16. Both gonorrhea and syphilis

   a. affect the immune system.
   b. are incurable.
   c. produce cold sores around the mouth.
   d. can be treated successfully with antibiotics if diagnosed early.

17. Chlamydia is

   a. a disease affecting 4.5 million men and women.
   b. a disease affecting the pelvic area in women.
   c. both a and b.
   d. neither a nor b.

MATCHING QUESTIONS

Match each term with the best description.

_____ 18. rape

_____ 19. AIDS

_____ 20. primary erectile failure

_____ 21. primary orgasmic dysfunction

_____ 22. sensate focus

_____ 23. syphilis

_____ 24. herpes

a. causes painful sores

b. is a male's long-term sexual problem

c. is a form of sex therapy

d. is forced sex

e. can be treated with antibiotics

f. is always fatal

g. is a female's long-term sexual problem

ANSWER KEY: SECTION IV

FILL IN THE BLANKS

1. rape

2. AIDS, acquired immune deficiency syndrome; immune system

3. erectile failure

4. primary erectile failure

5. secondary erectile failure

6. premature ejaculation; psychological; physical

7. inhibited ejaculation

8. anorgasmia; primary orgasmic dysfunction

9. secondary orgasmic dysfunction

10. sensate focus

MULTIPLE CHOICE

11. b

12. a

13. b

14. c

15. d

16. d

17. c

MATCHING QUESTIONS

18. d

19. f

20. b

21. g

22. c

23. e

24. a

INTEGRATING THE MATERIAL

1. How has your understanding of the processes of motivation and emotion acquired through reading Chapter 9 helped you in understanding the material on sexuality presented in Chapter 10?

ACTIVITIES FOR CHAPTER REVIEW

1. Look in the children's and teens' sections of your local bookstore for books introducing children to sexuality and sexual functioning. After examining a few books, think about how the sexual concepts are introduced and described. Do the books communicate differently to older children than to younger children? In what ways? Do the books present sexuality accurately and appropriately? What impact do you believe that understanding versus not understanding sexuality as a child can have on development into adulthood?

2. List the steps you would take to locate a competent sex therapist. What types of questions would you ask the therapist as an informed consumer?

CHAPTER
11
STATES
OF
CONSCIOUSNESS

CHAPTER OVERVIEW

Chapter 11 examines consciousness and its different states. Consciousness refers to our awareness of the sensations, thoughts, and feelings we are experiencing at a given moment. It includes our subjective understanding of the environment as well as our private internal world. It ranges from being wide awake to entering the deepest stages of sleep. By studying altered states of consciousness, those which differ from normal wakefulness, psychologists and biologists have uncovered different levels of consciousness.

   Chapter 11 is divided into three sections.

I.   The first section of the chapter examines the processes of sleep and dreaming. A person progresses through four distinct stages of sleep during the night. Stage 1 is characterized by relatively rapid, low-voltage brain waves. Stage 2 is characterized by a slower, more regular wave pattern with momentary interruption of sharp-pointed waves called sleep spindles. In stage 3, the brain waves become slower; in stage 4, the pattern is even slower, and people are least responsive to outside stimulation. Several times during the night, after sleepers cycle from higher stages back to stage 1, rapid eye movement (REM) sleep and dreaming occur. The body seems to require a certain amount of REM sleep to function properly. The physiological changes that occur during sleep and during dream activity as indicated by brain waves are measured by the electroencephalograph. Although there are theories about why we dream, the issue remains unresolved. Daydreams, or fantasies that we construct while awake, are a typical part of waking consciousness. Sleep disturbances such as insomnia and narcolepsy are described, as are methods for overcoming insomnia.

II.   The second section of the chapter covers altered states of consciousness, including meditation and hypnosis. Hypnosis is a state of heightened susceptibility to the suggestions of others. Although a person who is hypnotized is suggestible, that person will not perform antisocial behavior or self-destructive acts. In addition, people cannot be hypnotized against their will. Controversy exists as to whether hypnosis is an altered state of consciousness. Outside the laboratory hypnosis has been used in medical care (for chronic pain), in law enforcement, and in professional sports (for increased concentration). Meditation is a learned technique for refocusing attention that brings about an altered state of consciousness.

III. The third and final section of the chapter focuses on drug use. The most dangerous drugs are those which are addictive. Addiction involves a biological or psychological dependence on the part of the user. Stimulants include caffeine, nicotine, and amphetamines as well as cocaine. The most common depressant is alcohol. Other depressants include barbiturates, heroin, and morphine. Hallucinogens—drugs capable of producing hallucinations—include marijuana, LSD, and PCP. The effects of all these drugs, withdrawal symptoms, and adverse and overdose reactions are described. The chapter ends with a list of signs and symptoms that indicate when drug use has become drug abuse.

STUDY STRATEGY

Follow this strategy for *each* section of the chapter.

   1. Review the CHAPTER OUTLINE up to Recap and Review I.

   2. Read the CHAPTER OVERVIEW, Section I.

   3. Read the chapter in the text up to Recap and Review I.

4. For any question you answered incorrectly or did not understand, go back to the parts of the text that cover that material.

5. Write your answers to the REVIEW QUESTIONS for Section I in the *Study Guide*. Consult the answer key only after you have finished. Then correct any mistakes.

6. After you have completed the REVIEW QUESTIONS for Section I and have corrected your mistakes, follow the STUDY STRATEGY for Section II. Do the same for each section until you have completed all REVIEW QUESTIONS.

7. Then, complete the INTEGRATING THE MATERIAL questions at the end of the *Study Guide* chapter. Answering these questions will help you see how the material fits together.

And, don't forget:

Go back to the parts of the text that cover material that was difficult for you. If you still don't understand a concept, ask your teacher for clarification. Your questions in class and your teacher's answers will help other students as well.

MASTERY QUESTIONS

After mastering Chapter 11, you will be able to answer the following questions:

What are the different states of consciousness?

What happens when we sleep, and what is the meaning and function of dreams?

How much do we daydream?

Are hypnotized people in a altered state of consciousness, and can they be made to do things against their will?

What are the major classifications of drugs, and what are their effects?

REVIEW QUESTIONS: SECTION I

FILL IN THE BLANKS

1. Your awareness of the sensations, thoughts, and feelings that you are experiencing at this moment is your _____.

2. Experiences of thought or sensation that differ from normal experience are known as _____ _____ of _____.

3. Most of our knowledge of what happens during sleep comes from measurement of _____ _____ in the brain taken by a(n) _____.

4. When people first go to sleep, they move into _____ _____ _____.

5. _____ _____, or momentary interruptions in the brain wave patterns, occur during _____ _____ _____.

6. You are sleeping as several fire engines race past your house with sirens blaring, yet you do not stir; you are probably in _____ _____ _____.

7. The sleep which occupies around 20 percent of an adult's sleeping time is known as _____ _____ _____ sleep.

8. Individuals awakened every time they show physiological signs of REM sleep are likely to show a _____ _____ when allowed to rest undisturbed.

9. According to Freud, the disguised meanings of dreams hidden by more obvious subjects are known as the _____ content.

10. The uncontrollable need to sleep for short periods during the day is known as _____.

11. Freud used dreams as a guide to the _____.

12. Sleep _____ may account for sudden infant death syndrome.

MULTIPLE CHOICE

13. Each night you dream of winning a marathon race, and your analyst tells you that this expresses your desire to succeed in life. This desire is, in Freudian terms, the

    a. manifest content of your dream.
    b. latent content of your dream.
    c. paradoxical content of your dream.
    d. REM content of your dream.

14. The stages through which you pass during the night as you sleep change around

    a. twice a night.
    b. every hour.
    c. three times a night.
    d. every ninety minutes.

15. The electroencephalograph is commonly referred to as an

    a. EEG.
    b. EKG.
    c. EEC.
    d. EEM.

16. Sleep spindles are characteristic of stage _____ sleep.

    a. 1
    b. 2
    c. 3
    d. 4

17. The heart rate increases, blood pressure rises, and males have erections during

    a. the rebound effect.
    b. sleep apnea.
    c. REM sleep.
    d. narcoleptic sleep.

18. The theory that, during REM sleep, the brain produces electrical energy which randomly stimulates memories in different parts of the brain is an attempt to explain

    a. dreaming.
    b. sleep disturbances.
    c. the rebound effect.
    d. sleep apnea.

19. A sleep disorder characterized by difficulty in breathing and sleeping simultaneously is known as

    a. narcolepsy.
    b. rebounding.
    c. insomnia.
    d. apnea.

20. It is *not* true that during REM sleep

    a. the eyes move back and forth.
    b. dream content is markedly reduced.
    c. major body muscles appear paralyzed.
    d. it is difficult to awaken the sleeper.

21. A friend comes to you concerned about his health after having stayed up for thirty-six hours straight studying without sleep. The most valid thing you could tell him is that

    a. if he is going to stay up like that, he should see a doctor regularly.
    b. if he continues to do that, he will probably get sick.
    c. there should be no long-term consequences of not sleeping for all that time.
    d. research has demonstrated that it will affect his ability to study.

22. Dreams are

    a. experienced by everyone during the night.
    b. experienced during paradoxical sleep.
    c. both a and b.
    d. neither a nor b.

23. Dreaming has been induced by injection with drugs similar to

    a. alcohol.
    b. cocaine.
    c. acetylcholine.
    d. dopamine.

24. Daydreams are

    a. a typical part of waking consciousness.
    b. usually indicative of psychological disturbance.
    c. both a and b.
    d. neither a nor b.

MATCHING QUESTIONS.

Match each term with the best description.

_____ 25. consciousness	a. is a transitional stage
_____ 26. altered state of consciousness	b. is the deepest stage
_____ 27. electroencephalograph	c. is when sleep spindles occur
_____ 28. stage 1 sleep	d. is the inability to stay asleep
_____ 29. stage 2 sleep	e. is difficulty sleeping and breathing
_____ 30. stage 3 sleep	f. affects sleeping infants
_____ 31. stage 4 sleep	g. is awareness of sensation and thought
_____ 32. REM sleep	h. measures brain waves
_____ 33. rebound effect	i. is when greater peaks and valleys are seen
_____ 34. latent dream content	j. is when dreams occur
_____ 35. manifest dream content	k. occurs after REM deprivation
_____ 36. insomnia	l. is the disguised meaning
_____ 37. narcolepsy	m. is the surface meaning
_____ 38. sleep apnea	n. differs from normal experience
_____ 39. sudden infant death syndrome	o. is uncontrollable sleep

ANSWER KEY: SECTION I

FILL IN THE BLANKS

1. consciousness
2. altered states; consciousness
3. electrical activity; electroencephalograph (EEG)
4. stage 1 sleep
5. sleep spindles; stage 2 sleep
6. stage 4 sleep
7. rapid eye movement
8. rebound effect
9. latent
10. narcolepsy
11. unconscious
12. apnea

MULTIPLE CHOICE

13. b
14. d
15. a
16. b
17. c
18. a

19. d
20. b
21. c
22. c
23. c
24. a

MATCHING QUESTIONS

25. g
26. n
27. h
28. a
29. c
30. i
31. b
32. j

33. k
34. l
35. m
36. d
37. o
38. e
39. f

REVIEW QUESTIONS: SECTION II

FILL IN THE BLANKS

1. _____ is a state of heightened susceptibility to the suggestions of others.

2. Every major religion, including Christianity and Judaism, has some form of _____.

3. Followers of the Maharishi Mahesh Yogi practice a form of _____ known as _____ _____ by repeating a _____ over and over.

4. A learned technique for refocusing attention that brings about an altered state of _____ is known as _____.

5. You join a TM group and are given a word or sound to repeat over and over while you meditate. This is known as your _____.

6. Some theorists reject the notion that _____ represents an altered state of consciousness.

MULTIPLE CHOICE

7. A person under hypnosis is in a state of heightened

   a. awareness.
   b. sensitivity.
   c. suggestibility.
   d. consciousness.

8. Which percentage of the population cannot be hypnotized at all?

   a. 25 to 50 percent
   b. 5 to 10 percent
   c. 15 to 20 percent
   d. 65 to 75 percent

9. Which one of the following statements concerning hypnosis is true?

   a. Some researchers have shown that people pretending to be hypnotized show behaviors nearly identical to those of truly hypnotized people.
   b. Recent research has found very little change in electrical activity in the brains of hypnotized people.
   c. Ernest Hilgard argues that hypnosis does not represent a significantly different state of consciousness.
   d. Psychologists feel that we are on the verge of a true understanding of the nature of the hypnotic state.

10. A friend of yours is always talking about TM and her mantra. She is probably a follower of

    a. Edgar Casey.
    b. Sigmund Freud.
    c. Maharishi Mahesh Yogi.
    d. Indira Gandhi.

11. As a state of meditation is reached, the meditator loses

    a. insight to problems.
    b. conscious awareness.
    c. the need for oxygen.
    d. feeling.

12. About 5 to 10 percent of the population

    a. cannot be hypnotized.
    b. practices TM.
    c. spends an unusual amount of time daydreaming.
    d. has some sleep disturbance.

13. Hypnosis has been used successfully in

    a. helping victims recall the details of an accident.
    b. relieving chronic pain.
    c. both a and b.
    d. neither a nor b.

14. Following meditation, people report

    a. difficulty breathing.
    b. new insights.
    c. both a and b.
    d. neither a nor b.

MATCHING QUESTIONS

Match each term with the best description.

_____ 15. hypnosis

_____ 16. meditation

_____ 17. transcendental meditation

_____ 18. mantra

_____ 19. Yogi

a. produces a state of heightened susceptibility

b. popularized TM

c. is repeated over and over

d. is a learned technique

e. relies on a mantra

ANSWER KEY: SECTION II

FILL IN THE BLANKS

1. hypnosis

2. meditation

3. meditation; transcendental meditation; mantra

4. consciousness; meditation

5. mantra

6. hypnosis

MULTIPLE CHOICE

7. c

8. b

9. a

10. c

11. b

12. a

13. c

14. b

MATCHING QUESTIONS

15. a

16. d

17. e

18. c

19. b

REVIEW QUESTIONS: SECTION III

FILL IN THE BLANKS

1. A friend of yours has had problems with stress and the doctor has prescribed a tranquilizer. The drug helps change behavior; so you know that it is a(n) _____ drug.

2. Substances that produce a physical or psychological dependence in the user are called _____ _____.

3. _____ in coffee, candy, and soda and _____ in cigarettes are two common _____.

4. If taken in too large a quantity, _____ can cause convulsions and death; hence the phrase ''speed kills.''

5. You are working in a hospital emergency room when a woman comes in for help with a drug problem. She tells you that the drug she uses gives her the confidence she needs on the job but that she has become obsessed with getting it, she is suspicious of others, and her life is practically tied to the drug. The drug is probably _____.

6. Drugs that slow down the nervous system are known as _____.

7. _____ is used medically to control pain and is derived from the _____ _____.

8. Although _____ gives an initial rush of good feeling when injected, it leads to anxiety and depression and is extremely addictive. Its addicts are treated with _____.

9. A(n) _____ is a drug capable of producing changes in perception or hallucinations.

10. _____ is a common hallucinogen that is usually smoked.

11. Barbiturates are classified as _____.

MULTIPLE CHOICE

12. Angel dust is the street name for

   a. lysergic acid.
   b. morphine.
   c. phencyclidine.
   d. methadone.

13. The effects of a heroin injection last

   a. 10 to 20 hours.
   b. 2 to 3 hours.
   c. 3 to 5 hours.
   d. 2 to 4 hours.

14. Nembutal, seconal, and phenobarbital are all depressants and forms of

    a. opiates.
    b. barbiturates.
    c. hallucinogens.
    d. hypnotics.

15. The primary drawback to treating heroin addiction with methadone is that

    a. it is replacing one addiction with another.
    b. it is very costly.
    c. methadone does not truly relieve the craving for heroin.
    d. methadone does nothing for the psychological aspects of heroine addition.

16. LSD and hash oil are types of

    a. stimulants.
    b. hallucinogens.
    c. depressants.
    d. amphetamines.

17. The typical effect in an average-size adult of an alcohol blood level of .50 is

    a. a carefree sensation.
    b. confused understanding.
    c. clumsy speech.
    d. a comatose state.

18. Which of the following might be a sign of drug abuse?

    a. being high more often than not
    b. failing at school
    c. becoming physically unhealthy
    d. all of the above

MATCHING QUESTIONS

Match each term with the best description.

_____ 19. psychoactive drugs

_____ 20. addictive drugs

_____ 21. stimulants

_____ 22. amphetamines

_____ 23. cocaine

_____ 24. barbiturates

_____ 25. morphine

_____ 26. heroin

_____ 27. methadone

_____ 28. hallucinogens

_____ 29. marijuana

a. is the most common hallucinogen

b. is used to treat heroin addiction

c. induce sleep

d. is an illegal depressant

e. produce physical dependence

f. are a class of drugs that affect emotions, perceptions, and behavior

g. include such drugs as PCP and LSD

h. include such drugs as nicotine and caffeine

i. is usually snorted

j. are strong stimulants

k. is a medical painkiller

ANSWER KEY: SECTION III

FILL IN THE BLANKS

1. psychoactive
2. addictive drugs
3. caffeine; nicotine; stimulants
4. amphetamines
5. cocaine
6. depressants

7. morphine; poppy flower
8. heroin; methadone
9. hallucinogen
10. marijuana
11. depressants

MULTIPLE CHOICE

12. c
13. c
14. b
15. a

16. b
17. d
18. d

MATCHING QUESTIONS

19. f
20. e
21. h
22. j
23. i
24. c

25. k
26. d
27. b
28. g
29. a

INTEGRATING THE MATERIAL

1. How has your mastery of the concepts of the biological foundations of behavior, as studied earlier, helped you in understanding the impact of various drugs and drug addiction?

2. In what ways can an individual's motivation and emotions be affected by drug abuse?

ACTIVITIES FOR CHAPTER REVIEW

1. Sleep for a few nights with a pad and pen or cassette recorder next to your bed so that you can write down or record your dreams if you wake up during the night. Before you fall asleep, give yourself

the suggestion that you will be able to wake up after dreaming, record the dream, and fall back to sleep with no problem. What stage of sleep are you in when waking up from a dream?

2. The next time you are in a drugstore, examine the ingredients on the labels of such over-the-counter medications as decongestants and pain relievers. Do you recognize any of the ingredients as stimulants or depressants?

CHAPTER
12
DEVELOPMENT:
THE BEGINNINGS OF LIFE

CHAPTER OVERVIEW

Chapter 12 is the first of three chapters in Part Five, "The Person Develops and Differentiates." Developmental psychology is the branch of psychology that studies the patterns of growth and change occurring throughout life. This chapter covers the beginnings of life through childhood.

Chapter 12 is divided into three sections.

I.   The first section of the chapter examines the nature-versus-nature debate: How much of what we are is due to heredity and how much is due to environmental influences? In most instances, environmental factors play a critical role in enabling people to reach the potential capabilities provided by their genetic background. Thus developmental psychologists take an interactionist position on the nature-nurture issue. Studies of twins have provided a great deal of useful information on separating out genetic from environmental factors. Studies using cross-sectional and longitudinal research methods are examined. Then the beginnings of development are described, starting with conception. The one-celled zygote, which results from the fertilization of the egg by the sperm, contains twenty-three chromosomes, each of which contains thousands of genes. The zygote divides and over time becomes an embryo. Beginning in the ninth week until birth, the developing individual is called a fetus. Genetic influences on the fetus can result in difficulties and birth defects, including phenylketonuria (PKU), sickle-cell anemia, Tay-Sachs disease, and Down's syndrome. Primary environmental influences on prenatal development and newborn health include the mother's nutrition and state of mind, illness of the mother, the mother's drug intake, and the way the baby is delivered.

II. The second section of the chapter examines physical and social development. The neonate is born with a number of reflexes—unlearned, involuntary responses that occur automatically in the presence of certain stimuli. Attachment, the positive emotional bond that develops between a child and primary care givers, is the most important form of social development during infancy. The phenomenon has been widely studied with animals and humans. Methods of measuring attachment have been devised. The roles of the father and of peers in the infant's and child's social development and well-being are discussed, as are the impact of day care and other varying child-rearing styles. The section ends with a description of Erikson's theory of psychosocial development, which includes four stages within childhood.

III. The third and final section of the chapter considers the course of cognitive development in childhood. Piaget's theory of cognitive development is described in detail. Piaget's four stages of development are examined: the sensorimotor stage (birth to 2 years), the preoperational stage (2 to 7 years), the concrete operational stage (7 to 12 years), and the formal operational stage (12 years to adulthood). The hallmarks of cognitive development, according to Piaget's theory, include the understanding of object permanence, a decline in egocentric thinking, an understanding of the principles of conservation and reversibility, and the development of logical and abstract thinking. Piaget's theory has been extremely influential and largely upheld. Some theorists argue, however, that development is a more gradual process resulting more from quantitative than qualitative cognitive changes. Information-processing theories focus on the quantitative changes in the way we take in, use, and store information. The chapter ends with a list of methods for maximizing children's cognitive development.

STUDY STRATEGY

Follow this strategy for *each* section of the chapter.

1. Review the CHAPTER OUTLINE up to Recap and Review I.

2. Read the CHAPTER OVERVIEW, Section I.

3. Read the chapter in the text up to Recap and Review I.

4. For any question you answered incorrectly or did not understand, go back to the parts of the text that cover that material.

5. Write your answers to the REVIEW QUESTIONS for Section I in the *Study Guide*. Consult the answer key only after you have finished. Then correct any mistakes.

6. After you have completed the REVIEW QUESTIONS for Section I and have corrected your mistakes, follow the STUDY STRATEGY for Section II. Do the same for each section until you have completed all REVIEW QUESTIONS.

7. Then complete the INTEGRATING THE MATERIAL questions at the end of the *Study Guide* chapter. Answering these questions will help you see how the material fits together.

And, don't forget:

Go back to the parts of the text that cover material that was difficult for you. If you still don't understand a concept, ask your teacher for clarification. Your questions in class and your teacher's answers will help other students as well.

MASTERY QUESTIONS

After mastering Chapter 12, you will be able to answer the following questions.

How do psychologists study the degree to which development is a joint function of heredity and environmental factors?

What is the nature of development prior to birth, and what factors affect a child during pregnancy?

What are the major milestones of physical, perceptual, and social growth after birth?

How can we best describe cognitive development, and what can parents appropriately do to promote the cognitive development of their children?

REVIEW QUESTIONS: SECTION I

FILL IN THE BLANKS

1. If you were earning your doctorate so that you could do research on the patterns of psychological growth and change throughout life, you would be studying _____ psychology.

2. Influences on behavior that occur in the world around us and include family, friends, and school are called the _____.

3. If one or both of your parents have a certain color hair and you have the same color hair, you have acquired this characteristic through _____.

4. The issue of the degree to which the environment and heredity influence behavior is known as the _____ - _____ controversy.

5. We are all affected by our inherited or _____ makeup.

6. The process of _____ involves the unfolding of biologically predetermined behavior patterns.

7. Identical twins not only look alike, they have identical _____ makeup.

8. Through the process of _____, an egg cell is fertilized by a sperm cell.

9. At the moment of conception, a one-celled _____ begins to develop.

10. The point at which a fetus can survive if born prematurely is known as the age of _____.

11. Once the zygote develops to the point of having a head, brain, and other organs, it is known as an _____.

12. The developing child from nine weeks to birth is called a _____.

13. Each chromosome contains thousands of _____.

14. Children born with the genetic disease _____ cannot produce an enzyme that is required for normal development.

15. About 10 percent of the American black population have the possibility of passing on _____ - _____ _____, a disease that gets its name from the abnormal shape of the red blood cells.

16. _____ - _____ _____, most often found among Jews of Eastern European ancestry, results in the body's inability to break down fat.

MULTIPLE CHOICE

17. Sickle-cell anemia is a disease of the blood that affects

    a. most blacks in the world.
    b. about 10 percent of American blacks.
    c. about 50 percent of American blacks.
    d. about 50 percent of blacks throughout the world.

18. A child born with an inherited disease that results in the accumulation of poisons causing profound retardation is suffering from

    a. rubella.
    b. Tay-Sachs disease.
    c. PKU.
    d. Down's syndrome.

19. If both parents carry the trait for Tay-Sachs disease, their child's chances of being born with the disease are

    a. one in four.
    b. one in two.
    c. two in three.
    d. three in four.

20. Rubella is also known as

    a. Down's syndrome.
    b. German measles.
    c. PKU.
    d. sickle-cell anemia.

21. As a child psychologist, you are asked to speak to a women's group in the community about fetal alcohol syndrome. You can tell the group that it results in

    a. genetic defects.
    b. physical and mental retardation.
    c. oxygen shortage.
    d. alcoholic babies.

22. A disorder caused by the presence of an extra chromosome that results in mental retardation is known as

    a. Down's syndrome.
    b. Tay-Sachs disease.
    c. phenylketonuria.
    d. rubella.

23. The belief that a combination of genetic and environmental factors determines the course of development is held by

    a. all psychologists.
    b. neuropsychologists.
    c. interactionists.
    d. social psychologists.

24. When the egg becomes fertilized by the sperm, a one-celled zygote begins to develop

    a. within two weeks.
    b. within nine weeks.
    c. immediately.
    d. within twenty-four hours.

25. The number of chromosome pairs in the zygote is

    a. twenty-three.
    b. twenty-five.
    c. twenty-two.
    d. twenty-four.

26. The fetus reaches the age of viability at about

    a. 90 days.
    b. 20 days.
    c. 120 days.
    d. 28 weeks.

27. All of the following are considered characteristics with strong genetic components *except*

    a. alcoholism.
    b. weight.
    c. tooth decay.
    d. sexual preference.

MATCHING QUESTIONS

Match each term with the best description.

_____ 28. environment

_____ 29. hereditary factors

_____ 30. nature-nurture question

_____ 31. genetic

_____ 32. maturation

_____ 33. interactionists

_____ 34. identical twins

_____ 35. conception

_____ 36. chromosomes

_____ 37. genes

_____ 38. embryo

_____ 39. fetus

_____ 40. age of viability

_____ 41. sickle-cell anemia

_____ 42. PKU

_____ 43. Tay-Sachs disease

_____ 44. Down's syndrome

_____ 45. rubella

a. typically causes death by age 3 or 4

b. is German measles

c. is a disease that affects American blacks

d. is the inability to produce an enzyme

e. is a form of retardation caused by an extra chromosome

f. occurs at about 28 weeks of age

g. is the developing individual from nine weeks after conception through birth

h. is a zygote with a heart, brain, and other organs

i. are rod-shaped structures

j. transmit genetic information

k. is the time at which the egg is fertilized by sperm

l. have identical genetic makeup

m. believe that both genetics and environment influence development

n. is the unfolding of biologically predetermined behavior patterns

o. pertains to the biological factors that transmit hereditary information

p. is the world around us

q. is the environment-versus-heredity issue

r. are biologically transmitted influences on behavior

ANSWER KEY: SECTION I

FILL IN THE BLANKS

1. developmental
2. environment
3. heredity
4. nature-nurture
5. genetic
6. maturation
7. genetic
8. conception

9. zygote
10. viability
11. embryo
12. fetus
13. genes
14. phenylketonuria (PKU)
15. sickle-cell anemia
16. Tay-Sachs disease

MULTIPLE CHOICE

17. b
18. c
19. a
20. b
21. b
22. a

23. c
24. c
25. a
26. d
27. d

MATCHING QUESTIONS

28. p
29. r
30. q
31. o
32. n
33. m
34. l
35. k
36. i

37. j
38. h
39. g
40. f
41. c
42. d
43. a
44. e
45. b

REVIEW QUESTIONS: SECTION II

FILL IN THE BLANKS

1. A newborn child is called a _____.

2. A white lubrication called _____ covers the fetus, protecting it during _____.

3. A soft fuzz covering the body of a newborn is known as _____.

4. The neonate is born with a number of unlearned, involuntary responses to certain stimuli called _____.

5. If you touch the cheek of a neonate, it will demonstrate its _____ _____ by turning its head toward your finger.

6. The infant will demonstrate its _____ _____ to things that touch its lips and its _____ _____ to clear its throat.

7. The reflex action in response to sudden noise is known as the _____ or _____ _____.

8. If you stroke the outside of an infant's foot, it will probably demonstrate its _____ _____ by fanning out its toes.

9. As the infant grows older, it will show a decrease in responding to repeated presentations of the same stimulus as _____ occurs.

10. The positive emotional bond between parents and their children is known as _____.

11. According to newly discovered evidence, _____ has benefits well beyond the communication of affection.

12. Erikson is known for his theory of _____ development.

13. During the first stage of Erikson's theory, infants learn to develop _____.

MULTIPLE CHOICE

14. Psychosocial development is a life-span theory put forth by

    a. Sigmund Freud.
    b. Erik Erikson.
    c. Carl Rogers.
    d. Albert Bandura.

15. Trust versus mistrust is the _____ stage of psychosocial development.

    a. first
    b. second
    c. third
    d. fourth

16. The 3- to 6-year-old child experiences conflict between independence of action and the sometimes-negative results of that action in the stage of

    a. autonomy versus shame and doubt.
    b. initiative versus guilt.
    c. trust versus mistrust.
    d. industry versus inferiority.

17. Autonomy versus shame and doubt occurs from

    a. 18 months to 3 years.
    b. 3 to 6 years.
    c. 2 to 4 years.
    d. birth to 18 months.

18. You notice that an infant is responding less and less to the presence of its once-favorite toy. As a psychologist, you can tell the child's concerned parents that what is occurring is

    a. attachment.
    b. rooting.
    c. habituation.
    d. reflexing.

19. An infant that flings its arms, arches its back, and spreads its fingers is probably reacting to

    a. a touch to its cheek.
    b. a stroke of its foot.
    c. its mother's presence.
    d. a sudden noise.

20. A neonate's eyes have

    a. difficulty seeing colors.
    b. difficulty distinguishing shapes.
    c. limited capacity to modify the shape of the lens.
    d. limited capacity to follow moving objects.

21. The typical baby can walk by

    a. the time it is 6 months old.
    b. the time it is just over 1 year old.
    c. 18 months.
    d. 24 months.

22. Harlow found that infant monkeys who were given the choice of a wire monkey that provided food or a soft terrycloth monkey that was warm but did not provide food preferred

    a. the wire monkey.
    b. neither monkey.
    c. the cloth monkey.
    d. both equally.

23. A securely attached 1-year-old child will

    a. explore independently but return to the mother occasionally.
    b. cling to the mother and refuse to explore.
    c. be comfortable when left alone with a stranger.
    d. grow up to be a competitive, aggressive adult.

24. When children from poor or disadvantaged homes experience day-care, they

    a. show loss of attachment for their mothers.
    b. have difficulty forming peer relationships.
    c. show an increase in intellectual achievement.
    d. cry more than middle-class children.

MATCHING QUESTIONS

Match each term with the best description.

_____ 25. vernix

_____ 26. lanugo

_____ 27. rooting reflex

_____ 28. sucking reflex

_____ 29. Moro reflex

_____ 30. habituation

_____ 31. attachment

_____ 32. psychosocial development

_____ 33. trust versus mistrust

_____ 34. autonomy versus shame and doubt

_____ 35. initiative versus guilt

_____ 36. industry versus inferiority

_____ 37. Babinski reflex

_____ 38. Erikson

a. is a stage from ages 6 to 12 years

b. is the response of fanned toes

c. is a stage from ages 3 to 6 years

d. is a stage from ages 18 months to 3 years

e. is a positive emotional bond

f. is a white lubrication

g. is a soft fuzz

h. is a response to touched lips

i. is a response to sudden noise

j. is a life-span theory

k. researched the stages of psychosocial development

l. is a stage from birth to 18 months

m. is a decrease in attention to a stimulus

n. results in the turn of the head toward touch

ANSWER KEY: SECTION II

FILL IN THE BLANKS

1. neonate

2. vernix; birth

3. lanugo

4. reflexes

5. rooting reflex

6. sucking reflex; gag reflex

7. Moro; startle reflex

8. Babinski reflex

9. habituation

10. attachment

11. touch

12. psychosocial

13. trust

MULTIPLE CHOICE

14. b

15. a

16. b

17. a

18. c

19. d

20. c

21. b

22. c

23. a

24. c

MATCHING QUESTIONS

25. f

26. g

27. n

28. h

29. i

30. m

31. e

32. j

33. l

34. d

35. c

36. a

37. b

38. k

REVIEW QUESTIONS: SECTION III

FILL IN THE BLANKS

1. The process through which a child's understanding of the world changes as a function of age and experience is known as _____ _____ .

2. According to Piaget, the period from birth to 2 years is the _____ stage of cognitive development.

3. _____ _____ is the awareness that objects and people continue to exist even if they are out of sight.

4. The development of internal representational systems occurs during the _____ stage.

5. You are a developmental psychologist observing 3-year-olds as they play hide-and-seek. Some of them hide by putting their faces against a wall, covering their eyes. They seem to be assuming that since they cannot see, no one else can see them. This is a demonstration of _____ thought.

6. The knowledge that quantity is unrelated to the arrangement and physical appearance of objects is known as the principle of _____ .

7. Children begin to think in a more logical manner and to overcome some of their egocentrism in the
   _____ _____ stage.

8. The idea that some changes can be undone by reversing an earlier action is known as
   _____.

9. According to Piaget, the _____ _____ stage from age 12 to adulthood is
   characterized by an increase in _____ and _____ thought.

10. Improvement in information processing is tied to advances in _____, the planning,
    monitoring, and revising of cognitive strategies.

MULTIPLE CHOICE

11. Most studies show that only between 40 and
    60 percent of college students and adults
    fully reach

    a. cognitive maturity.
    b. the formal operational stage.
    c. the concrete operational stage.
    d. the preoperational stage.

12. Children who think that a given quantity of
    water changes as it is poured from a small
    glass into a large glass do not yet
    understand

    a. concrete thought processes.
    b. object permanence.
    c. the principle of conservation.
    d. sensorimotor principles.

13. A child who cannot yet represent the
    environment using images, language, or
    other symbols is probably in the

    a. sensorimotor stage.
    b. preoperational stage.
    c. concrete operational stage.
    d. formal operational stage.

14. Piaget's theory is one of

    a. psychosocial development.
    b. sensorimotor development.
    c. maturation.
    d. cognitive development.

15. A child who knows that he or she can roll a
    piece of clay into a long "sausage" yet still
    undo this by reversing the operation
    understands the concept of

    a. object permanence.
    b. conservation.
    c. reversibility.
    d. maturation.

16. The period characterized by logical thought
    and loss of egocentrism is the

    a. sensorimotor stage.
    b. preoperational stage.
    c. formal operational stage.
    d. concrete operational stage.

17. Language development in the period from
    age 2 to 7 years is characteristic of the

    a. preoperational stage.
    b. sensorimotor stage.
    c. formal operational stage.
    d. concrete operational stage.

18. Of the following, the *least* important factor
    in maximizing a child's cognitive growth is

    a. holding high expectations for the child.
    b. providing the child with a vast quantity
       of toys.
    c. being emotionally responsive to and
       involved with the child.
    d. giving the child a chance to make
       mistakes.

19. Critics of Piaget's theory claim that it is too

    a. quantitative.
    b. comprehensive.
    c. cognitive.
    d. disconnected.

20. According to the formation-processing approach to cognitive development,

    a. memory improves dramatically with age.
    b. computers are superior to the human mind.
    c. children progress from concrete to abstract thinking in stages.
    d. attention decreases with age.

MATCHING QUESTIONS

Match each stage of cognitive development with the best description.

_____ 21. sensorimotor stage

_____ 22. preoperational stage

_____ 23. concrete operational stage

_____ 24. formal operational stage

a. is the stage in which logical and abstract thinking becomes firmly established

b. is the stage during which language development and symbolic thinking take place

c. is the stage during which object permanence becomes understood but there is no capacity for symbolic representation

d. is the stage during which the child develops the concepts of conservation and reversibility

ANSWER KEY: SECTION III

FILL IN THE BLANKS

1. cognitive development

2. sensorimotor

3. object permanence

4. preoperational

5. egocentric

6. conservation

7. concrete operational

8. reversibility

9. formal operational; abstract; logical

10. metacognition

MULTIPLE CHOICE

11. b   16. d

12. c   17. a

13. a   18. b

14. d   19. d

15. c   20. a

MATCHING QUESTIONS

21. c   23. d

22. b   24. a

INTEGRATING THE MATERIAL

1. Many psychologists believe that the study of development is the study of all of psychology, that all psychological concepts are contained in the study of development. Why might they believe this?

2. Do you view development as a continuous process or a discontinuous process? Explain. Do you believe that proposing stages of development means conceptualizing development as a discontinuous process? Explain.

ACTIVITIES FOR CHAPTER REVIEW

1. Debate the following statement: Infants are very passive during the first 6 months of life. In debating this statement, include information on early reflexes and reactions to internal states, sensorimotor activities, and early social functioning. After reviewing this information, how would you describe the average infant that is under 6 months of age?

2. Make a two-column list of genetic factors and environmental factors that might influence the course of physical, social, and cognitive development.

   Genetic factors   *Environmental factors*

Explain the interactionist viewpoint on the nature-nurture controversy.

3. Call or write to the day-care centers and nursery schools in your community for written information about the programs they offer. At what ages are children grouped together? How are the programs structured in terms of time, activities, and goals? Which of the programs do you like the best? Why? Which do you like the least? Why? If you have the opportunity, visit one or two day-care centers to get a feel for how they operate.

4. Observe a child under 1 year of age and record the child's activity on an ongoing basis for five minutes. Make a list in advance of the types of behaviors you are going to record. Your list might include smile, laugh, talk, touch, look, play with toy, play with person, or any other categories of interest to you. At the end of five minutes, add up the number of total behaviors and the number by category. What types of questions of interest are raised by your data?

CHAPTER

13

DEVELOPMENT: ADOLESCENCE TO THE END OF LIFE

CHAPTER OVERVIEW

Chapter 13 is the second chapter of Part Five, "The Person Develops and Differentiates." This chapter examines the process of development from adolescence through young adulthood, middle age, and old age. Development is a lifelong process.

Chapter 13 is divided into three sections.

I. The first section of the chapter covers development during adolescence: physical, moral, cognitive, and psychosocial. Physical changes are dramatic during adolescence and are largely the result of the secretion of hormones. Puberty is the time during which sexual organs mature and begins at about age 11 or 12 for girls and 13 or 14 for boys. A well-known theory of moral development was advanced by Lawrence Kohlberg, who used Piaget's theory of cognitive development as a guide to describe the evolution of moral judgments. According to Kohlberg, there are six stages of moral development which become increasingly abstract and sophisticated. A theory of moral development in women was researched by Carol Gilligan, who maintains that women's morality is centered on individual well-being rather than moral abstractions. The chapter expands Erikson's theory of psychosocial development, whose early stages were described in Chapter 12, to include stages 5 through 8, which account for psychosocial development from adolescence through late adulthood. During adolescence, people enter the stage of identity versus role confusion, which might include an identity crisis. As it turns out, the characterization of adolescence as a "story time" is largely a myth. Over the last two decades, the occurrence of teenage suicide has tripled.

II. The second section of the chapter covers the periods of early and middle adulthood. For most people, early adulthood marks the peak of physical health. Social and developmental transitions take place in the middle years. Around age 40 or 45, people generally question their lives and may experience a midlife crisis. During the last stages of middle adulthood, the fifties, people generally become more accepting of themselves and others. Although many marriages end in divorce, marriage is still highly valued by society and most people get married. The proportion of women who work has increased, but the division of household roles between husband and wife has not changed very much.

III. The third and final section of the chapter examines the process of growing old. There are changes in physical stamina and decreases in sensory acuity. Two major theories try to account for the physical decline: genetic preprogramming and wear-and-tear. Cognitive processes affected by aging include fluid and crystallized intelligence and memory. Fluid intelligence decreases but crystallized intelligence increases. Changes in social activity are explained by disengagement theory and activity theory. People approaching death move through a series of stages, as do people mourning another's death: They move from shock and denial and disbelief to depression to coming to terms and acceptance.

STUDY STRATEGY

Follow this strategy for *each* section of the chapter.

1. Review the CHAPTER OUTLINE up to Recap and Review I.

2. Read the CHAPTER OVERVIEW, Section I.

3. Read the chapter in the text up to Recap and Review I.

4. For any question you answered incorrectly or did not understand, go back to the parts of the text that cover that material.

5. Write your answers to the REVIEW QUESTIONS for Section I in the *Study Guide*. Consult the answer key only after you have finished. Then correct any mistakes.

6. After you have completed the REVIEW QUESTIONS for Section I and have corrected your mistakes, follow the STUDY STRATEGY for Section II. Do the same for each section until you have completed all REVIEW QUESTIONS.

7. Then, complete the INTEGRATING THE MATERIAL questions at the end of the *Study Guide* chapter. Answering these questions will help you see how the material fits together.

And, don't forget:

Go back to the parts of the text that cover material that was difficult for you. If you still don't understand a concept, ask your teacher for clarification. Your questions in class and your teacher's answers will help other students as well.

MASTERY QUESTIONS

After mastering Chapter 13, you will be able to answer the following questions:

What major physical changes mark the onset of adolescence, and how do our bodies continue to change as we grow?

What principal kinds of social and intellectual changes occur in early adulthood, middle adulthood, and old age, and what are their causes?

How does moral development proceed?

What are the stages of psychosocial development in adolescence and adulthood?

How can we adjust to death and mourning?

REVIEW QUESTIONS: SECTION I

FILL IN THE BLANKS

1. _____ is the developmental period between _____ and adulthood during which many physical, cognitive, and social changes take place.

2. The maturation of sexual organs takes place during _____.

3. According to Erikson, there is a time in adolescence when one tests to determine one's own unique qualities; this is known as the stage _____ _____ _____ _____.

4. Your roles, capabilities, and distinguishing character are known as your _____.

5. The period during early adulthood which focuses on developing close relationships is known as the _____ - _____ - _____ stage.

6. The _____ - _____ - _____ stage is the period during middle adulthood in which we take stock of our contributions to family and society.

7. Kohlberg developed a theory of _____ development.

8. According to Gilligan, women's morality is centered more on individual _____ - _____ than on moral abstractions.

9. Ego-integrity versus despair is a stage during _____ adulthood.

MULTIPLE CHOICE

10. The stage of development which begins just before the teenage years and ends just after them is known as

   a. adolescence.
   b. late childhood.
   c. early adulthood.
   d. puberty.

11. Puberty usually begins at age

   a. 14 or 15.
   b. 11 or 12 for girls and 13 or 14 for boys.
   c. 13 or 14 for girls and 11 or 12 for boys.
   d. 13 or 14 for both boys and girls.

12. Stages of moral development have been studied by

   a. Piaget.
   b. Erikson.
   c. Kohlberg.
   d. Gardner.

13. Adolescents have typically reached Piaget's

   a. concrete operational stage.
   b. preoperational stage.
   c. conventional morality stage.
   d. formal operational stage.

14. You are 15 years old and testing yourself for those things which you like and are good at; you are probably in the stage of

   a. generativity versus stagnation.
   b. identity versus role diffusion.
   c. industry versus inferiority.
   d. ego integrity versus despair.

15. According to Erikson, you will focus on developing close relationships in the stage of

   a. intimacy versus isolation.
   b. generativity versus stagnation.
   c. identity versus role diffusion.
   d. industry versus inferiority.

16. The generativity versus stagnation stage occurs in

   a. adolescence.
   b. early adulthood.
   c. middle adulthood.
   d. late adulthood.

17. According to Kohlberg, preconventional morality is based on

   a. morality of principles and conscience.
   b. maintenance of authority and social order.
   c. morality of contract.
   d. reward and punishment.

18. According to Kohlberg's system,

   a. people move through the six stags by age 10.
   b. people move through stages in a fixed order.
   c. both a and b are true.
   d. neither a nor b is true.

19. Carol Gilligan studied the growth of morality in

   a. women.
   b. children.
   c. only older adults.
   d. handicapped people.

20. Over the last two decades, teenage suicide has

   a. declined.
   b. tripled.
   c. doubled.
   d. been overreported.

MATCHING QUESTIONS

Match each of the following stages of development with the best description.

_____ 21. generativity versus stagnation

_____ 22. identity versus role diffusion

_____ 23. intimacy versus isolation

_____ 24. ego-integrity versus despair

_____ 25. conventional morality

_____ 26. postconventional morality

_____ 27. preconventional morality

a. is the highest level of moral thinking, according to Kohlberg

b. is the psychosocial stage in which testing for unique qualities is predominant

c. is the psychosocial stage during late adulthood

d. is a stage of morality that is the most concrete

e. is the psychosocial stage in which people focus on relationships

f. is a stage proposed by Kohlberg in which people are interested in pleasing others by acting as good members of society

g. is the psychosocial stage during middle adulthood

ANSWER KEY: SECTION I

FILL IN THE BLANKS

1. adolescence; childhood
2. puberty
3. identity versus role confusion
4. identity
5. intimacy-versus-isolation
6. generativity-versus-stagnation
7. moral
8. well-being
9. late

MULTIPLE CHOICE

10. a
11. b
12. c
13. d
14. b
15. c
16. c
17. d
18. b
19. a
20. b

MATCHING QUESTIONS

21. g
22. b
23. e
24. c
25. f
26. a
27. d

REVIEW QUESTIONS: SECTION II

FILL IN THE BLANKS

1. The point at which women stop menstruating is known as _____, generally occurring at around age _____.

2. Individuals begin to realize that life is finite at around age _____, during the _____ _____.

3. Individuals who have strong negative feelings over not accomplishing what they had hoped in life may experience a _____ _____.

4. The psychic timepiece that indicates the major milestones in adult life has been called the _____ _____.

MULTIPLE CHOICE

5. For most people, adulthood marks the peak of

   a. physical health.
   b. cognitive development.
   c. maturation.
   d. accomplishment.

6. Adulthood is generally considered to last from

   a. around age 18 to 35.
   b. around age 25 to 45.
   c. around age 20 to 40 or 45.
   d. around age 25 to about age 50.

7. A model of adult development composed of six major stages has been proposed by

   a. Erikson.
   b. Piaget.
   c. Kohlberg.
   d. Levinson.

8. A 45-year-old woman who has stopped menstruating is experiencing

   a. a midlife crisis.
   b. menopause.
   c. a midlife transition.
   d. puberty.

9. Levinson's model is based on a study of

   a. women.
   b. adolescents.
   c. men.
   d. men and women.

10. The proportion of married women with children who are employed outside the home is about

   a. 50 percent.
   b. 60 percent.
   c. 70 percent.
   d. 95 percent.

11. The proportion of people who eventually get married is

    a. 65 percent.
    b. 75 percent.
    c. 85 percent.
    d. 95 percent.

12. Most research suggests that compared with children raised in two-parent families, those raised in one-parent families are

    a. as well-adjusted.
    b. more intelligent.
    c. less aggressive.
    d. more anxious.

MATCHING QUESTIONS

Match each term with the best description.

_____ 13. menopause

_____ 14. midlife crisis

_____ 15. midlife transition

_____ 16. Levinson

    a. is associated with a theory of development
    b. is the result of negative evaluation
    c. is the end of menstruation
    d. is a point at which life is examined

ANSWER KEY: SECTION II

FILL IN THE BLANKS

1. menopause; 45

2. 40; midlife transition

3. midlife crisis

4. social clock

MULTIPLE CHOICE

5. a

6. c

7. d

8. b

9. c

10. c

11. d

12. a

MATCHING QUESTIONS

13. c

14. b

15. d

16. a

REVIEW QUESTIONS: SECTION III

FILL IN THE BLANKS

1. Developmental psychologists who study aging are known as _____.

2. Some theories suggest that there is a built-in time limit to the production of human cells; these are known as _____ _____ _____ of aging.

3. Some theories that suggest that the body, in effect, wears out are called _____ - _____ - _____ theories of aging.

4. When you are confronted with a new problem, your ability to deal with it is known as _____ _____.

5. In contrast to fluid intelligence, _____ _____ does not decline in old age; it actually _____.

6. _____ is a(n) _____ term typically applied to elderly people who experience progressive deterioration of mental abilities.

7. _____ _____ is a progressive brain disease leading to a(n) _____ _____ in mental and physical abilities.

8. The _____ _____ of aging sees aging as a gradual withdrawal from the world on physical, psychological, and social levels.

9. According to _____ _____, old age should reflect a continuation, as much as possible, of the kinds of activities in which people participated during the earlier parts of their lives.

10. According to Kübler-Ross, when people are facing death, the first stage is _____ and the last stage is _____.

MULTIPLE CHOICE

11. Individuals who face death move through each of the following stages *except*

    a. mourning.
    b. denial.
    c. anger.
    d. acceptance.

12. The pioneering work on death was done by

    a. Kohlberg.
    b. Erikson.
    c. Kübler-Ross.
    d. Levinson.

13. You are a gerontologist speaking to a group of students. In your remarks you tell them that aging is a gradual withdrawal from the world on physical, psychological, and social levels. Your remarks are in keeping with

    a. activity theory.
    b. disengagement theory.
    c. wear-and-tear theory.
    d. Erikson's theory.

14. Disengagement theory has been criticized for

    a. being too broad.
    b. suggesting that the elderly stop developing.
    c. being too psychological and subjective.
    d. suggesting that disengagement is an automatic process.

15. One of your friends tells you that his father is suffering from a brain disease which is causing an irreversible decline in physical and mental abilities. He is probably talking about

    a. Alzheimer's disease.
    b. brain cancer.
    c. sickle-cell anemia.
    d. phenylketonuria.

16. Most gerontologists view the term "senility" as

    a. synonymous with Alzheimer's.
    b. one that has outlived its usefulness.
    c. helpful in describing certain problems.
    d. still accurate.

17. Most evidence suggest that memory change in the aging process is

    a. rapid.
    b. slow but progressive.
    c. not inevitable.
    d. pervasive.

18. Changes in fluid intelligence begin to appear in

    a. old age.
    b. early adulthood.
    c. adolescence.
    d. middle adulthood.

19. One difference between crystallized and fluid intelligence is that

    a. fluid intelligence is useful only in certain situations.
    b. fluid intelligence improves with age.
    c. crystallized intelligence improves with age.
    d. crystallized intelligence is better in women.

20. Genetic preprogramming theories suggest that

    a. there is a built-in time limit to the reproduction of human cells.
    b. the human body wears out.
    c. our lives are preprogrammed.
    d. our emotions are preprogrammed.

MATCHING QUESTIONS

Match each term with the best description.

_____ 21. gerontologists

_____ 22. genetic preprogramming theories

_____ 23. wear-and-tear theories

_____ 24. fluid intelligence

_____ 25. crystallized intelligence

_____ 26. senility

_____ 27. Alzheimer's disease

_____ 28. disengagement theory

_____ 29. activity theory

_____ 30. Kübler-Ross

a. outlined the stages of dying

b. states that successful aging depends on activities

c. is a broad, imprecise term concerning deteriorating function

d. suggest that human cell production is predetermined

e. states that aging is a gradual withdrawal

f. is the ability to deal with new problems

g. improves with age

h. study aging

i. claim that the body wears out

j. is a disease that causes irreversible decline

ANSWER KEY: SECTION III

FILL IN THE BLANKS

1. gerontologists

2. genetic preprogramming theories

3. wear-and-tear

4. fluid intelligence

5. crystallized intelligence; improves

6. senility; imprecise

7. Alzheimer's disease; increasing decline

8. disengagement theory

9. activity theory

10. denial; acceptance

MULTIPLE CHOICE

11. a

12. c

13. b

14. d

15. a

16. b

17. c

18. b

19. c

20. a

MATCHING QUESTIONS

21. h

22. d

23. i

24. f

25. g

26. c

27. j

28. e

29. b

30. a

INTEGRATING THE MATERIAL

1. Explain how social development is a lifelong process from infancy through old age. How do social decisions and experiences at one point in life affect social functioning later in life?

2. How can the way in which a person functions and makes decisions throughout life affect acceptance of death at the end of life?

ACTIVITIES FOR CHAPTER REVIEW

1. Interview one or more people in the middle years of life and find out their views on life-span development. Do they view themselves as continuing through a developmental process physically, socially, cognitively, or in any other way? What are the major issues to be faced during the middle years and how do these issues differ from earlier years that had to be faced?

2. Visit a nursing home to see what it is like. What is the age group? What are the facilities like? What types of activities are available?

CHAPTER 14

PERSONALITY

CHAPTER OVERVIEW

The study of personality involves understanding the characteristic ways in which people behave. How people are the same and how they are different from one another are both areas of interest. Chapter 14 discusses a number of theories of personality and tools for assessing personality.

Chapter 14 is divided into three sections.

I.   The first section of the chapter describes Freud's psychoanalytic theory, which is based on the hypothesis that unconscious forces act as determinants of personality. The discussion of Freud's theory includes the role of the unconscious, instinctual drives, the pleasure and reality principles, the structure of personality (id, ego, superego), and the stages of personality development according to Freud. These stages include the oral stage (birth to 12–18 months), the anal stage (12–18 months to 3 years), the phallic stage (3 to 5–6 years), the latency stage (5–6 years to adolescence), and the genital stage (adolescence to adulthood). An important underlying dynamic in the way personality functions is the use of defense mechanisms—unconscious strategies that people adopt to reduce anxiety by concealing the source of anxiety from themselves and others. These defense mechanisms include repression, regression, rationalization, denial, projection, and sublimation. Neo-Freudians, Freud's successors, placed greater emphasis on the ego and on social factors. Among the neo-Freudians are Jung, who developed the concepts of the collective unconscious and archetypes; Adler, who coined the term ''inferiority complex''; and Horney, who viewed personality development in terms of social relationships.

II.   The second section of the chapter explores three further approaches to the study of personality: trait theory, learning theory, and humanistic theory. Trait theory hypothesizes that we have enduring characteristics that differentiate us from one another. Major trait theorists include Allport, Cattell, and Eysenck. Rather than explaining behavior, traits merely provide descriptive labels. After reviewing the literature on trait theory, Walter Mischel argued that people do not consistently demonstrate traits over different situations. Mischel's work led personality theorists to focus more directly on the nature of person-situation interactions. In contrast, learning theories of personality ignore the inner person and focus only on what is observable—the outer person and the environment. Skinner is a strict learning theorist who focuses on stimuli and responses. Dollard and Miller applied the principles of stimulus-response learning to Freud's constructs. Social learning theorists, such as Bandura, emphasize the role of observation in the development of personality. Humanistic theories, such as those proposed by Maslow and Rogers, focus on the value of unconditional positive regard, the development of the self-concept and the role of self-esteem in personality.

III.   The third and final section of the chapter considers various approaches to assessing personality. Reliability and validity allow for consistent and objective measurement. Self-report measures, including the Minnesota Multiphasic Personality Inventory (MMPI), ask people to report on a range of their own behaviors; inferences about their personalities are then made from the self-reports. Projective personality tests, including the Rorschach Test and the Thematic Apperception Test (TAT), present ambiguous stimuli onto which people can project their feelings and personality dynamics. Behavioral assessments are direct measures of observable behavior. It is important when assessing personality to keep in mind what the instruments are designed to measure and not to rely on any single measure by itself.

STUDY STRATEGY

Follow this strategy for *each* section of the chapter.

1. Review the CHAPTER OUTLINE up to Recap and Review I.

2. Read the CHAPTER OVERVIEW, Section I.

3. Read the chapter in the text up to Recap and Review I.

4. For any question you answered incorrectly or did not understand, go back to the parts of the text that cover that material.

5. Write your answers to the REVIEW QUESTIONS for Section I in the *Study Guide*. Consult the answer key only after you have finished. Then correct any mistakes.

6. After you have completed the REVIEW QUESTIONS for Section I and have corrected your mistakes, follow the STUDY STRATEGY for Section II. Do the same for each section until you have completed all REVIEW QUESTIONS.

7. Then complete all INTEGRATING THE MATERIAL questions at the end of the *Study Guide* chapter. Answering these questions will help you see how the material fits together.

And, don't forget:
Go back to the parts of the text that cover materials that was difficult for you. If you still don't understand a concept, ask your teacher for clarification. Your questions in class and your teacher's answers will help other students as well.

MASTERY QUESTIONS

After mastering Chapter 14, you will be able to answer the following questions:

How do psychologists define and use the concept of personality?

What is the structure and development of personality according to Freud and his successors?

What are the major aspects of trait, learning, and humanistic theories of personality?

How can we most accurately assess personality, and what are the major types of personality measures?

REVIEW QUESTIONS: SECTION I

FILL IN THE BLANKS

1. According to psychoanalytic theory, a person is unaware of that part of his or her personality called the _____.

2. The part of personality most in touch with reality is the _____.

3. Newborn babies seek immediate satisfaction of needs, and their personalities operate according to the _____ principle.

4. _____ refers to behavior reflecting an earlier stage of development.

5. The part of the superego that motivates us to do the right thing is called the

    _____-_____.

6. Refusing to believe the truth is a defense mechanism called _____.

7. The first stage of personality development, according to Freud, is the _____ stage.

8. According to Freud, a child's interest centers around the genitals during the _____ stage of development.

9. According to Freud, during the _____ stage, sexual concerns are largely unimportant.

10. The purpose of the _____ is to reduce the tension caused by the primary drives and by irrational impulses.

11. The collective unconscious is a concept developed by _____.

12. Alfred Adler believed that the primary human motivation is the striving for _____.

MULTIPLE CHOICE

13. Three-year-old Tommy is biting his nails and overeating. According to Freud, Tommy's problem would most likely be

    a. an unresolved Oedipal conflict.
    b. fixation at the oral stage.
    c. repression of unacceptable impulses.
    d. projection of his inadequacies.

14. Jane wants to tell off her boss but knows she could get fired for losing control in that way; so she controls her impulses. According to psychoanalytic theory, Jane's decision reflects

    a. displacement of feelings.
    b. sublimation.
    c. the reality principle.
    d. neurotic anxiety.

15. Alfred Adler is most closely associated with

    a. archetypes.
    b. sublimation.
    c. the inferiority complex.
    d. the ego-ideal.

16. When Bill found out that he did not get the job he had applied for and really wanted, he said he didn't care. Bill's thinking reflects

    a. repression.
    b. rationalization.
    c. regression.
    d. projection.

17. The ability to love is a characteristic we share with our ancestors and the human race as a whole. According to Jung, the ability to love is part of our

    a. collective unconscious.
    b. libido.
    c. ego-ideal.
    d. conscience.

18. Infants spend the first year of life in the stage of development known as

    a. oral.
    b. anal.
    c. phallic.
    d. Oedipal.

19. Instinctual drives are infantile wishes and drives contained in the

   a. ego.
   b. conscience.
   c. superego.
   d. unconscious.

20. The part of personality that is most active when a person feels guilty is the

   a. id.
   b. ego.
   c. superego.
   d. libido.

MATCHING QUESTIONS

Match each term with the best description.

_____ 21. id

_____ 22. ego

_____ 23. conscience

_____ 24. superego

_____ 25. collective unconscious

_____ 26. projection

a. is a defense mechanism

b. is a concept originated by Jung

c. is the raw, unorganized part of personality

d. is the moral part of personality

e. is the part of personality that uses the reality principle

f. is part of the superego

ANSWER KEY: SECTION I

FILL IN THE BLANKS

1. unconscious
2. ego
3. pleasure
4. fixation
5. ego-ideal
6. denial
7. oral
8. phallic
9. latency
10. id
11. Jung
12. superiority

MULTIPLE CHOICE

13. b
14. c
15. c
16. b
17. a
18. a
19. d
20. c

MATCHING QUESTIONS

21. c

22. e

23. f

24. d

25. b

26. a

REVIEW QUESTIONS: SECTION II

FILL IN THE BLANKS

1. A _____ is an enduring dimension of personality.

2. A person's preference for chocolate candy would be considered a(n) _____ trait.

3. According to Eysenck, _____-_____ and _____-_____ are two important dimensions of personality.

4. Observational learning is the concept underlying _____ _____ theory.

5. _____ is the view that behavior is shaped by factors external to us.

6. Supportive behavior from another person, regardless of one's worth or actions, is called _____ _____ _____.

7. According to humanistic theory, we have both a real self-concept and a(n) _____ self-concept.

8. Cattell found that sixteen _____ _____ represented the basic dimensions of personality.

9. According to Allport's trait theory, _____ _____ such as honesty and sociability make up the core of personality.

10. Mischel underscored the importance of considering _____.

11. _____ and _____ tried to integrate psychoanalytic theory and stimulus response theory to explain personality.

MULTIPLE CHOICE

12. Dollard and Miller expanded learning theory to include

    a. a collective unconscious.
    b. Skinner's findings.
    c. Freudian notions.
    d. self-actualization.

13. Humanistic personality theories emphasize the

    a. striving individual.
    b. individual in conflict.
    c. individual in relation to the family.
    d. individual as an observer.

14. According to Bandura, we can modify our own personalities through the use of

    a. defense mechanisms.
    b. drive reduction.
    c. psychoanalysis.
    d. self-reinforcement.

15. John is so achievement-oriented that he gets depressed when he gets any grade less than A. This description of John constitutes a

    a. central trail.
    b. cardinal trait.

    c. situational factor.
    d. surface trait.

16. Ben is so moody that you never know how he will react. How might Ben score on Eysenck's measures of personality?

    a. high on introversion
    b. high on extroversion
    c. high on neuroticism
    d. high on stability

17. Which name does not belong with the other three?

    a. Bandura
    b. Eysenck
    c. Cattell
    d. Allport

18. According to Rogers, anxiety can be caused by

    a. unconscious conflicts.
    b. a discrepancy between one's experiences and one's self-concept.
    c. an absence of positive reinforcement for good behavior.
    d. factors that inhibit the expression of central traits.

MATCHING QUESTIONS

Match each psychologist with the best description.

_____ 19. Rogers

_____ 20. Dollard and Miller

_____ 21. Bandura

_____ 22. Skinner

_____ 23. Cattell

a. developed traditional learning theory
b. developed social learning theory
c. measured surface and source traits
d. believed in unconditional positive regard
e. translated Freudian concepts to expand learning theory

ANSWER KEY: SECTION II

FILL IN THE BLANKS

1. trait
2. secondary
3. introversion-extroversion; neuroticism-stability
4. social learning
5. determinism
6. unconditional positive regard
7. ideal
8. source traits
9. central traits
10. situations
11. Dollard; Miller

MULTIPLE CHOICE

12. c
13. a
14. d
15. b
16. c
17. a
18. b

MATCHING QUESTIONS

19. d
20. e
21. b
22. a
23. c

REVIEW QUESTIONS: SECTION III

FILL IN THE BLANKS

1. A test has _____ if it measures what it is supposed to measure.

2. Tests on which people answer questions about their own behavior are called _____-_____ measures.

3. MMPI stands for _____ _____ _____ _____.

4. The Rorschach is an example of a(n) _____ test.

5. The _____ _____ _____ involves telling stories while looking at a series of pictures.

6. A test is considered _____ if it measures what it is trying to measure consistently.

7. Standards of test performance are called _____.

MULTIPLE CHOICE

8. Which one of the following tests is most appropriately used in the employment setting?

   a. TAT
   b. Edwards Personal Preference Schedule
   c. MMPI
   d. Rorschach

9. Which one of the following tests is designed to uncover unconscious content?

   a. MMPI
   b. TAT
   c. California Psychological Inventory
   d. Edwards Personal Preference Schedule

10. Test stimuli are the most ambiguous on the

   a. TAT.
   b. California Psychological Inventory.
   c. Rorschach.
   d. MMPI.

11. If an individual's test scores vary greatly from one session to the next, it is likely that the test itself is

   a. unreliable.
   b. invalid.
   c. both a and b.
   d. neither a nor b.

12. The MMPI was originally developed to

   a. identify personality patterns.
   b. uncover unconscious thoughts.
   c. locate traits.
   d. perform none of the above.

13. When personality assessments are evaluated, it is important to keep in mind that

   a. tests are infallible.
   b. decisions should not be based solely on the results of any one test.
   c. projective measures are more valid than other measures because they delve beneath the surface.
   d. most people lie on self-report measures.

MATCHING QUESTIONS

Match each term with the best description.

_____ 14. Rorschach

_____ 15. MMPI

_____ 16. California Psychological Inventory

_____ 17. TAT

a. involves telling stories based on pictures

b. is used in employment settings

c. uses inkblots as stimuli

d. is a self-report measure

ANSWER KEY: SECTION III

FILL IN THE BLANKS

1. validity
2. self-report
3. Minnesota Multiphasic Personality Inventory
4. projective
5. Thematic Apperception Test (TAT)
6. reliable
7. norms

MULTIPLE CHOICE

8. b
9. b
10. c
11. c
12. a
13. b

MATCHING QUESTIONS

14. c
15. d
16. b
17. a

INTEGRATING THE MATERIAL

1. What do you feel that each theory of personality contributes to the understanding of the development of personality?

2. How has your mastery of learning theory earlier in the text helped you to understand personality theory?

3. What are the advantages and pitfalls of personality assessment?

ACTIVITIES FOR CHAPTER REVIEW

1. Write four descriptions of someone's personality, each based on a different theory of personality: (a) trait theory, (b) psychoanalytic theory, (c) learning theory, and (d) humanistic theory. You may choose a friend, a family member, or a fictional character. With friends and family members, it is not a good idea to share the information with the subjects described. In your trait description, make a list of central and secondary traits; include situational variables if you like. In your psychoanalytic description, include hypotheses about unconscious conflicts and motivations and the use of defense mechanisms. With learning theory, include the role of early experiences and reinforcement. Your humanistic description might include the person's strivings, level of self-actualization obtained, and self-concept. Which theoretical framework did you find the most useful to work with? Explain.

CHAPTER 15

HEALTH PSYCHOLOGY: STRESS, COPING, AND HEALTH

CHAPTER OVERVIEW

Chapter 15 explores the field of health psychology—the area of psychology applied to the prevention, diagnosis, and treatment of medical problems. Because the mind and the body are clearly linked, physical health is influenced by psychological factors.

Chapter 15 is divided into three sections.

I. The first section of the chapter deals with the causes and outcomes of stress and the ways we can reduce and cope with stress. Health difficulties that can be made worse by stress are described. Illnesses can be predicted from past stress factors to a certain extent. The general adaptation syndrome (GAS) model has been used to characterize stress and its impact. Hans Selye, who developed this model, believes that continued exposure to stress results in a decline in the body's overall level of biological functioning because of the continued secretion of stress-related hormones. Various types of stressors are described and are categorized as cataclysmic, personal, or background stressors. Stress that is out of control can lead to learned helplessness, a concept developed by Martin Seligman. When someone feels so overwhelmed and unable to control events, that person may stop trying to cope and enter a state of learned helplessness. Coping is comprised of the efforts to control, reduce, or learn to tolerate stress. Coping techniques may take the form of using defense mechanisms, turning threat into challenge, reducing the perception of threat, changing goals, and preparing for stress through inoculation before it happens.

II. The second section of the chapter deals with the psychological aspects of major health problems, including heart disease, cancer, and smoking. Type A individuals are competitive, show a continual sense of urgency about time, are aggressive, exhibit a driven quality about their work, and are hostile when interrupted on a task; Type B individuals display an opposite pattern. Type A behaviors have been repeatedly linked to coronary heart disease. Research on the impact of psychological factors on cancer has shown that the emotional response of the patient may have an impact on the course of the disease; stress can suppress the immune system. Research on smoking indicates that smokers go through four basic stages that result in the smoking habit: preparation, initiation, becoming a smoker, and maintaining the smoking habit. Quitting smoking has proved difficult. Long-term successful treatment occurs in only 15 percent of those trying to quit.

III. The third and final section of the chapter deals with the doctor-patient relationship and how it relates to the prevention and course of physical illness. Although doctors and patients have been communicating for many years, researchers are just beginning to investigate ways in which the quality of communication can be improved. Barriers to effective communication with the physician take their toll on patients' ability to recover. Patient compliance can be increased when patients feel that they are in a partnership with the doctor and have some control over their medical condition; compliance also increases when the doctor is warm and friendly and keeps the patient well-informed. "Good" patients are cooperative on the surface, but may be overly dependent and reluctant to discuss their concerns.

STUDY STRATEGY

Follow this strategy for *each* section of the chapter.

1. Review the CHAPTER OUTLINE up to Recap and Review I.

2. Read the CHAPTER OVERVIEW, Section I.

3. Read the chapter in the text up to Recap and Review I.

4. For any question you answered incorrectly or did not understand, go back to the parts of the text that cover that material.

5. Write your answers to the REVIEW QUESTIONS for Section I in the *Study Guide*. Consult the answer key only after you have finished. Then correct any mistakes.

6. After you have completed the REVIEW QUESTIONS for Section I and have corrected your mistakes, follow the STUDY STRATEGY for Section II. Do the same for each section until you have completed all REVIEW QUESTIONS.

7. Then complete all INTEGRATING THE MATERIAL questions at the end of the *Study Guide* chapter. Answering these questions will help you see how the material fits together.

And, don't forget:

Go back to the parts of the text that cover material that was difficult for you. If you still don't understand a concept, ask your teacher for clarification. Your questions in class and your teacher's answers will help other students as well.

MASTERY QUESTIONS

After mastering Chapter 15, you will be able to answer the following questions:

What is stress, how does it affect us, and how can we best cope with it?

How do psychological factors affect such health-related problems as smoking, coronary heart disease, and cancer?

What are the best ways to encourage behavior that improves health?

Does the nature of our interactions with physicians affect our health?

How can we ensure patient compliance to medical advice?

REVIEW QUESTIONS: SECTION I

FILL IN THE BLANKS

1. A formal definition of stress is the _____ to events that _____ or _____ a person.

2. Circumstances known as _____ produce _____ to our well-being.

3. _____ _____, which often result from stress, are caused by an interaction of psychological, emotional, and physical difficulties.

4. Selye's model of the _____ _____ _____ suggests that a person's response to stress occurs in three stages: _____ and _____, _____, and _____.

5. Stressors which take the form of natural disasters such as tornadoes and plane crashes are known as _____ _____.

6. _____ _____ are major life events such as the death of a parent and the loss of one's job.

7. Standing in a long line at a bank and getting stuck in traffic are examples of daily hassles, known more formally as _____ _____.

8. People who believe that nothing they try to do to remedy or avoid a situation makes any difference are demonstrating _____ _____.

9. Individuals who are _____ are making efforts to control, reduce, or learn to tolerate the threats that lead to _____.

10. On an unconscious level, we use _____ _____ as a means of dealing with _____.

MULTIPLE CHOICE

11. A technique for dealing with a stressful situation which involves the conscious regulation of emotions is known as

    a. general adaptation syndrome.
    b. a defense mechanism.
    c. emotion-focused coping.
    d. problem-focused coping.

12. The management of stressful problems or stimuli as a coping technique is known as

    a. problem-focused coping.
    b. adaptation and resistance.
    c. alarm and mobilization.
    d. learned coping.

13. An elderly person who gives in to the loss of control that is experienced when being placed in a nursing home may be living in a state of

    a. psychosomatic illness.
    b. cataclysmic stress.
    c. learned helplessness.
    d. emotion-focused coping.

14. Background stressors do not require much coping or response, but continued exposure to them may produce

    a. an inability to use problem-focused techniques.
    b. as great a toll as a single, more stressful incident.
    c. as great a toll as a cataclysmic event.
    d. psychosomatic illness.

15. In Selye's GAS model, preparation to fight the stressor occurs in the

    a. alarm and mobilization stage.
    b. exhaustion stage.
    c. adaptation stage.
    d. resistance stage.

16. Psychosomatic illness would be more likely to occur in the stage of the GAS model known as

    a. exhaustion.
    b. alarm and mobilization.
    c. resistance.
    d. adaptation.

17. A rise in certain hormones secreted by the adrenal glands, a rise in heart rate and blood pressure, and changes in how well the skin conducts electrical impulses are all reactions to

    a. psychosomatic illness.
    b. learned helplessness.
    c. emotion-focused coping.
    d. stress.

18. Overall, it appears that for someone to consider an event as stressful, that person must perceive the event as

    a. important.
    b. frightening.
    c. threatening.
    d. dangerous.

19. According to Selye, to totally avoid stress, a person would have to

    a. remain in the resistance stage.
    b. use problem-focused coping.
    c. remain in the alarm and adaptation stage.
    d. cease living.

20. The efforts to control, reduce, or learn to tolerate the threats that lead to stress are known as

    a. defense mechanisms.
    b. personal stressors.
    c. coping.
    d. background stressors.

Part Six: PHYSICAL AND MENTAL HEALTH

MATCHING QUESTIONS

Match each term with the best description.

_____ 21. stress

_____ 22. stressors

_____ 23. psychosomatic disorders

_____ 24. general adaptation syndrome

_____ 25. cataclysmic events

_____ 26. personal stressors

_____ 27. background stressors

_____ 28. learned helplessness

_____ 29. coping

_____ 30. inoculation

_____ 31. defense mechanisms

a. involves preparation for stress

b. involves efforts to control, reduce, or learn to tolerate a threat

c. is the belief that one has no control over the environment

d. is the response to threatening events

e. are caused by an interaction of psychological, emotional, and physical difficulties

f. occur suddenly and affect many people at once

g. are daily hassles

h. are unconscious strategies to reduce stress

i. are major life events, such as the death of a family member

j. is a three-stage model of stress

k. are circumstances that produce threats to our well-being

ANSWER KEY: SECTION I

FILL IN THE BLANKS

1. response; threaten; challenge

2. stressors; threats

3. psychosomatic disorders

4. general adaptation syndrome; alarm; mobilization; resistance; exhaustion

5. cataclysmic events

6. personal stressors

7. background stressors

8. learned helplessness

9. coping; stress

10. defense mechanisms; stress

MULTIPLE CHOICE

11. c	16. a
12. a	17. d
13. c	18. c
14. b	19. d
15. d	20. c

MATCHING QUESTIONS

21. d	27. g
22. k	28. c
23. e	29. b
24. j	30. a
25. f	31. h
26. i	

REVIEW QUESTIONS: SECTION II

FILL IN THE BLANKS

1. _____ _____ _____ is a pattern characterized by competitiveness, impatience, and a tendency toward frustration and hostility.

2. A heightened risk of _____ _____ _____ is generally associated with the _____ _____ _____ pattern.

3. Individuals who are not usually aggressive, driven, or hostile and who are less competitive and not especially time-oriented may be displaying _____ _____ _____.

4. The evidence linking _____ _____ _____ and _____ _____ _____ is correlational; so we cannot say that one _____ the other.

5. According to the U.S. Surgeon General, _____ is the greatest _____ cause of _____ in America.

6. Psychologists have determined that smokers go through _____ _____ _____ which culminate in the smoking habit.

7. The most effective treatments for smokers who want to quit have been _____ _____, which view smoking as a learned habit and concentrate on changing the smoking response.

8. Some studies suggest that a patient's emotional response may have an effect on the course of a disease; this is evidence that emotional state may affect the _____ _____.

MULTIPLE CHOICE

9. Of those trying to quit smoking, long-term success occurs in

   a. 50 percent.
   b. 15 percent.
   c. 20 percent.
   d. 10 percent.

10. Which of the following is *not* one of the four stages leading to the formation of the smoking habit?

    a. organization
    b. preparation
    c. initiation
    d. maintaining

11. Smokers develop a physiological dependence on

    a. cigarettes.
    b. tar.
    c. nicotine.
    d. relief from anxiety.

12. There is some evidence suggesting that, rather than focusing on Type A behavior as the cause of heart disease, we should concentrate on

    a. Type A behaviors that affect the immune system.
    b. Type B behaviors which appear critical in the prevention of heart disease.
    c. Type A behaviors which can be altered instead of eliminated.
    d. Type B behaviors that work with the immune system.

13. Type A behaviors would be of little more than passing interest to health psychologists were it not for the fact that

    a. clinical psychologists do not want to deal with Type A's.
    b. Type A behavior is very difficult to spot.
    c. Type B's are healthier and more satisfying to work with.
    d. Type A behavior has been linked to heart disease.

14. Research suggests that cancer patients

    a. generally have a very positive attitude.
    b. suppress their anger about having the disease.
    c. have Type A personalities.
    d. have Type B personalities.

15. What is likely to prove most effective in reducing the amount of smoking in this country are

    a. better medical programs for people who want to quit.
    b. scare tactics concerning the health consequences of smoking.
    c. changing societal attitudes about smoking and people who smoke.
    d. family pressure.

MATCHING QUESTIONS

Match each term with the best description.

_____ 16. immune system

_____ 17. coronary heart disease

_____ 18. Type A behavior

_____ 19. Type B behavior

_____ 20. smoking

a. has psychological and biological causes

b. appears to be a critical pattern in the prevention of heart disease

c. involves competitiveness and impatience

d. may be linked to Type A behavior

e. may be affected by emotional states

ANSWER KEY: SECTION II

FILL IN THE BLANKS

1. Type A behavior

2. coronary heart disease; Type A behavior

3. Type B behavior

4. Type A behavior; coronary heart disease; causes

5. smoking; preventable; death

6. four basic stages

7. behavioral strategies

8. immune system

MULTIPLE CHOICE

9. b

10. a

11. c

12. b

13. d

14. b

15. c

MATCHING QUESTIONS

16. e

17. d

18. c

19. b

20. a

REVIEW QUESTIONS: SECTION III

FILL IN THE BLANKS

1. There are important _____ _____ that influence a physician's effectiveness in diagnosing and treating medical problems.

2. The view held by many patients that doctors are _____-_____ results in serious _____ problems.

3. Research has shown that about one-_____ of all patients cannot accurately report how long they are to continue taking a medication and about one-_____ do not even know the purpose of the drug.

4. Patients typically construct their own _____ about their illnesses, which may have little basis in reality.

5. One major consequence of patient-physician communication difficulties is a lack of _____ with medical advice.

6. A patient's degree of _____ with his or her medical care is linked to how well and how accurately the physician is able to convey the nature of the medical problem and treatment.

7. Physicians who are most successful in bringing about patient _____ are perceived as friendly, likable, and interested in their patients.

MULTIPLE CHOICE

8. Which one of the following statements about patients' perceptions of physicians is *not* true?

    a. Many patients feel that physicians are intentionally trying to frighten them.
    b. Many patients believe that physicians are so skilled that they can easily identify a medical problem through little more than an examination.
    c. Patients may feel intimidated by the physician's relatively high prestige and power.
    d. Many patients believe that physicians are all-knowing.

9. Each of the following is a reason for poor patient-physician communication *except*

    a. the patient's view that the physician is all-knowing.
    b. the patient's compliance needs.
    c. the physician's use of medical jargon.
    d. the fact that patients construct their own theories of illness.

10. Research indicates that up to _____ of all patients cannot accurately report how long they are to continue taking a medication prescribed for them.

    a. three-quarters
    b. two-thirds
    c. one-quarter
    d. one-half

11. Theories that patients construct about their illnesses

    a. may have little basis in reality.
    b. may be relatively accurate.
    c. can aid in patient-physician communication.
    d. help patients comply with treatment.

12. One major consequence of difficulties in patient-physician communication is

    a. an increase in patient theories.
    b. distorted patient perceptions.
    c. lack of compliance with medical advice.
    d. lack of agreement as to the patient's problem.

MATCHING QUESTIONS

Match each term with the best description.

_____ 13. compliance
_____ 14. patient theories
_____ 15. medical jargon
_____ 16. psychological forces

a. are at work in the compliance process
b. can make communication difficult
c. have little basis in reality
d. is a complex social process

ANSWER KEY: SECTION III

FILL IN THE BLANKS

1. psychological dimensions
2. all-knowing; communication
3. half; quarter
4. theories
5. compliance
6. satisfaction
7. compliance

MULTIPLE CHOICE

8. a
9. b
10. d
11. a
12. c

MATCHING QUESTIONS

13. d
14. c
15. b
16. a

INTEGRATING THE MATERIAL

1. Explain both positive and negative ways in which psychological factors can influence physical health.

2. What information that you have mastered concerning learning theory may be applied to creating stress and coping with stress?

ACTIVITIES FOR CHAPTER REVIEW

1. Look through newspapers and magazines for follow-up stories on survivors of cataclysmic events. In what ways is stress visible in the lives of the people involved? What types of measures should be taken to help the survivors and their families?

2. Using the general adaptation syndrome as your model, observe yourself in class when a paper is due or a test is approaching. At what point do you experience alarm and mobilization? When do you prepare to "fight" the stressor? How do you do these things? Do you reach the exhaustion stage? Under what circumstances?

3. Select an upcoming stressor in your life (such as a job interview or moving) and inoculate yourself for the stress. Describe the process of inoculation. How successful were you?

CHAPTER

16

ABNORMAL BEHAVIOR

CHAPTER OVERVIEW

Chapter 16 deals with defining and describing abnormal behavior. The most significant disorders are discussed.

Chapter 16 is divided into four sections.

I. The first section discusses the difficult task of distinguishing abnormal from normal behavior. Rather than being distinct entities, normality and abnormality may be viewed as a continuum of behavior patterns. In an attempt to define legally which cases of abnormal behavior require treatment, most states have adopted four criteria. The person must be (1) dangerous to himself or herself; (2) incapable of providing for basic physical needs; (3) unable to make reasonable decisions about whether treatment is required; and (4) in need of treatment or care. Whether and at what point an individual meets these criteria is difficult to determine. One mental health survey revealed that close to 20 percent of adults queried had a mental disorder.

II. The second section of the chapter examines a variety of models of abnormality. Historically, there have been many views on abnormality. Today, various models are used to describe and account for it. The medical model views abnormal behavior as a biological disease. The psychoanalytic model considers the role of internal conflicts. The behavioral model emphasizes the external manifestations of abnormality. The humanistic model maintains that the person is in control and views people as basically rational. The sociocultural model views society as a major contributor to abnormality. These models are applied to the case of Joyce Brown. It is noted that people studying abnormal behavior often feel that they suffer from these problems themselves.

III. The third section of the chapter begins to examine how abnormal behavior is classified. A standard system has been developed by the American Psychiatric Association and is known as the *DSM-III-R*—the *Diagnostic and Statistical Manual of Mental Disorders, Third Edition–Revised*. This publication provides precise definitions for more than 230 separate diagnostic categories and evaluates a person's behavior according to five dimensions or axes. Three types of disorders are described in this section of the chapter: anxiety disorders, somatoform disorders, and dissociative disorders. Anxiety disorders occur when anxiety is so great that it impedes people's everyday functioning. The four types of anxiety described include generalized anxiety disorder, panic disorder, phobic disorder, and obsessive-compulsive disorder. Somatoform disorders are psychological problems that take on a physical form. Somatoform disorders include hypochondriasis and conversion disorder. Dissociative disorders occur when there is a splitting apart of normally integrated parts of personality. Three types include multiple personality, psychogenic amnesia, and psychogenic fugue.

IV. The fourth and final section of the chapter continues describing major disorders classified in the *DSM-III-R*. The disorders are mood disorders, including major depression and mania and bipolar disorders; schizophrenia; and personality disorders. Mood disorders are characterized by affective disturbances that are so great they impede daily living. Major depression is one of the most common forms, and the rate of depression is increasing. Other types of mood disorders include mania and bipolar disorders. Schizophrenia is the most severe form of mental disturbance, and schizophrenics make up the largest percentage of those hospitalized for mental disorders. This class of disorders is characterized by severe distortions of reality. Symptoms include delusions, perceptual disorders, emotional disturbances, withdrawal, disturbances of thought and language, and decline from a previous level of functioning. Personality-disordered individuals may appear to function well, but under the surface lies a set of inflexible, maladaptive personality traits that do not permit appropriate functioning in society. Other forms of abnormal behavior include sexual disorders, psychoactive-substance-use disorders, and organic mental disorders. The chapter concludes with a list of signals that suggest the need for outside intervention.

STUDY STRATEGY

Follow this strategy for *each* section of the chapter.

1. Review the CHAPTER OUTLINE up to Recap and Review I.

2. Read the CHAPTER OVERVIEW, Section I.

3. Read the chapter in the text up to Recap and Review I.

4. For any question you answered incorrectly or did not understand, go back to the parts of the text that cover that material.

5. Write your answers to the REVIEW QUESTIONS for Section I in the *Study Guide*. Consult the answer key only after you have finished. Then correct any mistakes.

6. After you have completed the REVIEW QUESTIONS for Section I and have corrected your mistakes, follow the STUDY STRATEGY for Section II. Do the same for each section until you have completed all REVIEW QUESTIONS.

7. Then complete all INTEGRATING THE MATERIAL questions at the end of the *Study Guide* chapter. Answering these questions will help you see how the material fits together.

And, don't forget:
   Go back to the parts of the text that cover material that was difficult for you. If you still don't understand a concept, ask your teacher for clarification. Your questions in class and your teacher's answers will help other students as well.

MASTERY QUESTIONS

After mastering Chapter 16, you will be able to answer the following questions:

How can we distinguish normal from abnormal behavior?

What are the major models of abnormal behavior used by mental-health professionals?

How can we apply these approaches to specific cases, such as that of Joyce Brown?

What is the classification system used to categorize abnormal behavior, and what are the major mental-health disorders?

What are the major indicators that signal a need for the help of a mental-health practitioner?

REVIEW QUESTIONS: SECTION I

FILL IN THE BLANKS

1. Rosenhan and each of his colleagues were diagnosed as _____.

2. The differences between normal and abnormal behavior are not as _____ as we might think.

3. One way to determine abnormality is to observe what behaviors are rare or infrequent and label these _____ as abnormal.

4. The fact that societal standards are not agreed upon, and change over time, leaves the deviation-from-the-ideal approach to defining abnormality as _____.

5. Another way of defining abnormality is through the degree of _____ _____ a person may experience.

6. Abnormality can also be seen as the inability to _____ effectively.

7. Since the distinction between normal and abnormal often remains indistinct, perhaps the best way to deal with the definition is to consider abnormal behaviors not as _____ _____, but rather as marking the two ends of a _____.

MUTLIPLE CHOICE

8. A continuum is

   a. a continuous measurement scale.
   b. the two end points of a scale.
   c. a kind of abnormal behavior.
   d. a definition for abnormal behavior.

9. The view of abnormal behavior which concentrates on the psychological consequences of the behavior for the individual is

   a. deviation from the ideal.
   b. sense of subjective discomfort.
   c. deviation from average.
   d. inability to function effectively.

10. The deviation-from-ideal approach to defining abnormal behavior takes into account

    a. behaviors that are rare or infrequent.
    b. the individual's inability to take proper care of himself or herself.
    c. the individual's deviation from societal standards.
    d. the individual's place on a continuum.

11. Observation of rare or infrequent behaviors is part of the

    a. deviation-from-average approach.
    b. deviation-from-ideal approach.
    c. sense-of-subjective-discomfort approach.
    d. continuum approach.

12. The continuum of normal and abnormal behavior looks at

    a. absolute states.
    b. severe abnormality on both ends.
    c. behavior as falling in between two extremes.
    d. behavior as always approaching abnormaltiy.

13. The best conclusions that can be made from the case of Joyce Brown is that

    a. her behavior is quite normal.
    b. she is clearly unable to take care of herself.
    c. she is a danger to society.
    d. abnormality is difficult to define.

14. In most states, which one of the following is *not* a criterion for abnormality?

    a. The person requires treatment.
    b. The person is dangerous to himself.
    c. The person suffers subjective discomfort.
    d. The person is not capable of providing for basic physical needs.

15. The number of Americans who have one or more mental disorders or have suffered from one within the past six months is

    a. 10 million.
    b. 18 million.
    c. 29 million.
    d. 50 million.

16. The number of Americans who abuse alcohol or other drugs is about

    a. 2 million.
    b. 5 million.
    c. 8 million.
    d. 10 million.

MATCHING QUESTIONS

Match each term with the best definition.

_____ 17. continuum

_____ 18. abnormal behavior

_____ 19. deviation from average

_____ 20. deviation from ideal

_____ 21. sense of subjective discomfort

a. allows us to look at behavior as falling in between two points

b. considers the standard toward which most people strive

c. considers rare, infrequent behaviors

d. considers the psychological consequences of behavior

e. is difficult to define

ANSWER KEY: SECTION I

FILL IN THE BLANKS

1. abnormal
2. apparent
3. deviations
4. inadequate

5. subjective discomfort
6. function
7. absolute states; continuum

MULTIPLE CHOICE

8. a
9. b
10. c
11. a
12. c

13. d
14. c
15. c
16. d

MATCHING QUESTIONS

17. a
18. e
19. c

20. b
21. d

REVIEW QUESTIONS: SECTION II

FILL IN THE BLANKS

1. When we speak of "mental illness" or the "symptoms" of abnormal behavior, we are using terminology related to the _____ _____.

2. The _____ _____ holds that abnormality stems from childhood conflicts over opposing wishes.

3. Those who look at the behavior itself as the problem are using the _____ _____.

4. Some psychologists concentrate on what is uniquely human and view people as basically rational. They are using the _____ _____.

5. _____ approaches to abnormal behavior make the assumption that people's behavior—both normal and abnormal—is shaped by the kind of _____ _____ and _____ or _____ in which they live.

6. Some students are susceptible to _____ _____ _____ in feeling that the symptoms and illnesses about which they are studying are characteristic of themselves. In most cases, of course, this is not the case.

MULTIPLE CHOICE

7. Criticism for reliance on unscientific, unverifiable information as well as vague concepts has been levied against the

   a. psychoanalytic model.
   b. humanistic model.
   c. sociocultural model.
   d. behavioral model.

8. The relationship of the individual to the world and the ways in which people view themselves in relation to others constitute the focus of the

   a. behavioral model.
   b. sociocultural model.
   c. humanistic model.
   d. medical model.

9. Which one of the following statements applies to the psychoanalytic model of abnormal behavior?

   a. Abnormality stems from childhood conflicts.
   b. Abnormal behavior itself is the problem.
   c. The symptoms of abnormal behavior are important.
   d. Humans strive toward self-fulfillment.

10. The medical model suggests that when a person shows symptoms of abnormality, the root cause will be found in

   a. the person's family.
   b. repressed childhood conflict.
   c. behavioral abnormalities.
   d. some physical aspect of the person.

11. The greatest strength as well as weakness of the behavioral approach to abnormal behavior lies in

   a. a refusal to see behavior as a symptom.
   b. emphasis on overt, observable behavior.
   c. emphasis on childhood conflict.
   d. attempts to blame abnormality on the family.

12. The idea that children pass through a series of stages in which sexual and aggressive impulses take different forms comes from

   a. Freud.
   b. Selye.
   c. Piaget.
   d. Skinner.

13. The extreme position that there really is no such thing as abnormal behavior is held by proponents of the

   a. psychoanalytic model.
   b. humanistic model.
   c. sociocultural model.
   d. behavioral model.

14. The most precise and objective model is

   a. humanistic.
   b. medical.
   c. behavioral.
   d. sociocultural.

15. Which model would focus on Joyce Brown's history of reward and punishment to explain her abnormal behavior?

    a. humanistic
    b. behavioral
    c. psychoanalytic
    d. sociocultural

16. Which model might look for a chemical imbalance to explain Joyce Brown's behavior?

    a. psychoanalytic
    b. behavioral
    c. humanistic
    d. medical

17. Which model would focus on Joyce Brown's personal choices in exploring her behavior?

    a. humanistic
    b. psychoanalytic
    c. behavioral
    d. medical

MATCHING QUESTIONS

Match each model with the best description

_____ 18. psychoanalytic model

_____ 19. sociocultural model

_____ 20. humanistic model

_____ 21. behavioral model

_____ 22. medical model

a. claims that behavior is shaped by family and society

b. is a physiological theory

c. views people as rational decision makers

d. emphasizes the here and now

e. is rooted in conflict

ANSWER KEY: SECTION II

FILL IN THE BLANKS

1. medical model

2. psychoanalytic model

3. behavioral model

4. humanistic model

5. sociocultural; family group; society; culture

6. medical student's disease

MULTIPLE CHOICE

7. b   13. c

8. c   14. c

9. a   15. b

10. d   16. d

11. b   17. a

12. a

MATCHING QUESTIONS

18. e   21. d

19. a   22. b

20. c

REVIEW QUESTIONS: SECTION III

FILL IN THE BLANKS

1. The _____ _____ _____ _____
_____ _____ _____ is commonly known as the *DSM-III-R*.

2. Without _____, most of us would not be terribly motiviated to study hard, to undergo physical examinations, or to spend long hours at our jobs.

3. The occurrence of anxiety that intrudes on daily functioning without obvious external cause is known as _____ _____.

4. When an individual experiences long-term, consistent anxiety without knowing why, he or she may be suffering from _____ _____ _____.

5. In another type of anxiety disorder, known as _____ _____, attacks lasting from a few seconds to several hours occur.

6. Intense, irrational fears of specific objects or situations are known as _____; people who have them are said to be suffering from _____ _____.

7. An individual who cannot get rid of an unwanted thought and repeatedly carries out some act that seems strange may be suffering from _____-_____ _____.

8. A constant fear of illness and misinterpretation of normal aches and pains is a condition known as
_____, which is one example of a class of disorders known as _____
_____.

9. Some of Freud's classic cases involved another type of disorder in which a _____
disturbance is characterized by an actual _____ disturbance such as the inability to
move one's arms. These disturbances are known as _____ _____.

10. Books and movies such as *Sybil* and *The Three Faces of Eve* portray individuals with
_____ _____. This is quite rare and falls under the heading of
_____ _____.

MULTIPLE CHOICE

11. The conditions of psychogenic fugue and psychogenic amensia fall under the heading of

    a. converson disorders.
    b. dissociative disorders.
    c. somatoform disorders.
    d. generalized anxiety disorders.

12. An urge to repeatedly carry out an act that seems strange and unreasonable even to the individual involved is known as

    a. an obsession.
    b. a phobic disorder.
    c. a compulsion.
    d. anxiety.

13. Each of the following is true of people experiencing an obsessive-compulsive disorder *except* that

    a. there is a reduction of anxiety from carrying out a compulsive ritual.
    b. they tend to repeatedly carry out strange acts.
    c. they are troubled by recurring thoughts.
    d. they tend to lead lives filled with unrelenting tension.

14. Generalized anxiety disorder may be defined as

    a. sudden anxiety characterized by heart palpitations, shortness of breath, sweating, faintness, and great fear.
    b. a feeling of apprehension or tension.
    c. psychological difficulties that take on physical form.
    d. the experience of long-term anxiety with no explanation.

15. All the following are criticisms of the *DSM-III-R except* that

    a. it has a tendency to view abnormal behavior in terms of some underlying physiological disorder.
    b. it pigeonholes people into inflexible categories.
    c. it is too comprehensive and exhaustive.
    d. it provides labels which are dehumanizing.

16. Intense irrational fears of specific objects or situations are called

    a. panics.
    b. phobias.
    c. obsessions.
    d. compulsions.

17. A person with an intense fear of heights is suffering from

    a. acrophobia.
    b. aerophobia.
    c. cynophobia.
    d. claustrophobia.

18. Xenophobia is the fear of

    a. water.
    b. cats.
    c. flying.
    d. strangers.

19. Hypochondriasis is an example of a class of disorders known as

    a. conversion disorders.
    b. anxiety disorders.
    c. somatoform disorders.
    d. mood disorders.

20. A dissociative disorder in which people take sudden, impulsive trips, sometimes assuming a new identity, is known as

    a. psychogenic fugue.
    b. psychogenic amnesia.
    c. multiple personality.
    d. obsessive-compulsive disorder.

21. The *DSM-III-R* provides

    a. labels.
    b. explanations.
    c. both a and b.
    d. neither a nor b.

22. All of the following are categories in the *DSM-III-R* except

    a. self-defeating personality disorder.
    b. somatoform disorder.
    c. mood disorder.
    d. sexual disorder.

MATCHING QUESTIONS

Match each term with the best description.

_____ 23. dissociative disorder

_____ 24. somatoform disorder

_____ 25. compulsion

_____ 26. obsessive-compulsive disorder

_____ 27. anxiety disorder

_____ 28. anxiety

_____ 29. acrophobia

_____ 30. phobic disorder

_____ 31. agoraphobia

_____ 32. panic attack

_____ 33. obsession

_____ 34. multiple personality

a. is a fear of open spaces

b. is a feeling of apprehension or tension

c. is a fear of heights

d. is two or more distinct personalities

e. is a recurring thought or idea

f. is characterized by heart palpitations, shortness of breath, and great fear

g. is a disorder in which psychological difficulties take on physical form

h. is characterized by obsessions or compulsions

i. is characterized by the splitting apart of personality facets

j. is characterized by unrealistic fear

k. is an urge to repeat a strange act

l. occurs when anxiety of unknown origin intrudes on daily functioning

ANSWER KEY: SECTION III

FILL IN THE BLANKS

1. *Diagnostic and Statistical Manual of Mental Disorders*
2. anxiety
3. anxiety disorder
4. generalized anxiety disorder
5. panic disorder

6. phobias; phobic disorder
7. obsessive-compulsive disorder
8. hypochondriasis; somatoform disorders
9. mental; physical; conversion disorders
10. multiple personalities; dissociative disorders

MULTIPLE CHOICE

11. b
12. c
13. a
14. d
15. c
16. b
17. a
18. d
19. c
20. a
21. a
22. a

23. i
24. g
25. k
26. h
27. l
28. b
29. c
30. j
31. a
32. f
33. e
34. d

REVIEW QUESTIONS: SECTION IV

FILL IN THE BLANKS

1. People with mood disturbances that are pronounced and long-lasting may be suffering from a(n)_____ _____.

2. One of the most common forms of affective disorders is _____ _____, which interferes with concentration, decision making, and sociability.

3. Unlike the despair of depression, another affective disorder known as _____ is an extended state of intense _____ and _____.

4. Individuals with _____ _____ typically experience
   _____ paired with bouts of _____.

5. People suffering from _____, which is characterized by severe distortion of
   _____, make up the largest percentage of those hospitalized for mental disorders.

6. Schizophrenics often have _____ or firmly held _____ with little or
   no basis in _____.

7. Perceptions of things that do not actually exist are known as _____.

8. The _____ hypothesis is one of the theories which suggests that
   _____ may be the result of a(n) _____ imbalance.

9. The _____-_____ hypothesis suggests that people suffering from
   _____ may have received simultaneous messages from their mothers that
   _____ one another.

10. The theory which suggests that schizophrenia is a learned behavior consisting of a set of
    inappropriate responses to social stimuli is known as the _____-_____
    theory of schizophrenia.

MULTIPLE CHOICE

11. The mental disorder characterized by
    inappropriate giggling, incoherent speech,
    and other strange behavior is known as

    a. catatonic schizophrenia.
    b. disorganized (hebephrenic)
       schizophrenia.
    c. paranoid schizophrenia.
    d. undifferentiated schizophrenia.

12. Delusions of persecution or greatness, loss
    of judgment, and unpredictable behavior are
    characteristic of

    a. paranoid schizophrenia.
    b. hebephrenic schizophrenia.
    c. catatonic schizophrenia.
    d. undifferentiated schizophrenia.

13. A mental disorder characterized by minor
    symptoms of schizophrenia following a
    severe case or episode is known as

    a. disorganized schizophrenia.
    b. catatonic schizophrenia.
    c. paranoid schizophrenia.
    d. residual schizophrenia.

14. The predisposition model of schizophrenia
    suggests that

    a. schizophrenic individuals received
       conflicting messages from their mothers.
    b. schizophrenia is biochemical in origin.
    c. certain individuals may have an inborn
       sensitivity to schizophrenia.
    d. schizophrenia is a learned set of
       behaviors.

15. Personality disorder is characterized by

    a. firmly held beliefs with little basis in reality.
    b. a mixture of symptoms of schizophrenia.
    c. a set of inflexible, maladaptive traits.
    d. an extended sense of euphoria and elation.

16. Individuals who display no reagard for the moral and ethical rules of society or for the rights of others may have a disorder known as

    a. antisocial personality.
    b. schizophrenia.
    c. bipolar disorder.
    d. double-bind disorder.

17. Each of the following is true concerning individuals with personality disorder except that

    a. they may have no concern for the rights of others.
    b. they have little ability to withstand frustration.
    c. they are personally distressed over their behavior.
    d. they may be manipulative.

18. Bipolar disorder used to be known as

    a. depression.
    b. manic-depressive disorder.
    c. schizophrenia.
    d. personality disorder.

19. The belief that Martians have hidden videocameras in the walls would be considered a(n)

    a. hallucination.
    b. compulsion.
    c. delusion.
    d. sign of withdrawal.

20. Schizophrenia may be caused by

    a. genetic factors.
    b. chemical factors.
    c. both a and b.
    d. neither a nor b.

MATCHING QUESTIONS

Match each term with the best description.

_____ 21. personality disorder

_____ 22. schizophrenia

_____ 23. dopamine hypothesis

_____ 24. double-bind hypothesis

_____ 25. hallucination

_____ 26. delusion

_____ 27. bipolar disorder

_____ 28. hebephrenic

_____ 29. affective disorder

_____ 30. undifferentiated

a. is a mixture of symptoms

b. is a belief with no basis in reality

c. includes states of euphoria and depression

d. includes mood disturbances

e. involves inappropriate giggling and incoherent speech

f. is characterized by severe distortion of reality

g. is a biochemical theory

h. is a perception with no reality

i. is characterized by a set of inflexible, maladaptive traits

j. involves the communication of simultaneous, contradictory messages

ANSWER KEY: SECTION IV

FILL IN THE BLANKS

1. affective disorder

2. major depression

3. mania; euphoria; elation

4. bipolar disorder; mania; depression

5. schizophrenia; reality

6. delusions; beliefs; reality

7. hallucinations

8. dopamine; schizophrenia; biochemical

9. double-bind; schizophrenia; contradicted

10. learned-inattention

MULTIPLE CHOICE

11. b

12. a

13. d

14. c

15. c

16. a

17. c

18. b

19. c

20. c

MATCHING QUESTIONS

21.	i	26.	b
22.	f	27.	c
23.	g	28.	e
24.	j	29.	d
25.	h	30.	a

INTEGRATING THE MATERIAL

1. Many disorders are described in this chapter and many distinctions are made among them because each disorder is unique. Even though they are all different, what do the disorders described in this chapter have in common?

2. In the previous chapter on health psychology an important point was made that the mind and the body work together and have an impact on each other. Discuss how the mind and body work together in the case of abnormal behavior.

ACTIVITIES FOR CHAPTER REVIEW

1. Interview a professional mental-health worker to find out more about the complexities of abnormal behavior. Design your interview to find out the types of people he or she works with, what a typical day is like in working with people who have mental-health problems, and the difficulties in diagnosis and treatment.

2. Select an abnormal behavior pattern described in the text and learn more about it by researching it in the library. Look up the abnormal behavior in the *DSM-III-R* and find journal articles that describe research on the disorder. *The Journal of Abnormal Psychology* and *The Journal of Clinical and Consulting Psychology* are good sources.

3. Review the various models of abnormality described in the text: medical, psychoanalytic, behavioral, humanistic, and sociocultural. Which model or models appeal to you the most? The least? Explain your views.

CHAPTER

17

TREATMENT OF ABNORMAL BEHAVIOR

CHAPTER OVERVIEW

Chapter 17 examines psychological and medical approaches to the treatment of abnormal behavior. Psychotherapy, the process in which a patient, or client, and a professional attempt to remedy problems, places emphasis on change as a result of discussions and interactions between therapist and client. Biologically based therapy uses drugs and other medical techniques to relieve psychological problems. Regardless of type of treatment, the goal is the same—relief from the psychological disorder and restoration of normal functioning.

Chapter 17 is divided into three sections.

I. The first section of the chapter covers psychodynamic and behavioral approaches to treatment. Psychodynamic therapy (including psychoanalysis) is based on the premise, first suggested by Freud, that the basic sources of abnormal behavior are unresolved past conflicts and anxiety over the possibility that unacceptable unconscious impulses will enter the conscious part of a person's mind. The goal of treatment is to work through these conflicts. In contrast, behavioral approaches are based on the premise that both normal and abnormal behaviors are learned through conditioning and reinforcement and that new behaviors can be learned in therapy through these same mechanisms. The most successful treatment based on classical conditioning is known as systematic desensitization. Cognitive-behavioral approaches and rational-emotive therapy set the goal of restructuring a person's faulty belief system to help the client maintain behavioral gains.

II. The humanistic approach gives the individual seeking treatment a more active role in both developing and reaching goals. Client-centered therapy, developed by Carl Rogers, is the best known and most frequently used type of humanistic therapy and is based on the principle of unconditional positive regard. Two other forms of humanistic therapy include existential therapy and gestalt therapy. Group therapy and family therapy are described briefly. The various forms of psychotherapy may be classifed along several dimensions, including directive versus nondirective, inner control of behavior versus outer control of behavior, long-term versus short-term, historical focus versus here-and-now focus, and cognitive change versus behavior change. Most psychologists agree that therapy does work. However, it is less clear whether one kind works better than another. The answer to this question depends on the nature of the psychological problem and the individual characteristics of therapist and client.

III. The third and final section of the chapter examines biological approaches to treatment, including drug therapy, electroconvulsive shock treatment, and psychosurgery. Of these three approaches, drug therapy is used with over 90 percent of all clients requiring a biological treatment. Drugs described include antipsychotic drugs (used to alleviate psychotic symptoms such as agitation and overactivity), antidepressant drugs (used in cases of severe depression to improve mood by allowing an increase in the concentration of certain neruotransmitters in the brain), lithium (which has been used successfully in cases of bipolar disorder and is used as a preventive treatment), and the minor tranquilizers, or antianxiety drugs (which are prescribed to help alleviate stress and anxiety on a short-term basis). Electroconvulsive shock therapy is still used today, but it has been improved. It remains a controversial technique. Psychosurgery became almost obsolete when successful drug therapy was introduced. However, it is still used occasionally in severe cases and remains another controversial technique. The use of community psychology is described as a preventive measure. The chapter ends with a discussion of how to choose the right therapist.

STUDY STRATEGY

Follow this strategy for *each* section of the chapter.

1. Review the CHAPTER OUTLINE up to Recap and Review I.

2. Read the CHAPTER OVERVIEW, Section I.

3. Read the chapter in the text up to Recap and Review I.

4. For any question you answered incorrectly or did not understand, go back to the parts of the text that cover that material.

5. Write your answers to the REVIEW QUESTIONS for Section I in the *Study Guide*. Consult the answer key only after you have finished. Then correct any mistakes.

6. After you have completed the REVIEW QUESTIONS for Section I and have corrected your mistakes, follow the STUDY STRATEGY for Section II. Do the same for each section until you have completed all REVIEW QUESTIONS.

7. Then complete the INTEGRATING THE MATERIAL questions at the end of the *Study Guide* chapter. Answering these questions will help you see how the material fits together.

And, don't forget:

Go back to the parts of the text that cover material that was difficult for you. If you still don't understand a concept, ask your teacher for clarification. Your questions in class and your teacher's answers will help other students as well.

MASTERY QUESTIONS

After mastering Chapter 17, you will be able to answer the following questions:

What are the differences between psychologically and biologically based treatment approaches?

What are the basic kinds of psychotherapies, and how do we evaluate them?

How are drug, electroconvulsive, and psychosurgical techniques used today in the treatment of mental disorders?

What is the best kind of therapy and therapist for a given situation?

REVIEW QUESTIONS: SECTION I

FILL IN THE BLANKS

1. A physician with an M.D. and postgraduate training in abnormal behavior is called a(n)

   _____ .

2. _____ _____ are psychological strategies that protect people from unconscious impulses.

3. A female patient who reacts to her psychiatrist as though he were her older brother is experiencing

   _____ .

4. The true message hidden within a dream is called the _____ content.

5. Aversive conditioning is a technique used to help people break unwanted habits by associating the habits with very _____ _____.

6. If a person made a list in order of increasing severity of things associated with his or her fear of flying, the list would be called a _____.

7. Learning by watching others' behavior and the consequences of that behavior is called _____ learning.

8. Ellis developed _____-_____ therapy, which restructures one's belief system.

9. A professional with a master's degree and specialized training in treating people in home and community settings is called a psychiatric _____ _____.

10. Systematic desensitization is based on _____ conditioning.

MULTIPLE CHOICE

11. The behavioral treatment approach uses all the following techniques *except*

    a. aversive conditioning.
    b. systematic desensitization.
    c. modeling.
    d. symptom substitution.

12. Psychodynamic therapy uses all of the following techniques *except*

    a. dream analysis.
    b. free association.
    c. contingency contracting.
    d. transference.

13. Defense mechanisms protect people from

    a. unconscious impulses.
    b. anxiety.
    c. both a and b.
    d. neither a nor b.

14. A psychiatric social worker has

    a. a Ph.D.
    b. an M.D.
    c. either a or b.
    d. neither a nor b.

15. According to Freud, the basic source of abnormal behavior are

    a. unresolved past conflicts and anxiety over the possibility that unacceptable unconscious impulses will enter the conscious mind.
    b. irrational cognitions which are mistaken by the individual as true facts, rather than beliefs, about the world.
    c. resistance to memories and the overuse of transference in the development of long-term relationships.
    d. early traumatic experiences that lead to making faulty associations.

16. Behavioral self-management involves all of the following concepts *except*

    a. getting goals.
    b. overcoming transference.
    c. modifying a response.
    d. being your own therapist.

17. Constructing a hierarchy of fears is a central part of the process of

    a. aversive conditioning.
    b. contingengy contracting.
    c. cognitive-behavioral therapy.
    d. systematic desensitization.

18. Clinical psychologists specialize in

    a. assessment of psychological problems.
    b. treatment of psychological problems.
    c. both a and b.
    d. neither a nor b.

MATCHING QUESTIONS

Match each term with the best description.

_____ 19. resistance

_____ 20. transference

_____ 21. defense mechanism

_____ 22. self-management technique

_____ 23. rational-emotive therapy

_____ 24. token system

_____ 25. free association

a. provides protection from unconscious impulses

b. is the unwillingness to discuss certain thoughts

c. was developed Albert Ellis

d. involves saying whatever comes to mind

e. provides rewards for desired behaviors; is used in institutional settings

f. is the process in which the client treats the therapist as a family member

g. allow you to design your own behavioral strategies for resolving a problem

ANSWER KEY: SECTION I

FILL IN THE BLANKS

1. psychiatrist

2. defense mechanisms

3. transference

4. latent

5. unpleasant stimuli

6. hierarchy

7. observational

8. rational-emotive

9. social worker

10. classical

MULTIPLE CHOICE

11. d   15. a

12. c   16. b

13. c   17. d

14. d   18. c

MATCHING QUESTIONS

19. b   23. c

20. f   24. e

21. a   25. d

22. g

REVIEW QUESTIONS: SECTION II

FILL IN THE BLANKS

1. _____ therapy draws upon the philosophical point of view of self-responsibility in developing treatment techniques.

2. _____ therapy is an approach that attempts to integrate thoughts, feelings, and behavior into a whole.

3. Supportive behavior from another person, regardless of one's own words or actions, is called _____ _____ _____.

4. _____ therapy is a humanistic approach that addresses the meaning of life.

5. Spontaneous remission refers to _____ without _____.

6. _____ counseling encourages the client to work out his or her own problems in a supportive atmosphere.

7. Client-centered therapy was developed by _____.

8. Existential therapy is based on the premise that freedom can produce _____, _____, and _____.

MULTIPLE CHOICE

9. Gestalt therapy was developed by

   a. Rogers.
   b. Chomsky.
   c. Perls.
   d. Ellis.

10. An underlying assumption of humanistic therapy is that people

    a. have control over their behavior.
    b. are driven by unconscious impulses.
    c. are capable of learning self-management techniques to control their behavior.
    d. believe the faulty cognitions that underlie their behavior.

11. Examine this therapist-client interaction:
    Client: "What good am I now that my children are on their own?"
    Therapist: "You feel that your family does not need you any more."
    The therapist's response is an example of

    a. behavior modification.
    b. nondirective counseling.
    c. psychoanalysis.
    d. rational-emotive therapy.

12. Fear of freedom and a search for meaning are most closely associated with

    a. nondirective therapy.
    b. existential therapy.
    c. gestalt therapy.
    d. client-centered therapy.

13. Completing unfinished business and reenacting specific conflicts experienced earlier are most clearly associated with

    a. nondirective therapy.
    b. existential therapy.
    c. gestalt therapy.
    d. cognitive-behavioral therapy.

14. The assumption that people are essentially responsible for solving their own problems underlies

    a. humanistic therapy.
    b. psychoanalysis.
    c. both a and b.
    d. neither a nor b.

15. The assumption that the goal of therapy is to help people resolve unconscious conflicts that create neurotic symptoms underlies

    a. client-centered therapy.
    b. humanistic therapy.
    c. both a and b.
    d. neither a nor b.

16. In humanistic therapy, unconditional positive regard is provided to the client

    a. as a reinforcement when goals have been met.
    b. as part of the contingency contract.
    c. no matter what the client says or does.
    d. to help resolve inner conflicts.

MATCHING QUESTIONS

Match each term with the best description.

_____ 17. gestalt therapy

_____ 18. existential therapy

_____ 19. spontaneous remission

_____ 20. client-centered therapy

_____ 21. nondirective counseling

_____ 22. group therapy

_____ 23. family therapy

a. was developed by Rogers

b. was developed by Perls

c. is for clients seeking a meaning to their lives

d. deals with a "system" rather than with separate individuals

e. involves working out your own problems in a supportive atmosphere

f. involves several unrelated people meeting with a therapist

g. is recovery without therapy

ANSWER KEY: SECTION II

FILL IN THE BLANKS

1. humanistic

2. gestalt

3. unconditional positive regard

4. existential

5. recovery; treatment

6. nondirective

7. Rogers

8. anguish; fear; concern

MULTIPLE CHOICE

9. c

10. a

11. b

12. b

13. c

14. a

15. d

16. c

MATCHING QUESTIONS

17. b

18. c

19. g

20. a

21. e

22. f

23. d

REVIEW QUESTIONS: SECTION III

FILL IN THE BLANKS

1. Chlorpromazine is an antipsychotic drug used in the treatment of _____.

2. _____ is a drug used in the treatment of bipolar disorders.

3. Minor tranquilizers alleviate _____.

4. _____ _____ is a controversial technique involving the administration of an electric current to a patient's head to treat depression.

5. Rarely used today, _____ is brain surgery to alleviate symptoms of mental disorder.

6. _____ _____ is the surgical destruction of certain areas of a patient's frontal lobes to improve the control of emotionality.

7. _____ psychology, which came of age in the 1960s, is aimed at minimizing and preventing psychological disorders.

MULTIPLE CHOICE

8. Antipsychotic drugs were successfully introduced during the

    a. 1950s.
    b. 1960s.
    c. 1970s.
    d. 1980s.

9. Which one of the following statements concerning antipsychotic drugs is true?

    a. They produce a cure in the same way that penicillin cures an infection.
    b. They function by increasing the production of dopamine at the sites where electrical impulses travel across nerve receptors.
    c. They are used for almost 90 percent of all hospitalized patients.
    d. None of the above statements is true.

10. Which one of the following drugs represents a preventive treatment?

    a. chlorpromazine
    b. lithium
    c. minor tranquilizer
    d. phenothiazine

11. The long-term side effects of antipsychotic drugs include

    a. dizziness.
    b. loss of muscle control.
    c. both a and b.
    d. neither a nor b.

12. It is *not* true that antianxiety drugs

    a. cause fatigue.
    b. can become lethal when taken in combination with alcohol.
    c. mask anxiety.
    d. are risk-free.

13. Disorientation, confusion, memory loss, and possible neurological damage are most closely associated with

    a. ECT.
    b. tranquilizers.
    c. lithium.
    d. antidepressants.

14. Chlorpromazine is a type of

    a. phenothiazine.
    b. preventive treatment.
    c. minor tranquilizer.
    d. neurotransmitter.

15. A common side effect of antidepressant medication is

    a. disorientation.
    b. hyperactivity.
    c. memory loss.
    d. drowsiness.

16. Exposure to light has been used in the treatment of

    a. depression.
    b. mania.
    c. schizophrenia.
    d. stress.

MATCHING QUESTIONS

Match each term with the best description.

_____ 17. lithium

_____ 18. antianxiety drug

_____ 19. chlorpromazine

_____ 20. prefrontal lobotomy

_____ 21. dopamine

_____ 22. ECT

a. may produce neurological damage

b. is a tranquilizer

c. is rarely used today

d. is used for treating bipolar disorders

e. is an antipsychotic drug

f. is a neurotransmitter

ANSWER KEY: SECTION III

FILL IN THE BLANKS

1. schizophrenia

2. lithium

3. anxiety

4. electroconvulsive therapy

5. psychosurgery

6. prefrontal lobotomy

7. community

MULTIPLE CHOICE

8. a	13. a
9. c	14. a
10. b	15. d
11. c	16. a
12. d	

MATCHING QUESTIONS

17. d	20. c
18. b	21. f
19. e	22. a

INTEGRATING THE MATERIAL

1. How has your understanding of the biological foundations of behavior, covered earlier in the text, helped you understand the origins and treatment of abnormal behavior?

2. What are some of the factors to take into account when seeking psychological services?

ACTIVITIES FOR CHAPTER REVIEW

1. Design a self-management program to deal with a problem that would lend itself to self-management. If you can't think of a problem that you would like to overcome, you might develop a program to deal with smoking, dieting, or some other behavior pattern. In designing your program, remember to set realistic goals (with subgoals along the way), provide appropriate reinforcement, and be specific in terms of a timeline.

2. Create a hierarchy of fears. Include steps beginning with the most feared object or situation and moving toward the least feared object or situation. For example, if you choose the fear of snakes, the most feared situation might be holding a snake and the least feared might be picturing a snake in your mind for five seconds, with a variety of steps in between. How would the hierarchy you created be used in a systematic desensitization program?

3. Make a list of questions that you would ask a therapist in order to find out if he or she could help a friend. Before writing your questions, be sure you know what you want to find out and the type of information you need about your friend's problem. Remember to ask about the therapist's credentials and orientation. Why is this type of information important?

4. Make a list of the drugs used for treating abnormal behavior. Next to the drug, write what it is used for, how it works, its effectiveness, and its possible side effects. This material could be written up in the form of a chart.

CHAPTER
18

SOCIAL PSYCHOLOGY: THE INDIVIDUAL IN A SOCIAL WORLD

CHAPTER OVERVIEW

Chapter 18 is the first of two chapters on social psychology, which is the study of how people's thoughts, feelings, and actions are affected by others. Social psychologists consider the nature and causes of individual behavior in social situations.

Chapter 18 is divided into three sections.

I.   The first section of the chapter explores attitudes—how they are formed and maintained, how persuasive techniques can be used to modify them, and how they fit or do not fit together with our behavior. Social psychologists generally consider attitudes to follow the ABC model, suggesting that attitudes have three components: affect, behavior, and cognition. Attitudes are learned predispositions to respond in a favorable or unfavorable manner to a particular object. Both classical conditioning and operant conditioning underlie attitude acquisition. The major factors promoting persuasion include message source, characteristics of the message, and characteristics of the recipient or target. People strive for consistency between their attitudes and their behavior. Inconsistency can lead to cognitive dissonance, a state of psychological tension. Self-perception theory states that people form attitudes by observing their own behavior.

II.   The second section of the chapter deals with our understanding and interpretation of the behavior of others—of the processes involved in social cognition. Rather than being haphazard, our impressions of others are learned (directly and indirectly) and follow regular, predictable patterns. We often form impressions of others by relying on basic, central traits to combine individual traits into an overall impression or by mathematically averaging individual traits into a general impression. Stereotypes are beliefs and expectations about members of a group formed simply on the basis of their membership in that group. Although stereotyping helps us make sense out of the world, it leads to inaccuracies that can be damaging to those who have been stereotyped.

III. The third and final section of the chapter explores the attribution process, through which we determine the meaning of other people's behavior—determinations which are often biased and inaccurate but which affect our impressions. One of the most common biases in our attributions is the tendency to attribute others' behavior to dispositional causes, but to attribute our own behavior to situational causes. We can increase the accuracy of impressions and reduce stereotyping by increasing contact, making positive values conspicuous, and providing information about the targets of stereotyping.

STUDY STRATEGY

Follow this strategy for *each* section of the chapter.

1. Review the CHAPTER OUTLINE up to Recap and Review I.

2. Read the CHAPTER OVERVIEW, Section I.

3. Read the chapter in the text up to Recap and Review I.

4. For any question you answered incorrectly or did not understand, go back to the parts of the text that cover that material.

5. Write your answers to the REVIEW QUESTIONS for Section I in the *Study Guide*. Consult the answer key only after you have finished. Then correct any mistakes.

6. After you have completed the REVIEW QUESTIONS for Section I and have corrected your mistakes, follow the STUDY STRATEGY for Section II. Do the same for each section until you have completed all REVIEW QUESTIONS.

7. Then complete the INTEGRATING THE MATERIAL questions at the end of the *Study Guide* chapter. Answering these questions will help you see how the material fits together.

And, don't forget:
    Go back to the parts of the text that cover material that was difficult for you. If you still don't understand a concept, ask your teacher for clarification. Your questions in class and your teacher's answers will help other students as well.

MASTERY QUESTIONS

After mastering Chapter 18, you will be able to answer the following questions:

What are attitudes and how are they formed, maintained, and changed?

How do we form impressions of what others are like and the causes of their behavior?

What are the biases that color the way in which we view others' behavior?

How can our judgments about others be made more accurately?

REVIEW QUESTIONS: SECTION I

FILL IN THE BLANKS

1. The branch of psychology concerned with how people's thoughts, feelings, and actions are affected by others is known as _____ _____.

2. Social psychologists who study _____ are interested in people's learned _____ to respond to a(n) _____ or _____ manner to a particular object.

3. Some of our attitudes develop through _____ _____ when we learn from watching others.

4. According to Festinger, _____ _____ occurs when a person holds two _____ or _____ that contradict each other.

5. Message interpretation characterized by thoughtful consideration of issues and arguments is known as _____ _____ _____.

6. _____ _____ _____ occurs when the source and related general information are considered rather than the message itself.

7. In cognitive dissonance theory, attitudes, thoughts, and beliefs are referred to as _____.

8. Bem has suggested an alternative to dissonance theory called the _____ _____ _____-_____.

9. The idea that people form attitudes by observing their own behavior, using the same principles that they use when they observe others' behavior, to draw conclusions about others' attitudes is put forth in the theory of _____-_____.

MULTIPLE CHOICE

10. The branch of psychology concerned with how people's thoughts, feelings, and actions are affected by others is

    a. counseling psychology.
    b. cognitive psychology.
    c. social psychology.
    d. clinical psychology.

11. Research has shown that attitudes can be acquired through

    , a. cognitive dissonance.
    b. classical conditioning.
    c. genetics.
    d. none of the above.

12. Advertisers often try to link a product they want consumers to buy to a

    a. positive feeling or event.
    b. cognition.
    c. peripheral route.
    d. dissonant stimulus.

13. An attempt to minimize dissonance by exposing oneself only to information that supports one's choice is known as

    a. dissonance reduction.
    b. cognitive reduction.
    c. cognitive dissonance.
    d. selective exposure.

14. According to Festinger's theory, if a smoker holds the cognitions "I smoke" and "Smoking causes cancer," he or she should be motivated to do all of the following *except*

    a. modify one or both cognitions.
    b. enter a stop-smoking program.
    c. make the attitudes consistent.
    d. change the importance of one cognition.

15. The conflict that arises when a person holds conflicting attitudes is known as

    a. classical conflict.
    b. central dissonance.
    c. cognitive dissonance.
    d. selective exposure.

16. A 5-year-old boy who overhears his father tell his mother that "Southerners are ignorant" may grow up to believe this opinion and adopt it as an attitude as a result of the process of

    a. direct reinforcement.
    b. vicarious learning.
    c. cognitive dissonance.
    d. persuasive communication.

17. Of the following, the best example of cognitive dissonance is

    a. stating that women should earn less money than men for doing the same job.
    b. exaggerating the merits of a product in order to promote sales.
    c. knowing that cigarette smoking is harmful, but doing it anyway.
    d. believing that handicapped people cannot hold good jobs and therefore not recommending them.

MATCHING QUESTIONS

Match each term with the best description.

_____ 18. social psychology

_____ 19. attitudes

_____ 20. vicarious learning

_____ 21. central route processing

_____ 22. peripheral route processing

_____ 23. cognitive dissonance

_____ 24. cognitions

_____ 25. selective exposure

a. includes attitudes, thoughts, or beliefs

b. is a means of minimizing dissonance

c. involves the conflict of contrasting attitudes

d. is the study of how people affect one another

e. are sets of learned predispositions

f. is the consideration of issues and arguments

g. involves the consideration of source and general information

h. happens by watching others

ANSWER KEY: SECTION I

FILL IN THE BLANKS

1. social psychology

2. attitudes; predisposition; favorable; unfavorable

3. vicarious learning

4. cognitive dissonance; attitudes; thoughts

5. central route processing

6. peripheral route processing

7. cognitions

8. theory of self-perception

9. self-perception

MULTIPLE CHOICE

10. c

11. b

12. a

13. d

14. b

15. c

16. b

17. c

MATCHING QUESTIONS

18. d

19. e

20. h

21. f

22. g

23. c

24. a

25. b

REVIEW QUESTIONS: SECTION II

FILL IN THE BLANKS

1. Individuals have highly developed _____, or sets of cognitions about people and social experience.

2. The processes that underlie our understanding of the social world are known as _____ _____.

3. An individual who organizes information about another person to form an overall impression of that person is said to be using the process of _____ _____.

4. In forming impressions of others, we pay particular attention to certain aspects of people known as _____ _____.

5. When beliefs and expectations about members of a group are held simply on the basis of their membership in that group, a kind of _____ known as a(n) _____ is being used.

6. Individuals having a combination of traits typically considered to be masculine and feminine are said to be _____.

7. The tendency to hold less favorable opinions about groups to which we do not belong while still holding favorable opinions about groups to which we do belong is known as _____-_____ _____.

8. If a person has an expectation about the occurrence of an event or behavior that increases the likelihood that the event or behavior will happen, he or she may be causing something to conform to a stereotype through _____-_____ _____.

MULTIPLE CHOICE

9. Groups to which an individual belongs are known as

    a. outgroups.
    b. subgroups.
    c. ingroups.
    d. central groups.

10. The processes that underlie our understanding of the social world are called

    a. social cognitions.
    b. schemas.
    c. central traits.
    d. stereotypes.

11. An androgynous person is one who

    a. makes good use of stereotypes.
    b. incorporates masculine and feminine traits.
    c. incorporates social cognitions with central traits.
    d. does not have ingroup-outgroup bias.

12. The finding that women's levels of achievement motivation are typically lower than those of males may be accounted for by

    a. self-fulfilling prophecy.
    b. ingroup-outgroup bias.
    c. sex-role stereotypes.
    d. social cognitions.

13. Sets of cognitions about people and social experiences are known as

    a. impression formations.
    b. biases.
    c. prophecies.
    d. schemas.

14. Being knowledgeable about illness and medicine, helping people get well, and understanding patients' needs are components of a

    a. bias about doctors.
    b. stereotype about doctors.
    c. schema about doctors.
    d. self-fulfilling prophecy about doctors.

15. Warm and cold are considered

    a. attributions that have little impact on first impressions.
    b. central traits.
    c. stereotyped descriptions of men and women.
    d. the basis for ingroup-outgroup bias.

MATCHING QUESTIONS

Match each term with the best description.

_____ 16. social cognition

_____ 17. impression formation

_____ 18. central traits

_____ 19. stereotype

_____ 20. ingroup

_____ 21. outgroup

_____ 22. androgynous

_____ 23. self-fulfilling prophecies

_____ 24. schemas

a. incorporates both the masculine and the feminine

b. are a set of cognitions

c. is the group to which one belongs

d. increase the likelihood of an event or behavior

e. underlies our understanding of the social world

f. can be formed on the basis of group membership alone

g. are considered in forming impressions of others

h. is the process of organizing information about another

i. is the group to which one does *not* belong

ANSWER KEY: SECTION II

FILL IN THE BLANKS

1. schemas

2. social cognition

3. impression formation

4. central traits

5. schema; stereotype

6. androgynous

7. ingroup-outgroup bias

8. self-fulfilling prophecy

MULTIPLE CHOICE

9. c

10. a

11. b

12. c

13. d

14. c

15. b

MATCHING QUESTIONS

16. e

17. h

18. g

19. f

20. c

21. i

22. a

23. d

24. b

REVIEW QUESTIONS: SECTION III

FILL IN THE BLANKS

1. _____ theory seeks to explain how we decide, on the basis of samples of an individual's behavior, what the specific causes of that behavior are.

2. Sources of behavior that are based on environmental factors are known as _____ _____.

3. _____ _____ of behavior are based on internal traits or personality factors.

4. The degree to which people behave similarly in the same situation is known as _____ information.

5. _____ information is the degree to which an individual behaves similarly in similar situations.

6. The extent to which a given behavior occurs across different situations is known as _____ information.

7. A common tendency known as _____ _____ _____ occurs when individuals attribute the behavior of others to dispositional causes but their own behavior to situational causes.

8. Trainees who read about an incident and are then given explanations for the behavior that occurred, only one of which is accurate, are being taught with an aid known as a(n) _____ _____.

9. Self-perception was developed by _____.

10. Assuming that others are similar to ourselves is known as the _____-_____ bias.

11. Inferring uniformly positive characteristics on the basis of knowing one positive trait of a person is called the _____ _____.

MULTIPLE CHOICE

12. A cultural assimilator is a

    a. teaching aid used to minimize prejudice.
    b. device used to check distinctiveness information.
    c. kind of consistency information.
    d. situational cause of behavior.

13. The tendency to attribute others' behavior to dispositional causes but our own behavior to situational causes is known as

    a. consistency information.
    b. fundamental attribution bias.
    c. dispositional attribution bias.
    d. distinctiveness information.

14. Which one of the following statements is the best example of dispositional attribution bias?

    a. John is being good because the teacher is watching.
    b. Even though I am not feeling sociable, I will go to the party if you do.
    c. Sue is staying up all night to study because she is a conscientious student.
    d. I become very anxious when criticized.

15. I put off visiting my aunt for such a long time that I decided I probably did not want to see her. Coming to this conclusion is an example of

    a. self-perception theory.
    b. cognitive dissonance theory.
    c. dispositional attribution bias.
    d. fundamental attribution bias.

16. The theory that seeks to explain, on the basis of samples of an individual's behavior, what the specific causes of that behavior are is known as

    a. situation theory.
    b. consensus theory.
    c. attribution theory.
    d. disposition theory.

17. The extent to which a given behavior occurs across different situations is known as

    a. distinctiveness information.
    b. consistency information.
    c. consensus information.
    d. attributional information.

18. Causes of behavior that are based on environmental factors are known as

    a. attributional causes of behavior.
    b. dispositional causes of behavior.
    c. consensual causes of behavior.
    d. situational causes of behavior.

MATCHING QUESTIONS

Match each term with the best description.

_____ 19. attribution

_____ 20. situational causes of behavior

_____ 21. dispositional causes of behavior

_____ 22. consensus information

_____ 23. consistency information

_____ 24. distinctiveness information

_____ 25. cultural assimilator

a. involves a given behavior occurring across different situations

b. can be used to reduce prejudice

c. include environmental factors

d. seeks to explain a behavior from a sample

e. include internal traits or personality factors

f. involves similar individual behavior in similar situations

g. involves similar behavior in the same situation

ANSWER KEY: SECTION III

FILL IN THE BLANKS

1. attribution

2. situational causes

3. dispositional causes

4. consensus

5. consistency

6. distinctiveness

7. fundamental attribution bias

8. cultural assimilator

9. Bem

10. assumed-similarity

11. halo effect

MULTIPLE CHOICE

12. a

13. b

14. c

15. a

16. c

17. a

18. d

MATCHING QUESTIONS

19. d

20. c

21. e

22. g

23. f

24. a

25. b

INTEGRATING THE MATERIAL

1. Attribution theory points out that we use different methods for evaluating ourselves and others, whereas self-perception theory points out that we use the same methods for evaluating ourselves and others. Discuss how each of these theories is useful in promoting our understanding of social functioning.

2. Using your knowledge of the processes of learning and memory, discuss where biases come from.

ACTIVITIES FOR CHAPTER REVIEW

1. Listen to politicians give speeches and to commercial ads on TV and make note of the techniques used to persuade you either to agree with the points made or to buy a product. What types of messages are you receiving through the auditory channel? Through the visual channel? What types of associations (methods of classical conditioning) are being made to increase the power of the messages? Make a note of these points. Also, think about the prejudices that you have that influence your judgment about the statements being made.

2. Examine yourself for inconsistencies in your thoughts, feelings, and behaviors regarding a particular issue. For example, do you smoke cigarettes and enjoy them even though you know this habit is damaging to your health? Do you feel uncomfortable among members of any particular minority group even though you know there is no logical reason to feel this way? Do you avoid seeking help for your problems even though you believe seeking help is a valid thing to do? These are just a few examples of inconsistencies that can create cognitive dissonance. Describe your experiences with cognitive dissonance. What types of dissonance are you motivated to reconcile and what types are you willing to live with? Explain.

3. Make a list of central traits that you feel apply to the following types of people: (a) politicians, (b) doctors, (c) Texans, (d) cat lovers, and (e) poets. Ask a friend to list central traits for the same groups, independent of your lists. How similar are you and your friend's lists? Now make a list of central traits that apply to yourself, and ask your friend to make a list of central traits to describe you. How closely do these lists correspond? Is it easier to list traits about groups or about yourself? Where did your beliefs and expectations (stereotypes) concerning the preceding groups come from? To what extent was vicarious learning involved? Would your list be different if you were a member of the group being described? Explain.

CHAPTER

19

SOCIAL PSYCHOLOGY: INTERACTING WITH OTHERS

CHAPTER OVERVIEW

Chapter 19 examines people's interactions and social relationships with one another. People have both positive and negative influences on one another's behavior, and these influences can be quite powerful. Chapter 19 is divided into three sections.

I.   The first section of the chapter deals with social influences—conformity, compliance, and obedience to authority. Conformity is a change in behavior or attitudes brought about by a desire to follow the beliefs or standards of other people. The classic study by Asch demonstrates the power of conformity and isolates the following variables as producing conformity: the nature of the group, the nature of the individual's response, the kind of task, and the unanimity of the group. Whereas conformity depends on indirect social influence, compliance occurs in response to direct, explicit social pressure. Obedience is a change in behavior resulting from a direct command. Strategies for remaining independent from group pressure include inoculation, forewarning, and consistency.

II. The second section of the chapter deals with interpersonal attraction and the processes of liking and loving other people as the foundation for the development of relationships. Among the most important factors considered by social psychologists for explaining the initial attraction between two people are proximity, exposure, similarity, need complementarity, and physical attractiveness. Love is differentiated from liking as a qualitatively different psychological state. Factors affecting the maintenance and the decline of love relationships are discussed.

III. The third and final section of the chapter explains aggressive and prosocial behavior. Aggression is defined as the intentional injury of or harm to another person; thus, the intent or purpose behind the behavior is a key factor. Instinct theories of aggression view aggression as the result of innate or inborn urges. Observational learning theory views aggression as learned by observing the consequences of aggressive behavior in others. Most experts agree that watching media violence can lead to a greater readiness to act aggressively. Each approach to the study of aggression suggests ways of reducing aggressive behavior. Instinct models use a catharsis approach; frustration-aggression and observational learning theories suggest removing frustration, employing nonaggressive models, and rewarding nonaggressive behavior. The opposite of aggression, prosocial or helping behavior, has also been studied by social psychologists. Helping behavior can be promoted by the provision of helpful models, the use of moral admonition, and the teaching of moral reasoning.

STUDY STRATEGY

Follow this strategy for *each* section of the chapter.

1. Review the CHAPTER OUTLINE up to Recap and Review I.

2. Read the CHAPTER OVERVIEW, Section I.

3. Read the chapter in the text up to Recap and Review I.

4. For any question you answered incorrectly or did not understand, go back to the parts of the text that cover that material.

5. Write your answers to the REVIEW QUESTIONS for Section I in the *Study Guide*. Consult the answer key only after you have finished. Then correct any mistakes.

6. After you have completed the REVIEW QUESTIONS for Section I and have corrected your mistakes, follow the STUDY STRATEGY for Section II. Do the same for each section until you have completed all REVIEW QUESTIONS.

7. Then complete the INTEGRATING THE MATERIAL questions at the end of the *Study Guide* chapter. Answering these questions will help you see how the material fits together.

And, don't forget:

Go back to the parts of the text that cover material that was difficult for you. If you still don't understand a concept, ask your teacher for clarification. Your questions in class and your teacher's answers will help other students as well.

MASTERY QUESTIONS

After mastering Chapter 19, you will be able to answer the following questions:

What are the major sources of social influence and the tactics that are used to bring them about?

What are the best strategies for resisting social pressure?

Why are we attracted to certain people?

What factors underlie aggression and prosocial behavior?

REVIEW QUESTIONS: SECTION I

FILL IN THE BLANKS

1. The area of social psychology concerned with situations in which the actions of an individual or group affect the behavior of others is known as _____ _____.

2. An individual who buys and begins to wear an article of clothing because everyone else does is exhibiting _____, or a change in behavior due to a desire to follow the beliefs or standards of other people.

3. Social rank held within a group is known as _____.

4. When two individuals in a group have dissenting views, the presence of a third person who shares one of the points of view, a _____ _____, may be just enough to reduce conformity in that group.

5. Individuals demonstrate _____ when their behavior is a response to direct social pressure.

6. _____ is a process involving exposure to arguments that oppose one's beliefs, thereby making the subject more resistant to later attempts to change those beliefs.

7. Telling people that a persuasive message is coming and what that message involves is a strategy known as _____.

8. A technique known as _____ is effective in reducing persuadability, but it can actually change the attitude of the _____.

9. A change in behavior due to the commands of others is known as _____.

MULTIPLE CHOICE

10. The procedure in which subjects are warned in advance that a persuasive message is coming is known as

   a. consistency.
   b. forewarning.
   c. inoculation.
   d. compliance.

11. A person who shares an unpopular belief, thereby encouraging nonconformity, is called

   a. a nonconformist.
   b. an inoculator.
   c. a social supporter.
   d. a status seeker.

12. People working on tasks and questions that are ambiguous are more susceptible to

   a. inoculation.
   b. compliance.
   c. forewarning.
   d. social pressure.

13. When people must make a response publicly, they are more likely to

   a. conform.
   b. look for social support.
   c. forewarn others.
   d. use inoculation.

14. The classic demonstration of pressure to conform comes from a series of studies carried out in the 1950s by

   a. Skinner.
   b. Asch.
   c. Zimbardo.
   d. Milgram.

15. The classic experiment demonstrating the power of authority to produce obedience was performed by

   a. Bandura.
   b. Asch.
   c. Milgram.
   d. Skinner.

MATCHING QUESTIONS

Match each term with the best description.

_____ 16. status

_____ 17. conformity

_____ 18. compliance

_____ 19. social supporter

_____ 20. inoculation

_____ 21. forewarning

_____ 22. consistency

a. is advance knowledge of persuasion

b. is the persistence of those holding an unpopular view

c. is one's social rank in a group

d. involves a change in behavior toward group norms

e. occurs in response to social pressure

f. shares an unpopular opinion

g. is a means of preparation to resist persuasion

ANSWER KEY: SECTION I

FILL IN THE BLANKS

1. social influence

2. conformity

3. status

4. social supporter

5. compliance

6. inoculation

7. forewarning

8. consistency; persuader

9. obedience

MULTIPLE CHOICE

10. b

11. c

12. d

13. a

14. b

15. c

MATCHING QUESTIONS

16. c

17. d

18. e

19. f

20. g

21. a

22. b

REVIEW QUESTIONS: SECTION II

FILL IN THE BLANKS

1. One of the best-established findings in the literature on interpersonal attraction is that proximity leads to _____.

2. The tendency to like those who like us and vice versa is known as the _____-_____-_____ effect.

3. Positive feelings for others are known as _____ _____.

4. By far the greatest amount of research in interpersonal attraction has focused on _____.

5. It is easier for researchers to produce states of _____ in strangers who have just met than to observe _____ _____ over long periods of time.

6. For most people, the equation "beautiful equals _____" is a very real one.

MULTIPLE CHOICE

7. The number of marriages ending in divorce and broken love affairs is

   a. one in three.
   b. one in two.
   c. two in three.
   d. three in five.

8. One of the most frequently given responses of husbands and wives, happily married for fifteen years or more, to the question of what has made their marriage last is

   a. perceiving the commitment as a lifelong one.
   b. feeling a sense of social responsibility.
   c. perceiving one's spouse as a best friend.
   d. perceiving one's spouse as a partner in a business venture.

9. Proximity is defined as

   a. nearness to another person.
   b. a tendency to like those who like us.
   c. a tendency of those whom we like to like us.
   d. distance from another.

10. According to Sternberg's theory of love, each of the following is a component of love except

    a. intimacy.
    b. passion.
    c. decision/commitment.
    d. individuation/separation.

11. Each of the following is a kind of love except

    a. empty love.
    b. compassionate love.
    c. fatuous love.
    d. companionate love.

12. A person decides to confront the partner and determine whether to attempt repair, redefinition, or termination of the relationship during the

    a. dyadic phase.
    b. social phase.
    c. grave-dressing phase.
    d. bonding phase.

MATCHING QUESTIONS

Match each term with the best description.

_____ 13. proximity	a. is qualitatively different from liking
_____ 14. reciprocity of liking	b. is nearness to another
_____ 15. love	c. is the result of proximity
_____ 16. liking	d. is liking those who like us

ANSWER KEY: SECTION II

FILL IN THE BLANKS

1. liking
2. reciprocity-of-liking
3. interpersonal attraction
4. liking
5. liking; loving relationships
6. good

MULTIPLE CHOICE

7. b
8. c
9. a
10. d
11. b
12. a

MATCHING QUESTIONS

13. b
14. d
15. a
16. c

REVIEW QUESTIONS: SECTION III

FILL IN THE BLANKS

1. Intentional injury or harm to another person is known as _____.

2. Instinct theories propose that _____ is primarily the outcome of _____ or inborn urges.

3. Konrad _____, a scientist who studied animal behavior, is the major proponent of the _____ approach.

4. The state produced by the thwarting or blocking of some ongoing goal-directed behavior is known as _____.

5. According to some researchers, whether or not aggression actually occurs depends on the presence of _____ _____, stimuli that have been associated with aggression in the past.

6. The _____ _____ expresses the notion that aggression is built up and must be discharged through violent acts.

7. When there is more than one witness to an emergency situation, there can be a sense of _____ _____ _____ among the bystanders.

8. A person who reasons that his or her perceived rewards for helping another must outweigh the cost of that help is using the _____-_____ approach.

9. Helping behavior that is beneficial to others while requiring sacrifice on the part of the helper is called _____.

10. One person's experiencing of another's emotions, leading to an increased likelihood of responding to the other's needs, is known as _____.

MULTIPLE CHOICE

11. Prosocial is a more formal way of describing behavior that is

   a. helping.
   b. cathartic.
   c. innate.
   d. aggressive.

12. Diffusion of responsibility can occur when

   a. aggressive cues are present.
   b. the catharsis hypothesis is in effect.
   c. there is more than one bystander to an incident.
   d. innate behaviors are operative.

13. The observational learning approach is sometimes called

   a. innate learning.
   b. cathartic learning.
   c. social learning.
   d. aggressive learning.

14. The most recent formulation of the frustration-aggression theory states that

   a. frustration always leads to aggression.
   b. frustration arouses an innate need for catharsis.
   c. frustration leads to aggression only when others are present.
   d. frustration produces anger, leading to a readiness to act.

15. To date, the most promising approach to reducing aggression comes from

    a. frustration-aggression theory.
    b. learning theory.
    c. the catharsis hypothesis.
    d. diffusion of responsibility.

16. Aggression can be effectively reduced by

    a. the use of punishment following aggressive behavior.
    b. the use of reward following nonaggressive behavior.
    c. both a and b.
    d. neither a nor b.

MATCHING QUESTIONS

Match each term with the best description.

_____ 17. altruism

_____ 18. empathy

_____ 19. rewards-cost approach

_____ 20. diffusion of responsibility

_____ 21. catharsis hypothesis

_____ 22. aggressive cue

_____ 23. frustration

_____ 24. aggression

_____ 25. innate

a. involves intentional injury or harm

b. is a stimulus

c. can result from blocked behavior

d. involves a helper's sacrifice for another

e. is used to predict the nature of bystander assistance

f. is the state of feeling the other's emotions

g. is a process through which responsibility is shared by all involved

h. states that built-up aggression must be discharged

i. means biologically determined, or inborn

ANSWER KEY: SECTION III

FILL IN THE BLANKS

1. aggression
2. aggression; innate
3. Lorenz, instinct
4. frustration
5. aggressive cues

6. catharsis hypothesis
7. diffusion of responsibility
8. rewards-cost
9. altruism
10. empathy

MULTIPLE CHOICE

11. a   14. d

12. c   15. b

13. c   16. b

MATCHING QUESTIONS

17. d   22. b

18. f   23. c

19. e   24. a

20. g   25. i

21. h

INTEGRATING THE MATERIAL

1. How is the nature of prosocial or helping behavior related to Kohlberg's theory of moral development discussed in Chapter 13?

2. In your evaluation of theories of aggression, which do you believe is more valid and why: innate theories or social learning theories?

ACTIVITIES FOR CHAPTER REVIEW

1. Observe a particularly popular item of clothing worn at your school or your place of work, and ask people their reasons for owning or wearing it. If you get the response "Just because I like it," try to elicit what the person likes about it. After asking six to ten people, examine the types of responses you have collected. Why do *you* think the item is popular? What might make the item become unpopular?

2. Think about how you became friends or acquaintances with the people you currently know. What roles were played by the following factors in the formation and maintenance of your relationships: proximity, mere exposure, similarity, physical attraction, the reciprocity-of-liking effect?

3. Watch some prime-time television and keep a log of violent incidents. How many violent incidents can you count in one hour? What is the nature of the violence? Do you believe that television violence leads to real violence? Explain.

CHAPTER
20
ORGANIZATIONS AND THE WORKPLACE

CHAPTER OVERVIEW

Chapter 20 discusses the nature of organizations and the workplace. Industrial-organizational psychologists study the workplace and the nature of organizations, specifically the relationship between the environment and people's well-being and behavior in that environment. In the workplace, relevant issues include the interactions of workers on the job, how jobs can be designed to prevent or reduce stress or fatigue, and how workers can be motivated and helped to maintain their morale.

Chapter 20 is divided into three sections.

I.   The first section of the chapter explores the nature of groups in organizations and their influence on individual responses to jobs. Groups are the building blocks of organizations and can have a major impact on an organization's climate and productivity. Groups have four characteristics: interaction among group members, perception of group membership among the members, shared goals and norms, and fate interdependence. Informal groups can exert as much influence as (or even more influence than) formal groups within an organization, which consists of groups of people working together to attain common goals. The Hawthorne studies in the 1930s revealed for the first time how sensitive workers are to the behavior of others in their work groups. Group cohesiveness is the degree to which group members are attracted to the group and its members. People have motives for working that go beyond the obvious one, making money. These include the Puritan work ethic, people's personal identity, and their social lives, values, and status in the community.

II. The second section of the chapter deals with the nature of decision making in organizations, including the ways in which decisions are made, how decisions may affect individuals in the organization, and improvements in the decision-making process. The value of using participative versus nonparticipative decision making depends on the nature of the specific situation as well as the type of participation. In general, group decision making is better for establishing objectives, evaluating alternatives, and choosing among alternatives when individuals are better at identifying alternatives and implementing decisions. There are a variety of techniques for improving the decision-making process, including brainstorming, nominal group techniques, and the promotion of controversy.

III. The third and final section of the chapter deals with the importance of job satisfaction and how to increase this central aspect of work. When company policies and procedures are perceived as fair and administered without bias, workers tend to feel greater satisfaction with their jobs. Thus, organizations with more decentralized decision making generally have higher worker satisfaction. Other issues related to job satisfaction include the supervisory style of the boss, the social context of work, job clarity, and role conflict. The chapter ends with a description of approaches to increasing job satisfaction.

STUDY STRATEGY

Follow this strategy for *each* section of the chapter.

1. Review the CHAPTER OUTLINE up to Recap and Review I.

2. Read the CHAPTER OVERVIEW, Section I.

3. Read the chapter in the text up to Recap and Review I.

4. For any question you answered incorrectly or did not understand, go back to the parts of the text that cover that material.

5. Write your answers to the REVIEW QUESTIONS for Section I in the *Study Guide*. Consult the answer key only after you have finished. Then correct any mistakes.

6. After you have completed the REVIEW QUESTIONS for Section I and have corrected your mistakes, follow the STUDY STRATEGY for Section II. Do the same for each section until you have completed all REVIEW QUESTIONS.

7. Then complete the INTEGRATING THE MATERIAL questions at the end of the *Study Guide* chapter. Answering these questions will help you see how the material fits together.

And, don't forget:

Go back to the parts of the text that cover material that was difficult for you. If you still don't understand a concept, ask your teacher for clarification. Your questions in class and your teacher's answers will help other students as well.

MASTERY QUESTIONS

After mastering Chapter 20, you will be able to answer the following questions:

What are the defining characteristics of groups and organizations?

How can we improve the quality of decisions made in organizations?

What are the characteristics of jobs that produce difficulties for workers?

How can we reduce job-related problems and stress?

REVIEW QUESTIONS: SECTION I

FILL IN THE BLANKS

1. Psychologists who study the workplace and organizations are known as
   _____-_____ psychologists.

2. A _____ is a collection of individuals in which there is _____ among members, perception of _____ _____, shared _____ and _____, and _____ interdependence.

3. The scientific study of groups and group processes is known as _____
   _____.

4. There is pressure on group members to adhere to _____, which are informal rules regarding the appropriateness of behavior.

5. A group of people working together to attain common goals is known as an _____.

6. A _____ _____ is a work unit set up by management to carry out a specific task.

7. Groups that develop as a result of interests and needs of the individuals making up an organization are _____ _____.

8. High levels of _____ _____ have a number of important consequences, including higher self-esteem for group members.

9. The _____ effect suggests that when subjects know they are in an experiment, their behavior may change simply as a function of the special attention they are receiving and not necessarily because of the experimental manipulations.

MULTIPLE CHOICE

10. Higher self-esteem for group members and higher likelihood of membership maintenance in a group are indicators of

    a. organizational socialization.
    b. high group cohesiveness.
    c. high group dynamics.
    d. low acceptance of group norms.

11. The company softball team is an example of a(n)

    a. formal group.
    b. dynamic group.
    c. socialized group.
    d. informal group.

12. Each of the following is characteristic of a group *except*

    a. perception of members as better.
    b. interaction among members.
    c. perception of group membership.
    d. fate interdependence.

13. A management study team set up to reduce costs is an example of a(n)

    a. dynamic group.
    b. formal group.
    c. informal group.
    d. normal group.

14. Informal rules regarding the appropriateness of behavior followed by group members are

    a. dynamics.
    b. policies.
    c. procedures.
    d. norms.

15. The Hawthorne studies were conducted during the

    a. turn of the twentieth century as part of the Industrial Revolution.
    b. 1930s.
    c. 1950s.
    d. 1970s.

16. The Hawthorne studies focused on

    a. changing organizational structure.
    b. promoting group cohesiveness.
    c. improving decision-making procedures.
    d. increasing worker productivity.

MATCHING QUESTIONS

Match each term with the best description.

_____ 17. group

_____ 18. group dynamics

_____ 19. norm

_____ 20. formal group

_____ 21. informal group

_____ 22. organization

a. is made up of groups working toward common goals

b. is set up to carry out a task

c. is a collection of individuals

d. is an informal rule

e. develops through need and interests

f. is the study of groups

ANSWER KEY: SECTION I

FILL IN THE BLANKS

1. industrial-organizational

2. group; interaction; group membership; norms; goals; fate

3. group dynamics

4. norms

5. organization

6. formal group

7. informal groups

8. group cohesiveness

9. Hawthorne

MULTIPLE CHOICE

10. b

11. c

12. a

13. b

14. d

15. b

16. d

MATCHING QUESTIONS

17. c

18. f

19. d

20. b

21. e

22. a

REVIEW QUESTIONS: SECTION II

FILL IN THE BLANKS

1. When the workers in a factory are involved in the decision to make some equipment changes, we can say that management is using _____ _____ _____.

2. A group is using a decision-making technique known as _____ when group members express as many new ideas as they can, no matter how outlandish, and no evaluation is made until all have spoken.

3. A group is using _____ _____ _____ to make decisions when suggestions are written in private and evaluation is made by secret ballot.

4. When experts are called in to complete questionnaires on a problem, the _____ _____ is being used.

5. Groups are _____ _____ at making decisions than individuals.

6. When individual members of a group share such a strong motivation to achieve consensus that they lose the ability to critically evaluate alternative points, a process known as _____ is occurring.

MULTIPLE CHOICE

7. Recent research suggests that better decisions are made under conditions of

   a. participation.
   b. controversy.
   c. brainstorming.
   d. groupthink.

8. In the phenomenon of groupthink, group members lose the ability to

   a. think.
   b. decide.
   c. evaluate.
   d. brainstorm.

9. Writing down ideas in private and using secret ballots are part of

   a. brainstorming.
   b. nominal group techniques.
   c. the Delphi method.
   d. groupthink.

10. When the Delphi method is used

   a. an expert is called in.
   b. secret ballots are taken.
   c. outlandish ideas are expressed.
   d. participative decision making is used.

11. Group decisions are more likely to be superior to individual decisions for each of the following *except*

    a. establishing objectives.
    b. identifying alternative solutions.
    c. evaluating alternatives.
    d. choosing an alternative.

12. For implementing a choice

    a. formal groups are better than informal groups.
    b. informal groups are better than formal groups.
    c. individuals are better than groups.
    d. individuals and groups are equally good.

13. The advantage of nominal group techniques is that they

    a. are nonpublic.
    b. involve open brainstorming.
    c. create powerful leadership.
    d. increase group cohesiveness.

MATCHING QUESTIONS

Match each term with the best description.

_____ 14. groupthink

_____ 15. nominal group technique

_____ 16. Delphi method

_____ 17. brainstorming

_____ 18. participative decision making

a. involves calling in an expert

b. is a process in which all decide

c. is a process in which there is no evaluation until the end

d. can employ secret ballots

e. sacrifices the ability to evaluate

ANSWER KEY: SECTION II

FILL IN THE BLANKS

1. participative decision making

2. brainstorming

3. nominal group technique

4. Delphi method

5. less efficient

6. groupthink

MULTIPLE CHOICE

7. b   11. b

8. c   12. c

9. b   13. a

10. a

MATCHING QUESTIONS

14. e   17. c

15. d   18. b

16. b

REVIEW QUESTIONS: SECTION III

FILL IN THE BLANKS

1. Decision making in which the distribution of authority extends throughout the organization is known as _____ _____ _____.

2. In _____ _____ _____, authority over decisions is controlled by a few people at the top of the organization.

3. If company _____ and _____ are perceived as fair and administered without bias, workers tend to feel greater _____ with their jobs.

4. The degree of explicitness of the rules which determine what is expected of a worker is called _____ _____.

5. _____ _____ arises when job expectations are defined in a way that makes it impossible to carry out the job properly.

6. Techniques for improving the quality of the activities involved in a job are known as _____ _____.

7. Individuals learn the rules and norms of appropriate behavior through a developmental process known as _____.

8. The process through which a worker learns to behave like others in an organization and to adopt similar attitudes is known as _____ _____.

MULTIPLE CHOICE

9. Techniques for improving the quality of the activities involved in a job are known as

   a. job enrichment.
   b. job satisfaction.
   c. job clarity.
   d. job conflict.

10. Role conflict occurs when

    a. people with two different job titles work together.
    b. clerical and management people work together.
    c. two or more sets of job demands contradict one another.
    d. individuals want to strike but cannot do so.

11. The degree of explicitness of the rules determining what is expected of a worker is known as

    a. role clarity.
    b. job clarity.
    c. role conflict.
    d. job conflict.

12. Increasing the variety of skills that must be used on a job is one method of

    a. job clarity.
    b. decision making.
    c. decentralization.
    d. job enrichment.

13. Decision making in which authority is controlled by a few people at the top of the organization is known as

    a. decentralized decision making.
    b. enriched decision making.
    c. centralized decision making.
    d. conflicting decision making.

14. When a worker learns to behave like others and adopts similar attitudes, the process is known as

    a. group socialization.
    b. fate interdependence.
    c. organizational socialization.
    d. group cohesiveness.

15. Japanese management strategies tend to be committed to

    a. the workplace and its goals.
    b. widespread recruitment.
    c. individual career advancement.
    d. labor unions.

MATCHING QUESTIONS

Match each term with the best description.

_____ 16. job clarity

_____ 17. role conflict

_____ 18. decentralized decision making

_____ 19. centralized decision making

_____ 20. job enrichment

a. results in impossible job expectations

b. occurs when the decisions are made at the top

c. leads to improved quality of activity

d. is the degree of explicitness of a role

e. occurs when there is decision authority throughout

ANSWER KEY: SECTION III

FILL IN THE BLANKS

1. decentralized decision making

2. centralized decision making

3. policies; procedures; satisfaction

4. job clarity

5. role conflict

6. job enrichment

7. socialization

8. organizational socialization

MULTIPLE CHOICE

9. a

10. c

11. b

12. d

13. c

14. c

15. a

MATCHING QUESTIONS

16. d

17. a

18. e

19. b

20. c

INTEGRATING THE MATERIAL

1. How do the concepts of conformity, compliance, and obedience apply to functioning in the workplace?

2. What are some cognitive dissonance issues that could arise in the workplace?

ACTIVITIES FOR CHAPTER REVIEW

1. If you have a job, list and describe some ways in which your job satisfaction could be improved. Would money alone do it? Distinguish between ways that you could enrich your job and ways that your employer could enrich your job. How would job enrichment affect other areas of your life? If you do not work, ask relatives or friends who work about the relationship between satisfaction on the job and productivity and about ways they can think of to enhance their lives at work.

2. Get a group of friends together and have a brainstorming session. Focus on an issue that is important to the group. In running the session, emphasize the necessity to say anything that comes to mind, even if it seems silly or irrelevant. Write down each idea so that the list is visible to everyone in the group. An appropriate topic might be how to help the homeless, how to improve the neighborhood, or how to solve any problem that has no obvious solution.

CHAPTER

21

TECHNOLOGY AND CONTEMPORARY SOCIETY

CHAPTER OVERVIEW

Chapter 21 considers the effects of technology and the environment on human functioning. Topics covered include the psychological impact of modern technology, the relationship between the environment and people's behavior and their sense of well-being (environmental psychology), and the psychological impact of both artificial and natural disasters and catastrophes.

Chapter 21 is divided into three sections.

I. The first section of the chapter explores ergonomics, the study of how people's behavior and abilities affect the design of tools, machines, and environments for effective use. Well-designed objects possess visibility, visual cues to their operation that are built into the design. Our adaptation to living with computers in the workplace, in educational settings, and in our everyday lives is examined. Some people have a fear of computers, called cyberphobia, and experience overwhelming anxiety when dealing with unfamiliar equipment. One of the most important issues raised by the use of computers throughout society is that of privacy. The magnitude and scope of data currently retained by various organizations is enormous.

II. The second section of the chapter explores psychological reactions to the social and physical environment, including the effects of crowding—one of the major social issues of our time. Environmental psychologists make a distinction between density and crowding. Density refers to the purely physical and spatial characteristics of an environment: the number of people per unit of space. In contrast, crowding is an unpleasant psychological and subjective state relating to how a person reacts to the physical density of the environment. Thus, high density alone does not lead to the experience of crowding. Specific factors that cause a certain density to be considered crowding include explanations based on stimulus overload, loss of control, focus of attention, and density intensity. Crowding can result in higher rates of illness and death, lower interpersonal attraction, decreases in helping, increases in aggression, and declines in performance levels, although crowding does not inevitably lead to negative consequences. Other environmental factors that influence behavior include heat, noise level, and air quality. Your personal environment can be made more livable by staking out your territory, personalizing your environment, and lowering the density of high-density settings.

III. The third and final section of the chapter covers the psychological impact of catastrophes and crises. The loss of the sense of control is one of the most critical results of a disaster. Research suggests that reactions to disasters tend to follow a fairly predictable course—rage followed by a state of daze and shock (denial) followed by dealing with the reality and getting on with life. Technological accidents provoke stronger reactions than natural accidents. The complexity of dealing with terrorism and hostage-taking is examined. The chapter ends with a discussion of psychological approaches to promoting peace and preventing war. It is pointed out that an arms buildup can act as a self-fulfilling prophecy. Important areas of research include attitudes toward other nations, defense-related decisions, behavior in times of crises, accidental war, and negotiation and prevention.

STUDY STRATEGY

Follow this strategy for *each* section of the chapter.

1. Review the CHAPTER OUTLINE up to Recap and Review I.

2. Read the CHAPTER OVERVIEW, Section I.

3. Read the chapter in the text up to Recap and Review I.

4. For any question you answered incorrectly or did not understand, go back to the parts of the text that cover that material.

5. Write your answers to the REVIEW QUESTIONS for Section I in the *Study Guide*. Consult the answer key only after you have finished. Then correct any mistakes.

6. After you have completed the REVIEW QUESTIONS for Section I and have corrected your mistakes, follow the STUDY STRATEGY for Section II. Do the same for each section until you have completed all REVIEW QUESTIONS.

7. Then complete the INTEGRATING THE MATERIAL questions at the end of the *Study Guide* chapter. Answering these questions will help you see how the material fits together.

And, don't forget:

Go back to the parts of the text that cover material that was difficult for you. If you still don't understand a concept, ask your teacher for clarification. Your questions in class and your teacher's answers will help other students as well.

MASTERY QUESTIONS

After mastering Chapter 21, you will be able to answer the following questions:

How does the design of everyday objects affect how we use them?

Why do some people fear computers, and what effects has the increased use of computers had on people's lives?

Why does crowding produce negative consequences?

What major aspects of the physical environment affect behavior?

What are the psychological consequences of surviving a disaster?

What contributions can psychologists make to the prevention of war and the promotion of peace?

REVIEW QUESTIONS: SECTION I

FILL IN THE BLANKS

1. The study of how people's behavior and abilities affect the design of tools, machines, and environments for effective use is known as _____.

2. Visibility enhances accurate _____ and cognitive understanding of mechanisms.

3. A central feature of visibility is _____ _____, a design that relies on an analogy between the physical appearance of a device and the physical actions that are required to operate it.

4. A computer _____ paralyzed computers around the United States.

5. Cyberphobia is fear of _____.

MULTIPLE CHOICE

6. A study conducted in the 1970s found that the federal government had close to 1000 data banks containing _____ records on individuals.

   a. about 5 million
   b. about 10 million
   c. between 1 million and 1 billion
   d. more than 1.25 billion

7. Ergonomics studies the interaction between

   a. people and machines.
   b. tools and machines.
   c. computers and technology.
   d. computers and the computer virus.

8. Designing a car dashboard so that a diagram of a person wearing a seatbelt lights up when seatbelts are not fastened is an example of

   a. cyberphobia.
   b. visibility.
   c. idiosyncrasy.
   d. ergonomics.

9. In the computer culture, hackers are often

   a. conforming.
   b. polite.
   c. adventurous.
   d. conventional.

10. Personal privacy is most threatened by

   a. the prevalence of computer viruses.
   b. the availability of information in computer data banks.
   c. the widespread application of ergonomics.
   d. the extensive use of computers in educational settings.

MATCHING QUESTIONS

Match each term with the best description.

_____ 11. ergonomics

_____ 12. visibility

_____ 13. natural mapping

_____ 14. cyberphobia

a. is the fear of computers

b. studies the interface between people and machines

c. is a design that relates the physical appearance of a device to the physical actions required to operate it

d. involves visual cues that facilitate operating a machine

ANSWER KEY: SECTION I

FILL IN THE BLANKS

1. ergonomics

2. perception

3. natural mapping

4. virus

5. computers

MULTIPLE CHOICE

6. d

7. a

8. b

9. c

10. b

MATCHING QUESTIONS

11. b

12. d

13. c

14. a

REVIEW QUESTIONS: SECTION II

FILL IN THE BLANKS

1. The number of people per unit of space is known as _____.

2. _____ is an unpleasant psychological and subjective state involving people's reactions to the density of their environment.

3. Physical attempts to withdraw from a crowded situation or to ignore the presence of others are accounted for by the _____-_____ explanation.

4. The _____-_____-_____ explanation suggests that the unpleasantness of crowding is due to the fact that people feel they cannot control their surroundings.

5. The _____-_____-_____ explanation is based on the fact that an attempt to determine what aspect of a stimulating situation is causing one's arousal can lead to a feeling of being crowded or of being comfortable.

6. The fact that "crowded" situations which seem negative become more negative, while those which seem positive become more positive, is the source of the _____-_____ explanation.

MULTIPLE CHOICE

7. The fact that crowding can lead to withdrawal from a situation is the basis of the _____ explanation of crowding.

   a. density-intensity
   b. focus-of-attention
   c. stimulus-overload
   d. loss-of-control

8. Density refers to the

   a. size of a crowd.
   b. number of people per unit of space.
   c. subjective reaction to a crowd.
   d. level of noise in a crowd.

9. The _____ explanation suggests that the unpleasantness of crowding is due to the feeling that people cannot control their surroundings.

   a. loss-of-control
   b. focus-of-attention
   c. density-intensity
   d. stimulus-overload

10. According to the focus-of-attention explanation, the person in a crowd who says "That guy sure is standing close to me" will

   a. become aggressive.
   b. withdraw from the crowd.
   c. experience crowding.
   d. deny the "guy's" presence.

11. According to the density-intensity explanation, if we do not like the people we are with at a party, high density will cause us to

   a. like them better.
   b. excuse ourselves from them.
   c. move around a lot.
   d. like them less.

12. The population of the world increases every year by

   a. 1 million people.
   b. 10 million people.
   c. 100 million people.
   d. 1 billion people.

13. Crowding leads to a decrease in

    a. helping behavior.
    b. task performance.
    c. both a and b.
    d. neither a nor b.

14. The presence of a higher-than-average number of negatively charged ions in the air increases

    a. aggression.
    b. crowding.
    c. density.
    d. cyberphobia.

MATCHING QUESTIONS

Match each term with the best description.

_____ 15. crowding

_____ 16. density

a. is the number of people per unit of space

b. is a psychological state

ANSWER KEY: SECTION II

FILL IN THE BLANKS

1. density
2. crowding
3. stimulus-overload
4. loss-of-control
5. focus-of-attention
6. density-intensity

MULTIPLE CHOICE

7. c
8. b
9. a
10. c
11. b
12. c
13. c
14. a

MATCHING QUESTIONS

15. b
16. a

REVIEW QUESTIONS: SECTION III

FILL IN THE BLANKS

1. The most critical result of disaster is a loss of one's _____ _____ _____.

2. Research suggests that reactions to disasters tend to follow a reasonably _____ course.

3. _____ accidents provoke stronger reactions than _____ accidents.

4. When our understanding of our enemies is distorted, the situation can lead to serious _____ _____.

MULTIPLE CHOICE

5. The first response to disaster is usually

   a. a state of daze and shock.
   b. defensiveness in the form of denial.
   c. an outcry of fear, sadness, or rage.
   d. a desire to work out the situation as best as possible.

6. Which one of the following is *not* a factor that distinguished those who showed the most symptoms from those who showed the least symptoms in the Three Mile Island accident?

   a. coping style
   b. social support received from others
   c. degree of responsibility assumed
   d. sense of loss of control

7. Which of the following events would cause the biggest psychological reaction?

   a. a brush fire
   b. a hurricane uprooting trees
   c. chemical waste floating near the shore
   d. a blizzard shutting off electricity

8. Which of the following events would cause the biggest psychological reaction?

   a. deer freezing to death in the winter
   b. 50-mile-an-hour winds causing a tree to fall on a house
   c. lightning causing a fire in an office building
   d. the announcement of a leak in a nuclear power plant

9. Which of the following distortions affected the United States' decision to enter the war in Vietnam?

   a. an image of the enemy as diabolical
   b. a moral self-image
   c. both a and b
   d. neither a nor b

10. An overconfident military and a lack of empathy for the enemy

   a. are distortions that can lead to war.
   b. are attitudes that can help the release of hostages.
   c. are necessary for survival.
   d. are attitudes that are not subject to change.

11. Beliefs about nuclear war

    a. have become less gloomy over the years.
    b. have remained remarkably stable over the past four decades.
    c. are not disclosed by most people.
    d. vary considerably from one person to the next.

12. Which of the following statements concerning people's attitudes toward nuclear war is the most accurate?

    a. People have become increasingly active in their attempts to prevent nuclear war.
    b. Most people take no concrete steps to stop the threat of nuclear war.
    c. People now feel more confident that they can survive a nuclear war than they did four decades ago.
    d. Most people do not think about the damage that could be caused by a nuclear war.

13. Deterrence leads to

    a. peace.
    b. arms buildup.
    c. nuclear freeze.
    d. trusting the enemy.

MATCHING QUESTIONS

Match each term with the best description.

_____ 14. deterrence

_____ 15. Personnel Reliability Program

_____ 16. mutually assured destruction

_____ 17. technological disasters

_____ 18. natural disasters

a. usually have a clear beginning and a clear end

b. have effects that may linger indefinitely

c. leads to arms buildup

d. is retaliation that would completely wipe out the attacking country

e. ensures appropriate training of people working with nuclear weapons

ANSWER KEY: SECTION III

FILL IN THE BLANKS

1. sense of control

2. predictable

3. technological; natural

4. strategic miscalculation

MULTIPLE CHOICE

5. c

6. d

7. c

8. d

9. c

10. a

11. b

12. b

13. b

MATCHING QUESTIONS

14. c

15. e

16. d

17. b

18. a

INTEGRATING THE MATERIAL

1. What is the most psychologically healthy way to deal with a natural disaster?

2. What kinds of roles will psychologists play in the twenty-first century that are different from what psychologists are doing now?

ACTIVITIES FOR CHAPTER REVIEW

1. Place yourself in a situation of high density—many people per unit of space. The environment may be a small elevator with many people, a store at peak time, or rush-hour traffic. Do you experience crowding? What does it feel like? Are you focused on the density, or are you able to distract yourself? How would you feel if the density increased?

2. Examine machines and pieces of equipment that you own (TV, VCR, stove, stereo, microwave, car dashboard), or machines and equipment owned by a friend or in a store. What features are well designed or poorly designed in terms of ease of usage? Do any of these machines or pieces of equipment have the feature of natural mapping? Can you think of ways to improve their design to facilitate usage?

3. Ask ten people whom you know how they feel about computers. Make sure that they are not all people who work with computers on a daily basis. Ask them about their comfort level with computers. Do you detect any cyberphobia?

APPENDIX

GOING BY THE NUMBERS: STATISTICS IN PSYCHOLOGY

Appendix: GOING BY THE NUMBERS: STATISTICS IN PSYCHOLOGY

CHAPTER OVERVIEW

The Appendix covers the topic of statistics and the application of statistical principles to the study of psychology. Statistics is the branch of mathematics concerned with collecting, organizing, analyzing, and drawing conclusions from numerical data. Basic approaches to statistical measurement are described throughout the Appendix.

The Appendix is divided into three sections.

I. The first section of the Appendix introduces descriptive statistics, the branch of statistics that provides a means of summarizing data. Summarizing data allows us to describe sets of observations based on collected information on individuals in the form of scores. Descriptive statistics shows us average (mean), middle (median), and most frequent (mode) performances or scores. The mean, median, and mode are the most common measures of central tendency.

II. The second section of the Appendix covers measures of variability. Once you have determined the central tendencies within a group, it is useful to know the degree of variability within the group. Variability can be measured as a range (highest to lowest scores) or, in a more sophisticated way, as a standard deviation from the mean.

III. The third and final section of the Appendix describes how statistics can be used to answer questions and make inferences about a population. The relationships between groups may be better understood when tests of statistical significance and correlation are performed. The section ends with useful strategies for evaluating statistical results as a consumer.

STUDY STRATEGY

Follow this strategy for *each* section of the chapter.

1. Review the APPENDIX OUTLINE up to Recap and Review I.

2. Read the APPENDIX OVERVIEW, Section I.

3. Read the Appendix in the text up to Recap and Review I.

4. For any question you answered incorrectly or did not understand, go back to the parts of the text that cover that material.

5. Write your answers to the REVIEW QUESTIONS for Section I in the *Study Guide*. Consult the answer key only after you have finished. Then correct any mistakes.

6. After you have completed the REVIEW QUESTIONS for Section I and have corrected your mistakes, follow the STUDY STRATEGY for Section II. Do the same for each section until you have completed all REVIEW QUESTIONS.

7. Then complete the INTEGRATING THE MATERIAL questions at the end of the *Study Guide* chapter. Answering these questions will help you see how the material fits together.

And, don't forget:

Go back to the parts of the text that cover material that was difficult for you. If you still don't understand a concept, ask your teacher for clarification. Your questions in class and your teacher's answers will help other students as well.

MASTERY QUESTIONS

After mastering the Appendix, you will be able to answer the following questions:

What are the various measures used to summarize sets of data?

How do they differ?

How are the basic statistical measures calculated?

What are the strengths and weaknesses of the basic statistical procedures?

What techniques are used to determine the nature of a relationship and the significance of differences between two sets of scores?

How can the key terms and concepts listed at the end of the Appendix be defined and applied?

REVIEW QUESTIONS: SECTION I

FILL IN THE BLANKS

1. _____ is the branch of statistics that provides a means of summarizing _____.

2. A(n) _____ is a bar graph.

3. The _____ is the average of all scores.

4. The mean, median, and mode are measures of _____ _____.

5. The _____ distribution of scores produces a bell-shaped, symmetrical curve.

6. The _____ is the point that divides a distribution in half.

7. The _____ is the most frequent score.

8. A(n) _____ distribution is an arrangement of scores from a sample that indicates how often a particular score is present.

MULTIPLE CHOICE

9. A distribution of scores that produces a bell-shaped curve is considered

    a. normal.
    b. bimodal.
    c. skewed.
    d. central.

10. Examine this set of numbers: 1, 2, 3, 4, 4, 4, 5, 5. What is the mean?

    a. 2.5
    b. 3.5
    c. 4
    d. cannot be determined with the information given

11. What is the mode of the set of numbers in question 10?

    a. 3
    b. 4
    c. 4.5
    d. both 4 and 5 (it is bimodal)

12. What is the median of the set of numbers in question 10?

    a. 3
    b. 3.5
    c. 4
    d. 4.5

13. What type of distribution would be formed by the set of numbers in question 10?

    a. normal
    b. symmetrical
    c. skewed
    d. modal

MATCHING QUESTIONS

Match each term with the best description.

_____ 14. mean

_____ 15. mode

_____ 16. median

_____ 17. normal distribution

_____ 18. histogram

a. forms a bell-shaped curve

b. is the average score

c. is a bar graph

d. is the midpoint

e. is the most frequent score

ANSWER KEY: SECTION I

FILL IN THE BLANKS

1. descriptive statistics; data
2. histogram
3. mean
4. central tendency
5. normal
6. median
7. mode
8. frequency

MULTIPLE CHOICE

9. a
10. b
11. b
12. c
13. c

MATCHING QUESTIONS

14. b
15. e
16. d
17. a
18. c

REVIEW QUESTIONS: SECTION II

FILL IN THE BLANKS

1. The highest score in a distribution minus the lowest score represents the _____.

2. A(n) _____ _____ is an index of how far an average score in a distribution of scores deviates from the distribution's center.

3. The standard deviation provides a means for converting _____ _____ on standardized tests, such as the SAT.

4. A distribution with closely packed scores will have a(n) _____ standard deviation than a distribution with widely dispersed scores.

MULTIPLE CHOICE

5. A deviation score is an original score minus the

   a. range.
   b. mode.
   c. square root.
   d. mean.

6. Which one of the following statements is true?

   a. When the means of two distributions are identical, the spread of scores must also be identical.
   b. The range of a distribution is the highest score plus the lowest score.
   c. The standard deviation is highly sensitive to extreme scores.
   d. The greater the spread of scores in a distribution, the greater the variability from the mean.

7. The final step in calculating a standard deviation is to

   a. subtract the resulting number from the mean.
   b. determine where the resulting number lies within the range of scores.
   c. take the square root of the resulting number.
   d. add the resulting number to the squared deviation scores.

MATCHING QUESTIONS

Match each term with the best description.

_____ 8. range

_____ 9. standard deviation

_____ 10. deviation score

_____ 11. variability

a. measures the spread or dispersion of a sample
b. is the highest score minus the lowest score
c. is not highly sensitive to extreme scores
d. equals the original score minus the mean

ANSWER KEY: SECTION II

FILL IN THE BLANKS

1. range

2. standard deviation

3. initial scores

4. lower

MULTIPLE CHOICE

5. d

7. c

6. d

MATCHING QUESTIONS

8. b

10. d

9. c

11. a

REVIEW QUESTIONS: SECTION III

FILL IN THE BLANKS

1. A(n) _____ _____ is a number that indicates the relationship between two variables.

2. A(n) _____ is a means of graphically illustrating the relationship between two variables.

3. A(n) _____ is a subgroup of a population of interest.

4. _____ statistics uses data from a sample to make predictions about the larger population from which the sample was drawn.

5. A(n) _____ relationship shows high values of one variable corresponding with low values of the other.

6. If high rates of liver disease correspond with high rates of alcohol consumption, these two variables have a(n) _____ relationship.

7. A correlation of .50 would indicate a(n) _____ relationship.

MULTIPLE CHOICE

8. In a comparison test on the effectiveness of two different brands of toothpaste, a marketing researcher found a difference between the two groups and a 96 percent probability that the results were due to a true difference between the groups and not to chance. It may be inferred from these findings that

   a. there was a positive correlation between the two groups.
   b. the results are statistically significant.
   c. the samples were drawn inappropriately.
   d. within-group performance was widely variable.

9. A correlation of .20 was found between glubbing and dibbing. This relationship would be considered

   a. almost nonexistent.
   b. slight.
   c. moderate.
   d. strong.

10. The correlation between mothers' and daughters' IQ scores is between

   a. .20 and .30.
   b. .40 and .50.
   c. .60 and .70.
   d. .80 and .90.

MATCHING QUESTIONS

Match each term with the best description.

_____ 11. significant outcome

_____ 12. perfect correlation

_____ 13. moderate negative correlation

_____ 14. not a significant outcome

   a. is -1.0
   b. is one in which the difference due to chance is under 5 percent
   c. is -0.45
   d. is one in which the difference due to chance is over 5 percent

ANSWER KEY: SECTION III

FILL IN THE BLANKS

1. correlation coefficient
2. scatterplot
3. sample
4. inferential
5. negative
6. positive
7. moderate

MULTIPLE CHOICE

8. b

9. b

10. d

MATCHING QUESTIONS

11. b

12. a

13. c

14. d

INTEGRATING THE MATERIAL

1. Research studies have been cited throughout the text. If you were to look up the articles referred to, how would you know if the findings were significant? What would a high correlation between two variables indicate?

2. What types of useful information can measures of central tendency yield about developmental milestones? About abnormal behavior?

ACTIVITIES FOR CHAPTER REVIEW

1. Weigh ten different people on a scale and record their weights. Calculate the mean, median, and mode of the set of scores (the weights). Is the distribution normal or skewed? How do you know? Calculate the standard deviation of the distribution. How variable was your sample?

2. Pay particular attention to TV commercials in which statistical findings are presented. When you hear a finding that is vague, write down the questions you would ask to obtain more accurate information. For example, the statement that ''more doctors recommend'' a particular product requires a lot more clarification in order to be meaningful. What type of clarification would you need for better evaluation of the product?